Spanish Verbs Wizard.

Everything you need to conquer Spanish verbs and speak Spanish fluently.

★Every Different Spanish Verb Type
Fully Explained and Conjugated:
Covers all regular and irregular verb types

★The 1001 Most Useful Spanish Verbs
each with translation and conjugation guide
linked to model verb

★ The 151 Best Spanish Verbs to Study First

★ The Lock-Step Learning Method
for Mastering All Spanish Verbs & Tenses

★ Fast Track your learning of Spanish verbs
with this clever guide as your companion.

By: Peter Oakfield

Riverbridge Books

ISBN 978-0-957493285

This edition published in the United Kingdom by
Riverbridge Books
192 Leckhampton Road, Cheltenham GL53 0AE   U.K.
Copyright © Peter Oakfield

About the author:
Peter Oakfield lives in the west of England and also writes about memory and topics related to the Spanish language. His other books include:

How to learn - Spanish - French - German - Arabic - any foreign language successfully.
 and
How To Transform Your Memory & Brain Power: Power-Learn, Memorize & Remember Anything.
 and
How I Learned To Speak Spanish Fluently In Three Months: Discover How You Can Conquer Spanish Easily The Same Way.
 and
Dual Language Spanish Reader. Level Beginner to Intermediate

Table of Contents

Introduction

Spanish verbs.
The rewards to be gained from learning Spanish are enormous, not just from the pleasure of being able to speak it but also from enjoying the literature and the culture.

But in order to be able to speak Spanish well it is essential to have a good knowledge of the verbs and to master their use. The verbs are the keystone of each and every sentence. They are the words that make things happen and without them a sentence would be just a collection of words without vitality and direction.

Accordingly for those learning Spanish, it is just as important to understand the verbs and to learn to use them, as it is to learn vocabulary generally. However, bearing in mind that there are 6 different persons for the conjugation of each tense, that there are 8 different tenses (i.e. including the imperative and the subjunctive, the latter having two forms, so 9 conjugations) as well as the compound tenses, it may at first seem that there is much to be mastered.

Luckily though, the work is in reality much less than might be imagined if it is approached in the right way and if you have the right tools and information. For example, as you will discover in this book the compound tenses can be very easy to learn; there is much regularity in the forms of the verbs; and whilst there are certainly seeming irregularities with many types of verbs, most of the irregular verbs in fact follow a rule or at least a sort of pattern; and the number of truly irregular verbs without any obvious pattern is really very small. And even these can be mastered if the clever learning techniques, which will be explained in this book, are applied.

Accordingly the scheme of this book is to present the subject as a workbook to fast track you to success and fluency with the Spanish verb. There are in four important parts in this book as follows.

Part 1 Understanding the Spanish Verb
You will discover here all the Spanish verb forms that you need to know so as to be able to understand and to learn them, however and

whenever they may be encountered or required. It will be appropriate for student at every level from beginner to advanced, and can be used both for learning and for simple reference purposes.

You will find full explanations of every type of regular verb; and of every type of irregular verb; both those that may follow a pattern in their irregularity, and also of all the other completely irregular verb forms.

Part 2 Examples of Every Different Spanish Verb Type Fully Conjugated
One hundred and four fully conjugated model Spanish verbs.
The explanations of the Spanish verb types are followed by 104 model verbs in fully conjugated form, covering every type of Spanish verb, both regular and irregular.

Part 3 The Most Useful and Essential Spanish Verbs
The one thousand and one most useful Spanish verbs.
By way of a further aid to the mastery of the Spanish verb, this book contains a collection of the 1001 most useful and important Spanish verbs for the student to learn. When you know these verbs you will be able to to speak Spanish more than comfortably in any likely situation. Every one of the 1001 is provided with a translation and a conjugation guide to a model verb amongst the 104 fully conjugated verbs that are set out in this book, so as to help you learn them easily.

Also included in this part of the book is a list of **the 151 Best Spanish Verbs to Study First** so as to be able to make yourself understood and to get by reasonably in the Spanish language.

Part 4 Mastering and Recalling Spanish Verbs and Tenses
Essential Memorizing Techniques for Memorising Spanish Verbs and The Lock-Step Learning Method for Mastering Spanish Verbs & Tenses; and also Memorising tips for different Spanish verb conjugations.
It is not enough to be able to understand Spanish verbs when they are encountered. It is essential also to be able to recall and to be able to conjugate them whenever required, Accordingly special attention has been given to the importance of learning and

memorising Spanish verbs, and there are 3 Chapters devoted specifically to proven memory techniques for learning and recalling verbs and their conjugations, including the Lock-Step Method for Spanish Verbs and Tenses, that will be found to be particularly valuable. A final chapter details numerous memorising tips patterns and pointers for different types of Spanish verb tenses.

How To Use This Book
You can use this book either for regular learning, or as a reference when uncertain as to a verb or its conjugation. However when learning the verbs initially (and for that matter, when learning the Spanish language generally) keep in mind the value of regular daily study. The importance of this cannot be overstated. Regular work at the study of the verbs (and especially the practical use of them) at least once a day will yield much better results than occasional study, for example just once a week, even if the amount of time devoted to the work is the same (e.g. by having one really long session at the weekends).

With the aid of this book you will soon be able to command the Spanish verb and achieve your goal of fluency with the Spanish language. Good luck with your study. If you have any comments you are welcome to email me at p.oakfield.spanish@gmail.com

Part One: Understanding the Spanish Verb

Chapter 1.
How To Pronounce Spanish Verbs Correctly

Knowing how to pronounce Spanish verbs, which requires a knowledge of how to pronounce Spanish letters and words, will help you to learn and remember the conjugations of the verbs more easily as will be seen. It will also help you both to speak the language correctly so that you will be understood, and in turn to be able to understand what is said to you.

The following simple rules are therefore an essential preliminary before Spanish verbs are studied.

1. How to pronounce the consonants.

b Sounds much as it does in English, but slightly softer.

c Sounds like the **c** in Call, except where it appears before the letters **e** or **i**. In these cases the **c** is pronounced **th** as in Think.

d Sounds much as it does in Dog, but is slightly softer. However where the **d** is at the end of a word or between two vowels the sound of the **d** is nearer to TH as in Think.

f Sounds as it does in English

g Sounds like the **g** in Goat, Got or Get, except where it appears before the letters **e** or **i**. In these cases the **g** sounds like the ch in Loch

gu Where **gu** appears before either **e** or **i** it sounds like **g** in Goat or Get and the **u** is then silent. However when the u after g has two little dots, ü, (a dieresis) then th u is pronounced. It sounds like Gooay as in bilingüe-(bilingual)

h This letter is always silent.

j Sounds like the **ch** in Loch (ie the same as the G before the letters e o i).

k Sounds like **k** in English. E.G. As in Kick.

l Sounds like the **l** in English E.G. As in Lot.

ll Sounds like the **lli** in Million.

m Sounds as it does in English. E.G. As in Metal.

n Sounds as it does in English. E.G. As in Now.

ñ Sounds like the **ny** in Canyon

p. Sounds as it does in English. E.G. As in Pit.

q This letter is **always** followed by the letter U and QU is pronounced like the K in Keen

r Where the **r** appears at the end of a word or between vowels it is pronounced like the R in Rig. At the beginning of a word the letter R is somewhat rolled.

rr The double **rr** is rolled almost with a purring sound.

s Sounds like the **s** in Snake. Think of a hissing snake. Note that the s should not be pronounced like the s in Treasure.

t Sounds like the **t** in Test. It is pronounced crisply.

v Has a sound somewhere between v and b and often just a less vigorous b sound.

y Sounds like the **y** in Yank. The y is only a consonant when it appears at the beginning of a word or syllable.

z Sounds the **th** in Think.

2. How to pronounce the vowels.

a Sounds like the **a** in Apple.

e Sounds like **ay** in Hay.

i Sounds like the **ee** in Need.

9

o Sounds like the **o** in Cope.

u Sounds like the **oo** in Loop.

y Is only a vowel when it is on its own (Y = and) sounds like the **ee** in Need, or at the end of a word.

Learn the sounds by listening and repeating.
To begin to grasp and to learn to speak the sounds correctly it is important not just to read about them (and bear in mind that written guidelines can only be an approximation) it is essential to listen to them as well. The best way is to listen repeatedly to audio recordings with a transcript, paying attention to each and every word, and repeating each sentence or phrase after you have heard it.

3. How to place the stress in the correct place with Spanish words.
Knowing how to place the stress correctly when speaking a Spanish word is of great importance, but luckily the rules are quite simple.

First: If the word has a letter with a written accent over it (EG **á** or **é** or **í** or **ó** or **ú**) the stress or accent is applied to the letter so written.
Examples: m**é**dico, p**á**rroco, combinaci**ó**n, est**é**ril.

Second: If the word has no written accent but ends in a consonant (but not if the word ends in **n** or **s**) then the last syllable is stressed.
Examples: comerci**a**l, desped**i**r, sal**u**d, prens**i**l.

Third: If the word has no written accent but ends with a vowel, or with **n** or **s,** then the syllable before the final syllable is stressed.
Examples: tort**i**lla, br**a**zo, c**a**mbio entr**a**da.

How essential is it to know where the stress should be? Would it for example matter if the word were not correctly pronounced? It is in fact very important to have the stress in the right place. Consider the following two Spanish words (the stress is shown bold):

Esp**e**ro = I hope/wait
Esper**ó** = He hoped/waited

As will be seen the different stress for each word results in a different meaning despite the similarities. The position of the stress can also explain a change in the spelling and pronunciation in the stem of a verb.

Chapter 2.
Understanding the language of verbs

Like many subjects, verbs have some specialist words which are used to refer to different aspects of verbs or the way in which they are used. This vocabulary is a form of shorthand which makes it easier to describe what is being spoken about, instead of having to use a longer explanation each time. Set out following are the most important examples of such words, with a short explanation of each.

There is no need to try and memorise these terms. Just read them over from time to time. Also whenever you come across any of the words in this book, you can check back quickly to refresh your understanding as to their meaning.

Note that the brief notes for each of the verbs are intended only as an introduction. All the different verb types will be dealt with fully further on.

Verb: This is included only for the sake of completeness. A verb is a word which indicates the action in a sentence. E.G. The dog **barked**. He **read** the book.

Infinitive verb: The infinitive of the verb is the verb in its basic form, before it has been altered in any way. All possibilities are still open as to the what will be done with it. In English the infinitive is recognizable because it includes the word "to". E.G. **To bark, to read**. In Spanish the verbs in the infinitive do not include the word "to" separately. The idea of the "to" is implied. All Spanish verbs in the infinitive end with the letters **ar**, or **er**, or **ir**.

Active: This indicates that the subject of the verb carries out the action referred to by the verb. E.G. The boy ran.

Passive: This indicates that the subject of the verb suffers the action referred to. E.G. The boy was stopped.

Reflexive verb. This is a verb in which the action turns back in some way on the subject. E.G. He stopped himself. English does not use reflexive forms much but in Spanish they are quite common. In Spanish a reflexive verb in the infinitive is recognizable by having

12

the letters "**se**" at the end. Examples: despedirse (to take one's leave: to say goodbye). Peinarse (to comb one's hair).

Persons: the different persons who may be the subject of the verb:
First person singular: I. In Spanish Yo
Second person singular: You (ie only one person). In Spanish Tú
Third Person singular: He. In Spanish Él or Ella if female. Usted (formal way of saying "you" to one person)
First person plural: We. In Spanish Nosotros or Nosotras if all are female.
Second person plural: You (ie more than one person). In Spanish Vosotros or Vosotras if all are female,
Third person plural: They. In Spanish Ellos or Ellas if all are female. Ustedes (formal way of saying "you" to more than one person)

Conjugate: to conjugate means to give the various inflections or parts of the verb in a desired tense. For example, taking the English verb 'to give', and conjugating it in the present indicative tense.
First person singular: I give
Seond person singular: You give
Third person singular: He gives
First person plural: We give
Second person plural; You give
Third person plural; They give

Present-Particle ('Present-P'): In English where the form of the verb ends with the letters ING, it is called the Present-Participle when it is part of a verb. E.G. The dog was barking: 'barking' is here the Present-Participle. Note also that the Present-Participle is sometimes used as an adjective. E.G. a barking dog.

The Present-Participle may also be used as a noun in English. For example: Running is a healthy sport. Smoking is bad for you. Etc. A Present-Participle used in this way it is known as a gerund. This does not occur in Spanish where the Present-Participle would not be used as a noun. (In Spanish the infinitive would be used instead: EG Smoking is bad for you.= Fumar es malo para ti.)

In Spanish the Present-Participle of a verb will generally end as follows:
Verbs ending in AR: drop AR and add..."ando". E.G. Hablar...Hablando = Speaking

13

Verbs ending in ER: drop ER and add...."iendo". E.G. Correr...Corriendo = Running

Verbs ending in IR ..drop IR and add..."iendo". E.G. Partiendo = Leaving/departing

Note that there are some irregular Present-Participles.

Past-Participle ('Past-P') : The verb is described as the Past-Participle when it is in the form in which it is added to another verb to give an indication of the past. E.G. He has stopped.

In Spanish the Past-Participle of the verb will usually end as follows:

Verbs ending in AR: drop AR and add "ado". E.G. Hablar ..Hablado = Spoken

Verbs ending in ER drop ER and add "ido"E.G. Correr...Corrido = Run

Verbs ending in IR drop IR and add "ido". E.G. Partir...Partido = Left/departed

Note that there are some irregular Past-Participles

Note that the Past-Participle may sometimes be used with the verb 'to be', not as part of the verb expressing the action, but as an adjective; and in these circumstances it will, like any adjective in Spanish, have to agree in gender and number with the noun which it modifies.

Personal pronouns for verbs in English and Spanish. (See Persons above)

I = Yo

You = (singular intimate form) Tú

He = Él. She+Ella.

You (singular: formal address) = Usted

We = Nosotros or if all are female Nosotras

You (plural intimate form) = Vosotros or if all are female Vosotras

They = Ellos or if all are female Ellas

You (plural: formal address) = Ustedes

Verb Stem: the form of the verb with the ending (AR, ER or IR) removed. For example: the infinitive of the Spanish verb Tomar (to take) with the infinitive ending AR removed, is Tom. This is called the stem, and different forms of the verb are created by adding letters onto the stem. For example Tomaba (I/he was taking).

Verb ending: the infinitive endings for all Spanish verbs are (as indicated above): **ar**. or **er**, or **ir**. The infinitive of every Spanish verb will end in one of those ways. For the various tenses the endings will be different as will be seen.

Tense: This word refers to the verb in a form which indicates the time of the action. E.G. The present, the past, the future etc.

Present Indicative tense: The verb is making a simple statement as to what is actually happening at the moment. E.G. He drinks. She reads. The dog barks.

Past historic or preterite tense: The verb is expressing a completed action. E.G. He read the book. They paid the bill. She scored the goal.

Imperfect tense: The verb is expressing something which was going on at some time in the past, but not completed, or which occured regularly. He was reading the book. They were paying the bill. She was scoring the goal. He was working every day last week.

Future tense: The verb is expressing something, which will certainly happen in the future. E.G. He will read the book. They will pay the bill. She will score the goal.

The conditional: The verb is expressing the idea of something in the future, which is uncertain. It suggests that the something might happen if some condition were to be met. E.G. He would read the book (if you asked him to do so). They would pay the bill (if they had the money). She would score a goal (if she is allowed to play).

Mood: The form of the verb that expresses the mode or manner or state of the action. E.G. **Indicative mood:** the verb when it just affirms or denies something. E.G. The boy ran. Other moods: The imperative and the subjunctive: see below.

Imperative mood: The verb when it expresses a command or advice. E.G. Shut up. Begin at once. Stop that.

Subjunctive mood; The verb when it expresses condition, hypothesis or contingency. E.G. If I were you. He may have arrived.

15

He should have arrived. In English the subjunctive mood is not much used but in Spanish it is in common usage.

Compound tense: A verb used together with another to form a single tense. In Spanish the verb Haber is mostly used only as an auxillary verb to form compound tenses. E.G. I have read. They should have paid the bill. She had scored the goal. However there are certain expressions related to the verb Haber which will be seen ahead. EG Hay: there is, there are, etc.

Irregular verbs: Verbs which do not conform to the general rules for the conjugation of verbs with their particular ending.

Radical Stem changing verbs: These are verbs which have a change in the vowel of the stem when the stress falls upon the usual vowel in the verb stem.

Othographic and Euphonic changes in verbs: These are verbs which may not be fully irregular but which have a change to accommodate the sound of the tense being used. With minor exceptions the sound follows what would be expected with the usual rule for the verb, or produces a more comfortable sound.

Chapter 3.
Conjugating Spanish Verbs: the different persons.

The different persons who may be speaking have already been introduced above. Yo, Tú, Él (Ella), Usted (Ud.), Nosotros (Nosotras), Vosotros (Vosotras), Ellos (Ellas), and Ustedes (Uds.).

Some comment with regard to the use of Usted and Ustedes is necessary so as to make the use of the appropriate verb ending clear.

The word Usted is a contraction of the words Vuestra Merced, meaning Your Grace. In the past in Spanish this form of address became common and because it is an address in the third person, it follows that the verb ending for it is also that for the third person. In other words it is exactly the same as for Él where there is one person (Usted); or the same as Ellos where there is more than one person (Ustedes).

This is much the same as it would be in English when addressing, for example a Judge. E.G. Not "you know" but "Your Honour knows"; or Royalty: E.g. "Your Majesty is welcome" and not "you are welcome".

The use of Usted was widespread at one time for addressing almost anyone other than children and family relations. It was used as a mark of respect, and even now it is not uncommon, but the use is diminishing, and the use of the familiar or more intimate Tú and Vosotros, is much more likely. The student should know how to use the correct verb ending for either style of address, and when in doubt it will be best to use Usted, as formal politeness is never going to cause offence. However when addressed as Tú or Vosotros, it will be appropriate to reply with similar address.

The conjugations of verbs in this book will always be set out in the traditional way, namely :
1st person singular (Yo),
2nd person singular (Tú),
3rd person singular (Él (Ella), Usted (Ud.)),

1st person plural (Nosotros (Nosotras)),
2nd person plural Vosotros (Vosotras),
3rd person plural (Ellos (Ellas), Ustedes (Uds.)).

For this reason the personal pronouns will not always appear next to the verb conjugations where they are set out in this book. Where they do not appear there is no need for them, because they will always be the same and the conjugations will always be in the same order.

Chapter 4.
The Present Tense

The present tense is a simple statement of what is occurring at the moment: the verb is referring to some action that is going on as the person speaks, or is something that is generally occurring.

E.G. He reads: Él lee. She speaks: Ella habla. They eat: Ellos comen. He walks to work: Él camina al trabajo.

As has been seen, the verb endings for the infinitive of all Spanish verbs are: AR, ER, and IR. When these are removed from the infinitive what remains is the verb stem. The endings for the tenses are added onto the stem.

Examples of stems.
**Hablar: to speak. Stem: Habl.....
**Beber: to drink. Stem Beb....
**Escribir: to write. Stem Escrib....

AR verbs. The verb endings for the present tense of AR verbs (in the order 1st person singular, 2nd person singular, 3rd person singular, 1st person plural, 2nd person plural, and 3rd person plural) are:
o, as, a, amos, áis, an.

ER verbs. With ER verbs the present tense endings are: o, es, e, emos, éis, en

IR verbs. With IR verbs the present endings are: o, es, e, imos, ís en

Examples

Present	Hablar AR verb	Beber ER verb	Escribir IR verb
Yo	hablo	bebo	escribo
Tú	hablas	bebes	escribes
Él/Ella/Ud.	habla	bebe	escribe
Nosotros/as	hablamos	bebemos	escribimos
Vosotros/as	habláis	bebéis	escribís
Ellos/as/Uds.	hablan	beben	escriben

Chapter 5.
The Imperfect Tense

The imperfect tense is a statement of something in the past that was in some sense continuing at the time being spoken of. The action went on for a while or was continuous in the past. What it does not do is to express one thing that occurred, specifically at one time, or just once.

Examples.
** He always read the paper....Siempre leía el periodico.
** She used to speak......Ella hablaba....
** The idea was not taking him by surprise ......La idea no le cogía de sorpresa
** While I was walking to work this morning....... Mientras caminaba al trabajo esta mañana
** My brother was sleeping when...............Mi hermano dormía cuando ....
** He used to travel by train........Viajaba en tren

By way of comparison note that the following would **not** be the imperfect but the past historic (preterite): I overslept last night. He read the paper and then gave it to me. Yesterday I travelled to work by train.

Sometimes in English the word "would" instead of indicating something conditional may refer to circumstrances which were occuring in the past. In Spanish the conditional would not be used to express the idea of something continuous in the past. The imperfect would be used.

** At the foot of a barrier where the small lizards would creep....Al pie de un vallado por donde serpeaban las largatijas...

Further examples will be found in Chapter 6 dealing with the Preterite or Past Historic, where some comparisions of both tenses are provided.

The Spanish imperfect tense is one of the easiest conjugations to learn as will now be seen.

AR Verbs: With AR verbs the endings in the imperfect are as follows:
aba, abas, aba, ábamos, abais, aban.

ER and IR verbs. ER and IR verbs each have the same imperfect tense endings which are: ía, ías, ía, íamos, íais, ían.

Examples.

Imperfect	Hablar AR verb	Beber ER verb	Escribir IR verb
Yo	hablaba	bebía	escribía
Tú	hablabas	bebías	escribías
Él/Ella/Ud.	hablaba	bebía	escribía
Nosotros/as	hablábamos	bebíamos	escribíamos
Vosotros/as	hablabais	bebíais	escribías
Ellos/as/Uds.	hablaban.	bebían	escribían

Note that the imperfect tense is completely regular for all Spanish verbs except for Ir (to go), Ver (to see) and Ser (to be).

The conjugations for these 3 verbs in the imperfect are as follows:-

Imperfect	Ser (to be)	Ver (to see)	Ir (to go)
Yo	era	veía	iba
Tú	eras	veías	ibas
Él/Ella/Ud.	era	veía	iba
Nosotros/as	éramos	veíamos	íbamos
Vosotros/as	erais	veíais	ibais
Ellos/as/Uds.	eran	veían	iban

Chapter 6.
The Preterite or Past Historic Tense.

The past historic tense is a statement of something that occurred just once. The tense is used to express an action which has been fully completed. This may be compared with the imperfect where the intention is to refer to an action which is in some way continuing.

Consider the following examples of use of both tenses.

Preterite
** He read the paper yesterday...Leyó el periódico ayer
** She spoke to me about it.......Ella me habló de ello
** I walked to work today..Anduve a trabajar hoy
** I learned Spanish at school... Aprendí español en la escuela
** He travelled by train yesterday ... Viajó en tren ayer
** He turned around....Se volvió

Imperfect
** We thought that you were in the garden.....Creíamos que estabas en el jardín.
** He was reading the paper when.... Leía el periodico cuando......
** She knew all the plants......Ella conocía todas las plantas.....
** He was an agreeable man.....Era un caballero muy agradable

Imperfect and Preterite
** Aun cuando el escondrijo daba (imperfect) espacio bastante, la pareja no se desunió (preterite) al encontrarse alli. .....Even when the hiding place gave sufficient space, the couple did not separate on finding themselves there.
** Ni menos se desviaron (preterite) sus rostros, tan cercanos, que él sentía (imperfect) el aletear de mariposa de los párpados de ella, y el cosquilleo de sus pestañas curvas....Nor less did they turn aside their faces, so close that he felt the butterfly flutter of her eyelids and the tickling of her curved eyelashes.

The Spanish preterite tense is not quite as easy to learn as the imperfect but should not present any real difficulty.

AR Verbs: With AR verbs the endings in the preterite are as follows:
...é, ...aste, ...ó, ...amos, ...asteis, ...aron.

ER and IR verbs. Both ER and IR verbs have the same preterite tense endings which are as follows: ...í ....iste, ...ió, ...imos, ...isteis, ...ieron.

Examples

Preterite	Hablar AR verb	Beber ER verb	Escribir IR verb
Yo	hablé	bebí	escribí
Tú	hablaste	bebiste	escribiste
Él/Ella/Ud.	habló	bebió	escribió
Nosotros/as	hablamos	bebimos	escribimos
Vosotros/as	hablasteis	bebisteis	escribisteis
Ellos/as/Uds.	hablaron	bebieron	escribieron

Chapter 7.
The Future Tense.

The future tense expresses something that will occur in the future, something that is going to happen. He will read the paper. She will speak to you. They will write a letter. The future tense in Spanish is much the same as in English.

Examples:
** Leeré el periodico mañana. I will read the newspaper tomorrow.
** El año que viene venderemos la casa. Next year we will sell the house.
** Tomarás una cerveza? Will you have a beer?
** Las personas que viven en esta casa serán ricas. The persons who live in that house will be rich. (Here the future indicates conjecture)

The Spanish future tense is one of the easiest tenses to learn because the endings are the same for all three types of verbs: AR, ER, and IR.

The endings are as follows: ...é, ...ás, ...á ...emos, ...éis, ...án.
However the verb endings for the future tense (and also for the conditional tense) are not added to the verb stem as with other verbs but are added to the infinitive.

Examples

Future	AR Hablar	ER Beber	IR Escribir
Yo	hablaré	beberé	escribiré
Tú	hablarás	beberás	escribirás
Él/Ella/Ud.	hablará	beberá	escribirá
Nosotros/as	hablaremos	beberemos	escribiremos
Vosotros/as	hablaréis	beberéis	escribiréis
Ellos/as/Uds.	hablarán	beberán	escribirán

Verbs which are irregular in the future and conditional tenses

Fortunately the number of Spanish verbs which are irregular in the future tense is limited to just twelve and all are easy to learn. Moreover the irregularity does not relate to the endings for the future tense but to what would otherwise be the infinitive form to

24

which they are attached. As will be seen from the follo
comprehensive list, the irregularities mostly consist of the dropping
of the final vowel for some of the infinitives, or the replacement of
the vowel with the letter d, and in only two cases, decir and hacer,
does the stem change completely.

Exactly the same changes occur for the conditional tense and so in
the following table both the future and the conditional are shown.
For each verb just the conjugation for the first person singular (yo)
is given. All the other persons have exactly the same variation to the
infinitive stem.

Infinit ive	Future (yo)	Conditional (yo)
Decir	dir-é	dir-ía
Poner	pondr-é	pondr-ía
Salir	saldr-é	saldr-ía
Valer	valdr-é	valdr-ía
Querer	querr-é	querr-ía
Tener	tendr-é	tendr-ía
Hacer	har-é	har-ía
Haber	habr-é	habr-ía
Poder	podr-é	podr-ía
Saber	sabr-é	sabr-ía
Caber	cabr-é	cabr-ía
Venir	vendr-é	vendr-ía

Chapter 8.
The Conditional Tense

The conditional tense (in English, something that I, you, he etc. *would* do if ...) generally expresses the idea, as the word conditional suggests, of something that is not certain: it is subject to a condition. Accordingly the use of the conditional generally implies or uses the words 'if', or 'but', or 'however', or similar qualification, or some explanation that the action proposed by the verb may not occur.

Examples:
** I would pass (conditional tense) the exams, if I could only find the energy to study more.
** I would read (conditional tense) the paper if I knew where it is.
** She would speak (conditional tense) to you, however she does not have time at the moment.

Also the conditional tense is often associated with the subjunctive: however this will be covered in a later chapter.

The conditional tense is especially easy to learn because it is so regular. The endings are as follows: ...ía, ...ías, ...ía, ...íamos, ...íais, ...ían; and these are simply added on to the infinitive.

Moreover just like the future tense, the endings are the same for all verbs types: ar, er and ir. Additionally, as has already been commented, the irregularities are confined to exactly the same 12 verbs as for the future tense. A table for these 12 has been set out in the chapter dealing with the future tense.

Examples of the conditional

Conditional	Ar hablar	Er beber	Ir escribir
Yo	hablaría	bebería	escribiría
Tú	hablarías	beberías	escribirías
Él/ella/Ud.	hablaría	bebería	escribiría
Nosotros/as	hablaríamos	beberíamos	escribiríamos
Vosotros/as	hablaríais	beberíais	escribiríais
Ellos/as/Uds.	hablarían	beberían	escribirían

As mentioned above the conditional is used:-

(a) to describe something that would occur if some condition is fulfilled.
** My sister would buy a car, if she had the money.
** Mi hermana compraría un coche, si tuviese el dinero.

** If she had a car she would lend it to you
** Si ella tuviese un coche, se lo prestaría a Ud.

The above two examples are both 'if/conditional' sentences, as to which see Chapter 13.

(b) to indicate approximation or probability with regard to some matter in the past.
** It would have been two o'clock at night.
** Serían las dos de la noche.

** She would have been ill because......
** Ella estaría enferma porque.....

(c) to express a wish, request or desire.
** She would like a coffee.
** Ella desearía un café.

** I would like to buy the book
** Me gustaría comprar el libro.

Note: when using querer, it may often be more appropriate to employ the imperfect subjunctive 'iera' form. The subjunctive imperfect is sometimes used in place of the conditional. For example: 'I should like a coffee.' 'quisiera un café.' This would be considered to be a more courteous form of expression than saying 'I would like a coffee.'

(b) after a past tense followed by que and expressing something, which, viewed from the past being spoken of, would be some time after that.
** I thought that you would write to me.
** Creía que me escribiría

** She said she would sell the book.

** Ella dijo que vendería el libro.

** He promised me that he would arrive tomorrow.
** Me prometió que llegaría mañana.

Such main clauses in a sentence of this type would be in the indicative and suggest saying, believing, knowing, affirming assuring, and other expressions of this nature.

The clause with the verb in the conditional may appear either before or after the clause with the verb in the indicative.

Compare the following sentences:-
1. He said that he would do it. Dijo que lo haría.
Note: past tense in main clause with the dependent conditional referring to what then would have been the future.

But
2. He says that he will do it. Dice que lo hará.
Note: present tense with the dependent clause referring to the future.

3. He says that he would not talk so much if he were in front of the judge.
Dice que no hablaría tanto si estuviese delante del juez.
Note: present tense introducing if/conditional clause with conditional and subjunctive.

Remember, as explained in relation to the imperfect tense, that although in English the conditional may sometimes be used to express the idea of something continuing in the past, in Spanish the imperfect would be used for this purpose and not the conditional.

Chapter 9.
Haber and the Compound Tenses.
Also: Hay, Habia, other forms derived from the verb Haber.

1.The Present-Perfect Tense: 2. The Pluperfect or Past-Perfect Tense. 3. The Preterite Perfect Tense. 4.The Future Perfect Tense. 5. The Conditional Perfect Tense. 6. The Present-Perfect Subjunctive Tense. 7. The Pluperfect Subjunctive Tense.

There are seven compound tenses as listed above and, despite the word "compound", they all are amongst the easiest tenses to learn. And with the exception of the two compound subjunctive forms, which admittedly require a little extra study, the compound haber tenses are also relatively easy to use in practice.

Note 1. All the compound tenses employ the auxillary verb Haber. Except for some purposes described below, this verb is always used, with the Past-Participle for the relevant activity, to form the required tense. Note also that the Past-Participle when conjugated with haber does not agree with its object (unlike an adjective). So, being part of the verb tense, with haber the Past-Participle will always end with o.

Note 2. Haber is translated as 'to have'. However the verb haber does not mean the same as the verb Tener, which means 'to hold' or 'to have to' etc.; and haber cannot generally be used on its own as Tener can be.

Note 3. It will be recollected that the verb is described as the Past-Participle when it is in the form in which it is added to another verb to give an indication of the past. E.G. He has stopped. 'Stopped' is here the Past-Participle.

In Spanish the Past-Participle of a verb will generally end as follows:
Verbs ending in AR: ...ado. E.G. Hablado = Spoken
Verbs ending in ER:.....ido. E.G. Corrido = Run
Verbs ending in IR ......ido. E.G. Partido = Left/departed
In each case the final two letters are removed from the infinitive and the ado or ido as appropriate tacked on.

There are some irregular Past-Participles, but not many and those that there are should not cause any difficulty. In the 104 Fully Conjugated Spanish Verbs and in the 1001 Most Useful Spanish Verbs provided with this book, the Past-Participle is always shown together with the infinitive, so again they will be easy to pick up and learn.

The tenses for Haber are given in the examples following and once they have been learned they can be used with the Past-Participle of <u>any verb</u>, so a great addition to the verb skills commanded will be achieved just by the modest amount of study required to master them.

These then are the conjugations of the seven compound haber tenses:-

1. The Present-Perfect Tense.
He, Has, Ha, Hemos, Habéis, Han.
English equivalent: "I have + Past-Participle". The tense is used to talk about some occurrence in the past, either at some uncertain time, or which in may some way still be continuing or is not quite complete. "I have passed my exams". "I have worked here for the last two years."

Examples
** He vendido el coche. I have sold the car.
** Él ha perdido su sombrero. He has lost his hat
** Hemos comprado una casa. We have bought a house.

2. The Pluperfect or Past-Perfect Tense.
Había, Habías, Había, Habíamos, Habíais, Habían.
English equivalent: "I had etc. + Past-Participle". Use of this tense is the same as it would be in English. It describes something that had occurred before some other event in the past (the other event not necessarily being mentioned because it is perhaps known or assumed or has been expressed previously).

Examples
**Antes de recibir tu carta yo había vendido el coche. Before receiving your letter I had sold the car.
**Antes de llegar a su despacho él había perdido su sombrero. Before arriving at his office he had lost his hat.

**Yo había leido el libro antes de darselo a mi hermano. I had read the letter before giving it to my sister.

3. The Preterite Perfect Tense.
Hube, Hubiste, Hubo, Hubimos, Hubisteis, Hubieron.
English equivalent: "I had etc.+ Past-Participle". This tense is really quite close in meaning to the pluperfect tense above. Whilst the student ought to know the conjugations of this tense so as to be able to understand them should they be encountered, it is not really necessary to worry about employing them in speech because the pluperfect will always suffice and the preterite perfect would not often be used in conversation.

4. The Future Perfect Tense.
Habré, Habrás, Habrá, Habremos, Habréis, Habrán.
English equivalent:"Will have" "shall have"+ Past-Participle. The tense is used just as it would be in English to express something that will occur in the future, subsequent to some other occurrence that is anticipated. The tense may also refer to the probability as to something that occurred recently.

Examples
** Habré vendido el libro antes de las dos. I will have sold the book before two o'clock.
** Habrá perdido su sombrero de nuevo. He will have lost his hat again.
** Supongo que habrán comprado una casa. I suppose that they will have bought a house.

5. The Conditional Perfect Tense.
Habría, Habrías, Habría, Habríamos, Habríais, Habrían.
English equivalent: "Would have." + Past-Participle. The tense indicates what would have happened if some condition had been satisfied. "I would have sent you a present with this letter if only I had remembered it was your birthday before I sealed the envelope."

Examples
** Habría vendido el coche si no lo hubiera* perdido. (* This is the pluperfect subjunctive.)I would have sold the car if I had not lost it.
** Él habría perdido su sombrero si ella no lo hubiera* encontrado. He would have lost his hat if she had not found it.

31

** Habríamos comprado una casa si hubieramos* tenido el dinero. (* This is the pluperfect subjunctive.) We would have bought a house if we had had the money.

6. The Present-Perfect Subjunctive Tense.

Haya, Hayas, Haya, Hayamos, Hayáis, Hayan.
English equivalent: There is no quite appropriate English equivalent to this tense because the subjunctive is so little used in English. The words "should have".. "may have"..."might have" + Past-Participle, are about the best translation that can be suggested, but these words are not always evident in English. The tense is more fully discussed in the chapter on the subjunctive.

Examples
** Temo que él haya vendido el coche. I fear that he may have sold the car.
** Dudo que él haya perdido su sombrero. I doubt that he might have lost his hat.
** Siento que ellos hayan comprado una casa. I am sorry that they have bought a house.

7. The Pluperfect (or Past-Perfect) Subjunctive Tense.

This tense has two forms.
Either: Hubiera, Hubieras, Hubiera, Hubiéramos, Hubierais, Hubieran.
Or: Hubiese, Hubieses, Hubiese, Hubiésemos, Hubieseis, Hubiesen.
English equivalent: As with the Present-Perfect subjunctive, there is no exact translation for this tense into English. "Might have " and "should have" + Past-Participle are again the nearest equivalents, but these are not to be regarded as close translations. More usually in English the simple pluperfect would be used where in Spanish the pluperfect subjunctive would be employed.

This tense is more fully discussed in the chapter on the subjunctive.

Examples
** Yo temia que él hubiera (hubiese) vendido el coche. I feared that he had sold the car.
** Ella dudaba que él hubiera (hubiese) perdido su sombrero. She doubted that he might have lost his hat.

** Él sentía que hubiéramos (hubiésemos) comprado una casa. He was sorry that we should have bought a house.

Hay, Habia, and expressions derived from the verb Haber

In addition to use as an auxillary verb, there are other forms derived from haber as follows:

1. Haber followed by de and an infinitive represents the following meanings: to have to, to be required to, to be to, etc.
Example: **Hemos de comer a las cuatro: We have to eat at four o'clock.

2.Haber used impersonally will mean: there is, there are, there were etc.
Examples
**Hay buenas noticias en el periodico: there are good news in the newspapers.
**Hay muchos huevos en la cocina?:...Are there many eggs in the kitchen?
**No hay nadie....: there is no-one....
**Habrá mucho sol este dia: there will be much sun today
**Había mucho sol ayer: there was much sun yesterday
**Habría ....there would be.....
**Hubo........there was....
**Ha habido......there has been.........

3. Haber used impersonally when followed by que and an infinitive denotes necessity or obligation.
Examples:
** Hay que leer el libro: It is necessary to read the book
** Había que perdonarle: It was necessary to forgive him.
** Que hay que hacer? : What is to be done?

Haber compound tenses illustrated with Hablar and Quejarse.

As has been seen, the conjugations of haber are always the same and only the Past-Participles are different between the verbs with which it is used as an auxiliary. Once you have learned the tenses of haber and used them with the Past-Participle for any verb, then you will be able to conjugate the compound forms for every verb for which you have learned the Past-Participle. See examples following.

33

Haber+ Hablar: to talk/to speak

Verb infinitive	Participles	
Haber/hablar compound tenses	Hablar: hablado	
Present-Perfect	**Present-Perfect subjunctive**	**Future Perfect**
yo he hablado	yo haya hablado	yo habré hablado
tú has hablado	tú hayas hablado	tú habrás hablado
él ha hablado	él haya hablado	él habrá hablado
nosotros hemos hablado	nosotros hayamos hablado	nosotros habremos hablado
vosotros habéis hablado	vosotros hayáis hablado	vosotros habréis hablado
ellos han hablado	ellos hayan hablado	ellos habrán hablado
Pluperfect	**Pluperfect subjunctive 1**	**Conditional Perfect**
yo había hablado	yo hubiera hablado	yo habría hablado
tú habías hablado	tú hubieras hablado	tú habrías hablado
él había hablado	él hubiera hablado	él habría hablado
nosotros habíamos hablado	nosotros hubiéramos hablado	nosotros habríamos hablado
vosotros habíais hablado	vosotros hubierais hablado	vosotros habríais hablado
ellos habían hablado	ellos hubieran hablado	ellos habrían hablado
Preterite Perfect	**Pluperfect-subjunctive 2**	
yo hube hablado	yo hubiese hablado	
tú hubiste hablado	tú hubieses hablado	
él hubo hablado	él hubiese hablado	
nosotros hubimos hablado	nosotros hubiésemos hablado	
vosotros hubisteis hablado	vosotros hubieseis hablado	
ellos hubieron hablado	ellos hubiesen hablado	

Haber/Quejarse: to complain

Verb infinitive	Participles	
Haber/quejarse compound tenses	quejado, quejándose	
Present-Perfect	**Present-Perfect subjunctive**	**Future Perfect**
me he quejado	me haya quejado	me habré quejado
te has quejado	te hayas quejado	te habrás quejado
se ha quejado	se haya quejado	se habrá quejado
nos hemos quejado	nos hayamos quejado	nos habremos quejado
os habéis quejado	os hayáis quejado	os habréis quejado
se han quejado	se hayan quejado	se habrán quejado
Pluperfect	**Pluperfect subjunctive 1**	**Conditional Perfect**
me había quejado	me hubiera quejado	me habría quejado
te habías quejado	te hubieras quejado	te habrías quejado
se había quejado	se hubiera quejado	se habría quejado
nos habíamos quejado	nos hubiéramos quejado	nos habríamos quejado
os habíais quejado	os hubierais quejado	os habríais hablado
se habían quejado	se hubieran quejado	se habrían quejado
Preterite Perfect	**Pluperfect-subjunctive 2**	
me hube quejado	me hubiese quejado	
te hubiste quejado	te hubieses quejado	
se hubo quejado	se hubiese quejado	
nos hubimos quejado	nos hubiésemos quejado	
os hubisteis quejado	os hubieseis quejado	
se hubieron quejado	se hubiesen quejado	

Chapter 10.
The Progressive Tenses

The progressives tenses are formed using the verb estar and the Present-Participle of the relevant verb. The action described by the verb is in progress at the time being spoken of. It is not something which has been completed.

It will be recalled that the Present-Participle form of the verb in English is recognizable by having the letters ING at the end. Running, walking, talking etc.

In Spanish the Present-Participle of a verb will end as follows:
Verbs ending in AR: drop AR and add..."ando". E.G. Hablar...Hablando = Speaking
Verbs ending in ER: drop ER and add...."iendo". E.G. Correr...Corriendo = Running
Verbs ending in IR ..drop IR and add..."iendo". E.G. Partiendo = Leaving/departing

The Spanish progressive tenses then are similar to the English progressive tenses which also use the verb 'to be' together with the Present-Participle, which makes remembering the Spanish form easier; although it should perhaps be added that some English speakers are in the habit of using the Past-Participle with these tenses, saying for example "He was/is sat" (instead of "sitting"), or "They were/are stood" (instead of "standing"). However the use of the Past-Participle for the progressive tenses is of course inappropriate in English, as it would also be in Spanish.

Note 1: The above comments should not be confused with the fact that the Past-Participle may sometimes be used with the verb 'to be', not as part of the verb expressing the action, but as an adjective; and in these circumstances it will, like any adjective in Spanish, have to agree in gender and number with the noun which it modifies.

Example:
** The flowers are dead: Las flores están muertas.
But: **The flowers are dying: Las flores están muriendo.

Note 2: There are some irregular Present-Participles. For example: pedir - pidiendo,

36

leer - leyendo, decir - diciendo, oir - oyendo, ir - yendo. Accordingly it is best always to learn the participles (present and past) when learning the verb. The participles for each verb shown conjugated in this book are shown alongside the infinitive in the verb tables in this book so learning them is straightforward.

The Present-Progressive tense is formed by adding the Present-Participle of the verb for the relevant acitivity as a separate word after the verb estar in the present tense.

For example: I am running. (Estoy corriendo.) I am dancing. (Estoy bailando).

The Past-Progressive is formed by adding the Present-Participle of the verb for the relevant activity as a separate word after the verb estar in the imperfect tense. Clearly the Past-Progressive has much in common with the use of the imperfect generally; and it may sometimes be preferable to use the imperfect of the relevant verb instead of the Past-Progressive.

For example: I was running. (Estaba corriendo.) I was dancing. (Estaba bailando).

Progressive tenses	Present-Progressive tense Correr	Past-Progressive tense Bailar
Yo	Estoy corriendo	Estaba bailando
Tú	Estás corriendo	Estabas bailando
Él/Ella/Ud.	Está corriendo	Estaba bailando
Nosotros/as	Estamos corriendo	Estábamos bailando
Vosotros/as	Estáis corriendo	Estabais bailando
Ellos/as/Uds.	Están corriendo	Estaban bailando

Other tenses of Estar may also be used with the Present-Participle.
In the table below only first person singular (Yo) in each case are shown, but of course the Present-Participle applies to all the persons.

Preterite	Yo estuve bailando
Future	Yo estaré bailando
Conditional	Yo estaría bailando

Use of the progressive tenses.
1.The progressive tenses in Spanish are used in more or less the same way as they would be in English, save that the the matter being spoken of is something **is** actually going on at that moment of speaking (Present-Progressive); or **was** actually going on at the moment being spoken of (Past-Progressive or preterite progressive); or will actually be going on in the future (future progressive); or would actually be going on (conditional progressive). So the tense is more deliberate than it would be in English where the progressive tenses are likely to be used in a less forceful way. Note also that the Spanish imperfect tense translates into English much as would the Spanish progressive past. IE I was....he was....etc.

2 Where a progressive tense is used, any object pronoun referred to by the verb will be tacked onto the end of the Present-Participle. EG Estoy comprandolo etc.

3. The Present-Progressive tense in Spanish would not be used to deal with some future event. For example in English one might say "I am driving home tomorrow". This use of the Present-Progressive tense would not be appropriate in Spanish where the present or future tense would employed instead. "I will drive home tomorrow"

4. As the Present-Participle used in a progressive tense is part of the verb, it does not have to agree in number or gender with the subject noun.

Chapter 11.
The Passive Voice

The passive voice is the use of a verb construction that avoids making the subject of the sentence the agent of the activity described, or that avoids having any clear subject.

Examples
** "The car was crashed by the drunken driver". In this sentence the car is the subject of the sentence but was not reponsible for the crash which was caused by the driver. By way of contrast consider the sentence in the active form. "The drunken driver crashed the car." Here the driver is the subject and carried out the action.

** "Fresh fish sold here". The sentence does not specify by whom the fish is sold.

** "Here they sell fresh fish" Again it is left unspecified who "they" may be.

** "It is not permitted to walk on the grass". The sentence does not make clear who may have made the order not to walk on the grass.

Before the different forms of the passive in Spanish are discussed it should be noted that, especially in spoken Spanish, the passive construction is avoided where practical, although where appropriate it will be used.

The Passive Using the verb Ser
One form of the passive voice in Spanish is by means of the verb Ser plus the Past-Participle of the relevant verb. The Past-Participle has already been discussed in relation to the compound tenses and so need not be further explained here. However it must be remembered that when the Past-Participle is used with Ser in the passive voice, it is like an adjective and must agree both as to number and as to gender with the subject of the sentence. (NB It will be recalled that the Past-Participle, when used not with Ser but in a compound tense with Haber, is always the simple Past-Participle and is **not** made to agree with the subject.)

Examples
** El pescado fue cocinado. The fish was cooked.

** Los huevos fueron cocinados. The eggs were cooked.
** Las patadas fueron cocinadas. The potatoes were cooked.

The agent or person responsible for the action in the passive sentence may be introduced after the verb, by the word 'por' followed the name of the agent.

Examples
** El pescado fue cocinado por el cocinero. The fish was cooked by the cook.
** Los huevos fueron cocinados por el cocinero. The eggs were cooked by the cook.
** Las patadas fueron cocinadas por el cocinero. The potatoes were cooked by the cook.

However bear in mind that it is preferable in Spanish to use the active voice if possible. Accordingly the above sentences could be better expressed as:
** El cocinero cocinó el pescado. etc.

The Passive using the reflexive form Se.
A futher use of the passive voice requires a reflexive form. The verb dealing with the action is expressed in the third person, either single or plural, preceded by the reflexive 'Se'.

Examples:
** Fresh fish sold here. Aqui se vende pescado fresco.
This is literally to say: 'Here fresh fish sells itself'. Of course it is understood that fresh fish does not really sell itself, and that it is sold by persons unidentified in the sentence.

** Se escribirán muchos libros. Many books will be written.
** Se pegó al muchacho. The boy was beaten.

Note that where the action is done to a human it will be necessary to use the "a" to make it clear that the person concerned did not do the thing to himself. For example: "Se pegó el muchacho" would mean that the boy beat himself.

Chapter 12.
The Subjunctive Mood.
When and how to use the subjunctive.

The subjunctive can be difficult to grasp when starting to learn Spanish, because it is not a mood which is much used, if at all, in English. Nonetheless the subjunctive form is in common use in in the Spanish language, and whilst an English speaker who does not use the subjunctive is unlikely to be seriously misunderstood when trying to express a relatively simple matter, to be able to speak good Spanish it is important to master the subjunctive.

The first point to note is that the subjunctive is mostly used only in dependent or subordinate clauses (unless used in imperative type sentences and expressions, which are dealt with in a later chapter). Accordingly (except with if/conditional clauses) the verb for the main clause in a sentence with a subjunctive will be in the indicative. The main clause in a sentence is that which expresses the main statement upon which any other clauses are dependant.

Example: ** 'I will come (main clause), though it may rain' (dependant clause with subjunctive).

N.B. The dependant clause may of course appear before the main clause.
Example: ** 'Though it may rain, I will come.'

Secondly, the subjunctive does not express anything which is certain, or factual. Its use is to indicate doubt or desire, hope, or a possiblity etc. The subjunctive then is likely to be seen in sentences or clauses that are dependant on some other sentence that has shown that there is uncertainty, desire, a demand, etc.

The following sentences provide examples of the types of expressions that would indicate use of the subjunctive mood.

** Anxiety/Distress: I fear that he is unwell. I regret that he may not be able to come.
** Desire/Hope: I hope you have passed the exam. I hope that you tidy your room.
** Demand/Prohibition: We insist that you stop. He demands that you surrender.

** Uncertainty/Possibility: Perhaps she missed the train. It is possible that he has the book.
** Doubt. I doubt that he will keep his word.
** Negation: It is doubtful that the train is on time.

The different forms of the subjunctive.
The subjunctives tenses are as follows:
The present subjunctive.
The imperfect subjunctive (which has two forms).
The perfect subjunctive.
The pluperfect subjunctive.
There is also a future subjunctive, but it is archaic and if encountered should be ignored.

The Present Subjunctive.
The endings for the present subjunctive are as follows:
AR verbs: ...e, ...es, ...e, ...emos, ...éis, ...en.
ER and IR verbs: ...a, ...as, ...a, ...amos, ...áis, ...an.

Examples of the present subjunctive.

Present Subjunctive	AR verb Hablar	ER verb Beber	IR verb Escribir
Yo	hable	beba	escriba
Tú	hables	bebas	escribas
Él/Ella/Ud.	hable	beba	escriba
Nosotros/as	hablemos	bebamos	escribamos
Vosotros/as	habléis	bebáis	escribáis
Ellos/as/Uds.	hablen	beban	escriban

Nearly always, but not in every case, irregular or stem changing verbs in the present subjunctive have the same stem as the verb in the first person present indicative. So when trying to recollect the present subjunctive it may be helpful to recall what the present indicative tense would be for Yo. Whether this is regular or irregular the same stem is generally used to add the endings for the present subjunctive.

The verbs Hablar, Beber and Escribir, in the table above are all regular, but now consider three irregular verbs: Estar, Venir and Valer.

Present Subjunctive	AR verb Estar	ER verb Valer	IR verb Venir
Yo	esté	valga	venga
Tú	estés	valgas	vengas
Él/Ella/Ud.	esté	valga	venga
Nosotros/as	estemos	valgamos	vengamos
Vosotros/as	estéis	valgáis	vengáis
Ellos/as/Uds.	estén	valgan	vengan

The Imperfect Subjunctive

The verb conjugations for the imperfect subjunctive are very easy to learn. The tense has two forms, either of which may generally be used. The endings for each are shown in the following table.

Imperfect subjunctive	AR Verbs ...ra etc.	ER& IR Verbs ...ra etc	AR Verbs ...se etc.	ER& IR Verbs ...se etc.
Yo	-ara	-iera	-ase	-iese
Tú	-aras	-ieras	-ases	-ieses
Él/Ella/Ud.	-ara	-iera	-ase	-iese
Nosotros/as	-áramos	-iéramos	-ásemos	-iésemos
Vosotros/as	-arais	-ierais	-aseis	-iesies
Ellos/as/Uds.	-aran	-ieran	-asen	-iesen

The imperfect subjunctive is formed by taking the third person plural (Ellos) of the preterite tense of the verb, removing the ending (which will be ARON for AR verbs and IERON for ER and IR verbs) and then applying the endings given above. This preterite rule for the formation of the imperfect subjunctive will be correct for all verbs, regardless as to whether the preterite is regular or irregular. This is why the imperfect subjunctive forms are easy to learn.

Note: The letters 'j', 'y' and 'ch' include the sound 'i' for this imperfect subjunctive rule so when these letters are left after removing the preterite ending, the 'i' in 'iera' and 'iese' is not used. The 'i' is already reflected in the j or y or ch. E.G. 'Leyeron' - 'leyesen' : 'Dijeron' - 'Dijesen': 'Hincheron' - 'Hinchesen'.

The Compound Subjunctive Tenses

The compound tenses have already been discussed and it will be recalled that the auxillary verb used for them is Haber. It is always used with the Past-Participle ('Past-P') for the verb which it accompanies. There are two compound subjunctive tenses: the Perfect Subjunctive and the Pluperfect Subjunctive, the latter having two forms. Both are easy to remember due to their regular format.

The Perfect Subjunctive.

Perfect Subjunctive	Haber plus Past-Participle:Haya etc.
Yo	haya + Past-P
Tú	hayas + Past-P
Él/Ella/Ud.	haya + Past-P
Nosotros/as	hayamos + Past-P
Vosotros/as	hayáis + Past-P
Ellos/as/Uds.	hayan + Past-P

The Pluperfect Subjunctive. The two forms.

Pluperfect Subjunctive	Haber plus Past-Participle: IERA etc.	Haber plus Past-Participle: IESE etc.
Yo	hubiera + Past-P	hubiese + Past-P
Tú	hubieras + Past-P	hubieses + Past-P
Él/Ella/Ud.	hubiera + Past-P	hubiese + Past-P
Nosotros/as	hubiéramos + Past-P	hubiésemos + Past-P
Vosotros/as	hubierais + Past-P	hubieseis + Past-P
Ellos/as/Uds.	hubieran + Past-P	hubiesen + Past-P

Circumstances in which the subjunctive would be used

1. Where the main clause indicates a request, an order, a prohibition etc.
Examples
** He tells me to come. Me dice que yo venga.
** I forbid them to dance. Prohibo que bailen.

44

** His mother has not allowed him to drink wine. Su madre no ha permitido que él bebiese vino.

2. Where the main clause indicates doubt, fear etc.
Examples
** I doubt that my brother will keep (may keep) his word. Dudo que mi hermano cumpla con su palabra.
** I fear that my father may speak to him about the matter. Temo que mi padre le hable del asunto.
** I am afraid the the teacher may not come. Temo que el profesor no venga.

3.Where the main clause indicates sorrow, joy, grief, surprise or other emotion..
Examples
** I am sorry that you should have troubled yourself. Siento que Ud se haya molestado.
** I am delighted that you have arrived. Me alegro que haya Ud llegado.
** I am glad that his exam has gone well. Celebro que le haya salido tan bien su examen.

4. Where the dependant clause begins with a conjunction, or a conjunctive expression and there is some uncertainty suggested. Typical conjunctions to look out for are: aunque, although, though: antes que, before: cuando, when: con tal que, on condition that: para que, in order that: como si, as if: por más que, however: sin que, without: dado que, provided that: á menos que, unless: puesto que, provided that: a fin que, in order: de modo que, so that: en caso de que, in case that.

Examples.
** I shall leave tomorrow though it may rain. Saldré mañana aunque llueva.
** I will not lend you my car unless you promise me to return it tomorrow. No le prestaré mi coche, á menos que me prometa devolverlo mañana.
** Whatever you may do, I will not forgive you. No te perdonaré, por más que hagas.

5. Where the dependant clause begins with a relative pronoun and there is some uncertainty suggested or implicit.

45

Examples.

** I want a teacher who speaks French. Quiero una profesora que hable francés.

** Show me a road that leads to Madrid. Enséñeme Ud un camino que salga para Madrid.

** If you want a drink that has no alcohol, I will supply it to you. Si Ud. quiere una bebida que no tenga alcohol, yo se la proporcionaré.

6. Where the main clause indicates a question or a denial/negative regarding the substance of the dependant clause.
Examples.

** Is there anyone who believes it? Hay alguien que lo crea?

** Do I say he is right? Digo yo que él tenga razon?

** Do you believe that they have arrived? Cree Ud que hayan llegado?

7. Where the main verb is impersonal and no certainty is indicated or implied.
Examples.

** It is right that he should know it. Es justo que lo sepa

** It may be that they know it. Puede ser que lo sepan.

** It is important that they should arrive on time. Importa que lleguen á tiempo.

8. The subjunctive may be used in a main clause for various declarations and expressions.
Examples.

**Long live Spain. Viva España

**Let no one go out. Que no salga nadie.

**God be with you. Vaya con Dios.

**I hope he comes soon. Ojalá venga pronto.

Which tense of the subjunctive should be used and when?
The answer to this will depend upon:-
a) the tense of the verb in the main clause
b) the time of the matter referred to in the dependant subjunctive clause.

The following table sets out typical circumstances in which each form of subjunctive would be appropriate assuming that the factors exist, as described above, which require the use of the subjunctive (other than in 'If'/Conditional clauses which are dealt with in Chapter 13). Examples of each are set out below the table.

46

Main clause tense	Time of action referred to in dependant clause	Subjunctive to be used if subj. circs exist	Examples
Present indicative	Same time or later than main verb.	Present Subj.	**1.** below
Future indicative	In the future.	Present Subj.	**2.** below
A past tense	At same time or later as main verb	Imperfect Subj	**3.** below
Present indicative	Before time of main verb	Imperfect Subj	**4.** below
Future indicative	Before time of main verb.	Perfect Subj.	**5.** below
Present indicative	In the (perfect tense) past	Perfect Subj.	**6.** below
A past tense	Earlier than time of main verb	Pluperfect Subj.	**7.** below

Examples: 1.
** Él prefiere que yo venga. He prefers that I should come.
** Siento que él no viva en la ciudad. I am sorry that he does not live in the town.
** Sugiero que duermas ahora. I suggest that you sleep now.

Examples: 2.
** Me dirá lo que escriban. He will tell me what they may write.
** Comeré lo que ella cocine. I will eat what she cooks.
** Terminaré este trabajo mañana si no vengan visitas. I will finish this work tomorrow, if no visitors come.

Examples: 3.
** Me extrañaba que no supieran cocinar. I was surprised that they did not know how to cook.
** Yo esperaba que ella cocinara. I expected that she should cook.
** Le dije al nino que se callase. I told the child to keep quiet.

Examples: 4.
** Temo que tuvieran que esperar un rato. I am afraid that they had to wait a while.

47

** Dudo que ella quisiera salir hoy. I doubt that she wanted to go out today.

** Parece imposible que el muchacho durmiera tanto. It seems impossible that the boy slept so much.

Examples: 5.

** Terminaré el trabajo cuando él haya pagado el dinero. I will finish the work when he has paid the money.

** Beberá cuando él haya comido. He will drink when he has eaten.

** Llegarán después de que hayan comprado un coche. They will arrive after they have bought a car.

Examples: 6.

** Dudo que él haya empezado su trabajo. I doubt that he has begun his work.

** Espero que ella haya dormido todo el dia. I expect that she has slept all day.

** Es un milagro que haya aprobado el examen. It is a miracle that he has passed the exam.

Examples: 7.

** Ella dudaba que él hubiera andado hasta la iglesia. She doubted that he had walked to the church.

** Ella esperaba que él hubiera mentido. She expected that he had lied.

** Parecía impossible que él no hubiera llegado. It seemed impossible that he had not arrived.

Chapter 13.
The Subjunctive and If/Conditional sentences.

If/Conditional sentences are those which contain both:

(a) An 'If-Condition' clause. This is a clause with a statement as to a condition. E.G. 'If I were you'. 'Si yo fuese Ud.'. ('If I were you', is incidentally, one of the few remaining uses of the subjunctive in English). Although we may call this clause the If-Condition clause, the verb in this clause will not be the conditional, but the subjunctive.
And
(b) A 'Would-Conclusion' clause. This is a clause with a statement as to what would occur if the condition set out in the If-Condition clause were to be satisfied. EG. 'I would buy the book'. 'Compraría el libro'. The verb in this Would-Conclusion clause will be in the conditional.

** If I were you I would buy the book. Si yo fuese Ud. compraría el libro.

Of course the above clauses may appear in either order. I.E. The If-Condition clause followed by the Would-Conclusion clause, or vice versa.

Although the If-Condition clause may frequently be commenced by if/si, other expressions such as 'aunque' may be used or implied.

Further examples of If/Conditional sentences:

** If I had time I would go to his house. Si yo tuviese tiempo, iría a su casa.
** I would not park the car here, if I were you. No aparcaría el coche aqui, si yo fuera Ud.
** If I had seen him, I would have asked him. Si lo hubiera visto, se lo habría preguntado.
** Even though he knew it, he would not have said it. Aunque lo supiera, no lo habría dicho.
** If I had given him money, he would have brought a new car. Si yo le hubiese dado dinero, él habría comprado un coche nuevo.

Which form of the subjunctive should be used in the If-Condition clause?

In general, as has previously been seen, either of the 2 forms of the imperfect subjunctive may be used, each generally being equal to the other. However the imperfect subjunctive forms ending in ARA etc. and IERA etc. (but not ASE etc. or IESE etc.) can be and often are used instead of the conditional.

Moreover as will be clear, the ideas that may be indicated by 'I/he etc. would' and 'I/he etc. should' run fairly close in some matters. For example, as explained earlier, instead of saying 'I would like a coffee' it is more usual both in English and in Spanish to say 'I should like a coffee.' 'Quisiera un café'.

For this reason the ARA and IERA forms of the imperfect subjunctive may be used in place of the conditional tense in the Would-Conclusion clause of an If/Conditional sentence (but never the ASE or IESE forms).

However the use of the same form of the subjunctive in both the If-Condition clause and the Would-Conclusion clause is avoided. So if the ARA or IERA form is used in the If-Condition clause then the usual conditional tense should be used in the Would-Conclusion clause. The following examples should make this clear.

If-Condition Clause	Would-Conclusion Clause
If I had time,	I would do it.
Si tuviese tiempo,	yo lo haría.
Si tuviera tiempo,	yo lo haría.
Si tuviese tiempo,	yo lo hiciera.

Chapter 14.
The Imperative.
When and how to use the imperative.
Also: The imperative and object pronouns.

The imperative, like the subjunctive, is called a mood. It does not describe something that is factual or certain, but rather something which the speaker wants another person to do. The imperative is what is used when a command is given. For example: Do this! Do that! Stop that at once! Write this down! Bring me the book! Get up! Go to sleep! Do not snore! Do not run! Etc.

Note that there is no imperative form for the first person singular (Yo) because a command would be given to someone else and not to oneself. Even when telling oneself to do something it will be as though someone else is speaking. Accordingly no 'Yo' imperative form exists. However the imperative does exist for the first person plural (nosotros) because it is possible to address oneselves in the imperative as a group: Let us stop. Let us start. Also obviously, since the imperative is only addressed directly to someone, for the third persons singular and plural only the Ud. and Uds. forms exist.

The regular imperative forms for verbs ending in AR, ER, and IR are as follows:

Imperative	Ar: Andar	Er: Beber	Ir: Escribir
tú	anda no andes	bebe no bebas	escribe no escribas
Ud.	ande no ande	beba no beba	escriba no escriba
nosotros	andemos no andemos	bebamos no bebamos	escribamos no escribamos
vosotros	andad no andéis	bebed no bebáis	escribid no escribáis
Uds.	anden no anden	beban no beban	escriban no escriban

Notes.

Second person singular (Tú)
1.Positive commands:
This is formed just by dropping the S from the Tú form of the present indicative.

2. Negative commands:
This is formed by borrowing from the Tú form in the present subjunctive.

3. Reflexive verbs: see below.

Third person singular (Ud.)
1. Positive and negative commands are both formed by borrowing from the Ud form in the present subjunctive.

2. Reflexive verbs: see below.

First person plural (Nosotros)
1.Positive and negative commands are both formed by borrowing from the Nosotros form in the present subjunctive.

2. Reflexive verbs: see below.

Second person plural (Vosotros)
1.Positive commands:
This is formed just by dropping the R from the infinitive of the verb and adding a D.

2. Negative commands:
This is formed by borrowing from the vosotros form in the present subjunctive.

3. Reflexive verbs: see below.

Third person plural (Uds)
1. Positive and negative commands are both formed by borrowing from the Uds form in the present subjunctive. This of course is the same as adding N on to the end of the singular imperative Ud form.

2. Reflexive verbs: see below.

Reflexive imperative forms.

Spanish, like some other languages, often employs reflexive verbs and this being the case, the form of the imperative, as might be guessed, changes slightly where the verb is reflexive.

The regular imperative forms for reflexive verbs ending in AR, ER, and IR (with examples: Peinarse:to comb one's hair. Meterse: to go/to enter into. Aburrirse: to be bored.) are as follows:

Imperative	Ar: Peinarse	Er: Meterse	Ir: Aburrirse
tú	péinate: no te peines	métete: no te metas	abúrrete: no te aburras
Ud.	péinese: no péinese	métase: no métase	abúrrase: no abúrrase
nosotros	peinémonos: no peinémonos	metámonos: no metámonos	aburrámonos: no nos aburramos
vosotros	peinaos: no os peinéis	meteos: no os metáis	aburríos: no os aburráis
Uds.	péinense: no péinense	métanse: no métanse	abúrranse: no abúrranse

Notes

1. Second person singular (Tú) reflexive form
Positive command:- The reflexive TE is added to the end of the verb.
Example:- Comb your hair. Péinate. Note that the accent is shown over the first syllable to show that the stress remains as it would do if the TE were separated from the verb.
Negative command:- The reflexive TE appears before the verb.
Example:- No te peines. Note: no need here for an accent because it is clear that the stress falls on the first syllable.

2. Third person singular (Ud.) reflexive form:
Positive command:- The reflexive SE is just added on the end of the verb.
Example: Péinese
Negative commands: Generally the reflexive SE remains at the end of the verb.
Example: No péinese

However there are some exceptions and sometimes the reflexive SE appears in front of the verb. Example: No se lave.

3. First person plural (Nosotros) reflexive form
Positive command: The final S is dropped and the reflexive is then added on the end of the verb.
Example: Peinémonos
Negative commands: Generally the same as the positive command with No appearing before the verb.
Example: No peinémonos
However there are some exceptions and sometimes the reflexive Nos appears in front of the verb. Example: No nos lavémos.

4. Second person plural (Vosotros) reflexive form
Positive command: The final D is dropped and the reflexive OS is added to the end of the verb.
Example:- Comb your hair. Peinaos.
Negative command: The reflexive OS appears before the verb.
Example: No os peinéis.

5. Third person plural (Uds) reflexive form
Positive command:- The reflexive SE is just added on the end of the verb.
Example: Péinense
Negative commands: Generally the reflexive SE remains at the end of the verb.
Example: No péinense
However there are some exceptions and sometimes the reflexive SE appears in front of the verb. Example: No se laven.

The imperative and object pronouns.
Where the imperative command is positive the object pronoun or pronouns are tacked onto the end of the verb. Where there are two or more pronouns they should appear in the following order: Reflexive pronoun, indirect pronoun, direct pronoun.
Examples.
** Throw it! (Tú) Tíralo!   Throw it to me! (Tú) Tíramelo!
** Sell it! (Tú) Véndelo!   Sell it to him! (Tú) Véndeselo!
** Give me it! (Tú) Démelo!   Tell me it! (Ud.) Dígamelo!
** Learn it! (Ud.) Apréndalo!   Forget it! (Ud.) Olvídelo

Where the imperative is in the negative, the object pronouns are placed in front of the verb. Again where there are two or more pronouns they should appear in the following order: Reflexive pronoun, indirect pronoun, direct pronoun.
Examples.
** Do not throw it! (Tú) No lo tíres!
** Do not throw it to me! (Tú) No me lo tíres!
** Do not sell it! (Tú) No lo véndas!
** Do not sell it to him! (Tú) No se lo véndas!
** Do not give me it! (Tú) No me lo des!
** Do not tell me it! (Ud.) No me lo digas!
** Do not learn it! (Ud.) No lo apréndas!
** Do not forget it! (Ud.) No lo olvides!

The circumstances in which the imperative should be used are straightforward, but the variations can be a trifle fiddly. Here then, for those in a hurry, is an easy way to deal with commands: turn them into polite requests. Instead of saying 'do this/do that', say 'please do this/do that'. The Spanish for 'please' is ((Tú) 'Hazme el favor de ......'; or (Ud.) 'Hagame el favor de...'

'Haz' and 'Haga' are the Tú and Ud. imperative forms for Hacer (to do). These can be used with an infinitive to request the matter desired.
Examples: 'Hazme el favor de abrir la puerta'. (Please open the door); or 'Hagame el favor de abrir la puerta'.

Chapter 15.
Spanish verbs and the preposition 'a' before a specific person etc.

In Spanish the preposition 'a' is in many cases inserted in the sentence with the verb in circumstances where this would not occur in English.

The basic rule is that if the direct object of the sentence is a specific person or some item treated as though it were a person, such as the family dog that is treated as one of the family, then the preposition 'a' is inserted before the direct object.

For example:
** El padre ama a su hijo. The father loves his son.
** La chica quiere a su perro. The girl loves her dog.

The following then are the main circumstances in which the preposition 'a' would be used:

1. Where the direct object is a noun being a definite person or personified object.
Examples.
** El maestro busca a su alumno. The teacher looks for his pupil.
** El abogado representa a su cliente. The lawyer represented his client.
** No vio a su tío. He did not see his uncle.

2. Before the proper name of things, *except* where the definite article is part of the name (e.g. *El* Prado)
Examples
** Él quiere ver a España. He wants to see Spain.
** *But*: Quiero visitar el Prado. I want to visit the Prado.

3. The preposition 'a' would **not** be used:
(a) before a common noun
Examples
** Me estrellé mi coche. I crashed my car.
** Quemó la cena. He burned the supper.

(b) Before a noun for a person in an indefinite sense:
Example
** I need a teacher. Necesito un profesor.
** *But*: He found his teacher. Encontró a su profesor.

4. The 'a' will also be used to avoid ambiguity in a sentence where both the subject and the direct object are nouns for things.
Example
** Summer follows the spring. Verano sigue a la primavera.

5. Note:
(a) Querer means to want. 'Querer a' means to love.
So:
** I want a mother. Quiero un madre.
** I love my mother. Quiero a mi madre.

(b) Tener would not take the 'a'
** So: I have a mother. Tengo una madre.

Chapter 16.
Defective, Incomplete and Impersonal Verbs

There are a number of Spanish verbs which, as will be seen, are defective or incomplete in that not all the expected conjugations exist or, whilst they may exist, generally only the third person is used. There are other verbs which are only ever used impersonally (ie only in the third person).

Impersonal Verbs
(a) Impersonal verbs are those which for logical reasons are limited to the infinitives, the participles, and the third person of the relevant tense. Whilst in theory constructions with other conjugations might be possible, they are in fact avoided.
** Llover: to rain. Llueve: it rains.
** Nevar: to snow. Nieva: it snows.
** Amanecer: to dawn. Amanece: dawn breaks
** Atardecer: to to get dark. Atardece: dusk falls

(b) Hacer. In addition to it's use generally, hacer is used impersonally in the third person of the relevant tense, to refer to the temperature, the weather, and to time (in the sense of time past, ago etc.)
Examples
** Hace buen tiempo: The weather is good.
** Hace calor: It is hot.
** Ocurrió hace diez años; It happened ten years ago.

Verbs used generally in just the third person.
There are some verbs that (although possibly available in other conjugations) are like the impersonal verbs and are used generally in the third person.

The most obvious example of such verbs is gustar, which is used to mean to like, but which more accurately translates as: to please or to be pleasing to. For example: 'Me gusta la crema'. This would be translated as 'I like cream', but really means 'cream pleases me'.

Other similar verbs:
** Encantar: to delight, to enchant.
** Bastar: to be enough, to be sufficient.
** Importar: to matter, to be important.

** Doler: to hurt, to distress.

Verbs which are incomplete.
These are some verbs for which with some tenses or persons, there is no conjugation available. This at least is the theory but sometimes an example will be heard of a conjugation which 'does not exist'. In Spanish as in English, the rules are not always absolute, especially for an inventive speaker.

Examples
** Abolir: to abolish. Only used in those forms in which the i of the infinitive is retained; (this includes the participles).
** Soler: to be accustomed to, to be in the habit of. Not available in the future, the conditional, the future perfect, the conditional perfect, and the imperative.
** Costar: to cost. In theory only available in the third person and the participles.
** Antojarse: to covet, to long for. Only available in the third person and the Present-Participle.
** Atañer: to concern, to have to do with. Only available in the third person and the participles.

Chapter 17.
Distinction between the verbs Estar and Ser (to be)

Both these verbs translate into English as the verb "to be". However in Spanish these two verbs are each used for different purposes and neither can be used in place of the other. This distinction obviously would not occur in English where the single verb "to be" would be used.

A basic guide to bear in mind is that generally **ser** is used to indicate something permanent and **estar** to indicate something which may not last.

The table below indicates various circumstances for appropriate use of the verbs.

	Ser examples	**Estar** examples
Progressive tenses		Estoy escribiendo, Estaba escribiendo
Passive voice	El pescado fue cocinado	
Permanent personal details	Ella es inteligente El hombre es albañil	
Temporary personal details		El muchacho está agotado
State of health		La chica está enferma
Time of day	Son las dos	
Date	Hoy es domingo	
Ownership	El coche es mío	
Location		Los platos sucios están sobre la mesa
Condition of things		La cocina está sucia La catedral está abierta
Permanent condition of things	Las paredes de la catedral son de ladrillo	

Chapter 18.
Some Spanish verbs having irregular or notable Past-Participles

The present and Past-Participles of all the verbs listed in this book are shown with those verbs. However here for convenience are some notable irregular forms of Past-Participles

Verb infinitive	Past-Participle
Abrir, to open	abierto
Bendecir, to bless	bendito
Cubrir, to cover	cubierto
Decir, to say	dicho
Descubrir, to uncover	descubierto
Escribir, to write	escrito
Hacer, to make, to do	hecho
Imprimir, to print	impreso
Ir, to go	ido
Maldecir, to curse	maldito
Morir, to die	muerto
Poner, to put	puesto
Romper, to break	roto
Ver, to see	visto
Volver, to return, to turn	vuelto

In verbs where the 'ido' of a Past-Participle follows the vowels a, e and o, the I of the ido will have an accent to show that it has the accent and is fully pronounced and that there is no diphthong.

Creer, to believe	creído
Roer, to gnaw	roído
Leer, to read	leído
Traer, to bring	traído

Chapter 19.
Examples of compound verbs derived from various irregular verbs

Compound verbs, that is verbs which are composed of some other verb plus a prefix, are conjugated in the same way as the verb without the prefix.

Examples with irregular verbs:-

The following verbs are conjugated in the same way as Hacer:-
Contrahacer, to copy, to counterfeit.
Deshacer, to undo.
Rehacer, to redo, to do again.

The following verbs are conjugated in the same way as Poner:-
Componer, to put together, to compose.
Deponer, to lay down, to remove, to depose.

The following verb is conjugated in the same way as Salir:-
Sobresalir, to project, to stand out

The following verb is conjugated in the same way as Valer:-
Equivaler, to be equal to, to rank the same as.

The following verb is conjugated in the same way as Traer:-
Retraer, to draw in, to retract.

The following verbs are conjugated in the same way as Venir:-
Convenir, to agree, to suit.
Revenir, to shrink, to come back.

The following verbs are conjugated in the same way as Ver:-
Prever, to foresee, to anticipate.
Rever, to see again, to review.

Note that some compound irregular verbs may have a different Past-Participle. Examples: Bendecir (bendito) and maldecir (maldito).

Chapter 20.
Reflexive Spanish Verbs

1. A reflexive verb is one where the object will be the same as the subject. In other words the person undertaking the action of the verb is the same as the object or person to whom the action of the verb occurs.

Examples.
** I shave myself. Yo me afeito.
** I stopped myself. Me detuve.
** They married: Se casaron.
** He undressed: Se desnudó.

2. The Spanish reflexive pronouns are as follows:
me (myself)
te (yourself)
se (him/her/(Ud) it's/self)
nos (ourselves)
os (yourselves)
se (them/(Uds) selves)

Example. Afeitarse: to shave oneself.

Present tense	Perfect tense
me afeito	me he afeitado
te afeitas	te has afeitado
se afeita	se ha afeitado
nos afeitamos	nos hemos afeitado
os afeitáis	os habéis afeitado
se afeitan	se han afeitado

3. In Spanish the use of the reflexive form is common, and will be normal wherever the action undertaken relates to the person undertaking it. This may be contrasted with English where the reflexive is not much used except where necessary to make quite clear that the action related to the object of the verb. "I hurt myself".

Bear in mind that the English 'myself'/ 'himself/ herself/themself' are often used not as a reflexive form but to reinforce or emphasise the identity of the person carrying out the action. For example 'I myself have read the book'. 'He drove the car himself'.

4. Spanish transitive verbs can generally be either reflexive or non reflexive.
Consider
** He shaved himself: Se afeitó.
** I shaved him. Le afeité
** He deceived me. Él me engañó
** I deceived myself . Me engañé a mí mismo.

5. However some Spanish verbs are used only reflexively.
** Alegrarse: to rejoice
** Atreverse a: to dare to

6. The third person reflexive would generally be used where possible instead of the passive form.
Examples:
** Fish is sold here. El pescado se vende aquí.
** How does one get to the bus station? Cómo se llega a la estación de autobuses?
** How are eggs cooked? Cómo se cocinan los huevos?

7. Reciprocal Reflexives Verbs.
Verbs will be described as reciprocal reflexives, when they refer to two or more people acting one upon the other.
Examples:
** They deceived each other. Se engañan unos a otros.
** They bathed each other. Se bañaban unos a otros.

Unos a otros, or uno as otro, as appropriate, may be added as above for greater emphasis.

8. Some verbs have a different meaning when used as reflexives.
Examples
** Dormir: to sleep. Dormirse: to fall asleep.
** Ir: to go. Irse: to go away (in effect: to take oneself away)
** Sentir: to be sorry, to feel regret. Sentirse: to feel, to suffer hurt/unwell etc.

Chapter 21.
Orthographic, Euphonic and Stress changes in Spanish verbs.

Note:
1. The following comments as to the changes for various verbs should **not** be regarded as something to be learned. What they are intended to do is to draw attention to what happens in the conjugation and to make the changes easier to appreciate. Read them to understand the verb types but not so as to learn as rules for conjugating them.

2. The verb classifications in this chapter and elsewhere (e.g. **4-O-Bullir-Empeller**) relate to the classification of the verbs in **Chapter 22. 104 Fully Conjugated Spanish Verbs**

Orthographic and Euphonic changes
Some types of verbs have changes for orthographic or euphonic reasons. The reason for the changes will generally be obvious, and a pattern may be evident.

4-O-Bullir-Empeller Verbs in which the infinitives IR and ER are preceded by LL.
Changes: to Present-Participle, to preterite and imperfect subjunctive
The i in ie or io is dropped when they would have occured in the conjugation

5-O-Bruñir-Tañer Verbs in which the infinitives IR and ER are preceded by Ñ.
Changes: to Present-Participle, preterite and imperfect subjunctive
The i in ie or io is dropped when it would have occured in the conjugation

6-O-Henchir **Verbs** in which the infinitive IR is preceded by CH.
Changes: to Present-Participle, preterite and imperfect subjunctive
1) The i in ie or io is dropped when they would have occured in the conjugation.
2) Henchir is also a verb that has stem or root changes unconnected with the CHIR rule. Note that the e in the root changes to i in the present, present subjunctive and imperative.

7-O-Rezar Verb with the ending zar.
Changes: to preterite, present subjunctive and imperative.
The z changes to c before e.

8-O-Creer Verbs with an unaccented i between two vowels.
Change: the i becomes y.

9-O-Tocar Verb with ending car.
Change: to preterite, present subjunctive and imperative.
C changes to qu before e.

10-O-Pagar Verb ending in gar.
Changes: to preterite, present subjunctive and imperative.
G changes to gu before e.

11-O-Averiguar Verb ending in guar.
Changes: to preterite, present subjunctive and imperative.
G changes to gü before e.

12-O-Escoger Verb ending in ger.
Changes: to present, present subjunctive and imperative.
G changes to j before a or o.

13-O-Dirigir Verb ending in gir.
Changes: to present, present subjunctive and imperative.
G changes to j before a or o.

14-O-Distinguir Verb ending in guir.
Changes: to present, present subjunctive and imperative.
Gu changes to g before a or o.

15-O-Delinquir Verb ending in quir,
Changes: to present, present subjunctive and imperative.
Qu changes to c before o and a.

16-O-Vencer Verb with the ending cer **which is preceded by a consonant.**
Changes: to present, present subjunctive and imperative.
C changes to z before o and a.

17-O-Esparcir Verb with the ending cir **which is preceded by a consonant.**
Changes: to present, present subjunctive and imperative.
C changes to z before o and a.

18-O-Conocer Verb with the ending cer **which is preceded by a vowel**
Changes: to present, present subjunctive and imperative.
Z is inserted before the c when followed by a or o.

19-O-Lucir Verb with the ending cir **which is preceded by a vowel**
Changes: to present, present subjunctive and imperative.
Z is inserted before the c when followed by a or o.

(Note: verbs ending in ducir, have further changes as to which see Producir below)

20-M-Producir Verb ending in ducir.
Changes: to present, present subjunctive, imperfect subjunctive and imperative
1) Z is inserted before the c when followed by a or o.
2) Change the c of their stem to j in the preterite,
3) Irregular preterite endings as follows- ....je, ...jiste, ...jo, ...jimos, ...jisteis, ...jeron. The two imperfect subjunctive forms are always drawn from the preterite el form, as has been seen already, and so these also are irregular

21-O-Instruir Verb ending in uir, in which the u is pronounced (but not those ending in guir, or güir in which the u is silent before the i)
Changes: to Present-Participle, preterite, present, present subjunctive, imperfect subjunctive and imperative
1) When accented or followed by a or o, the u becomes uy.
2) The i in terminations beginning with ie or io changes to y when unaccented (following the unaccented i between two vowels rule, as in **8-O. Creer**)

22-O-Argüir Verb ending in üir, in which the u is pronounced (but not those ending in guir, or güir in which the u is silent before the i
Changes: to present, present subjunctive, imperfect subjunctive and imperative
1) When accented or followed by a or o, the ü becomes uy.
2) The i in terminations beginning with ie or io changes to y when unaccented (following the unaccented i between two vowels rule, as in **8-O. Creer**)

23-O-Caer Verb ending in aer.
Changes: to present, present subjunctive, imperfect subjunctive and imperative
1) Change the first person singular (yo) present tense to aigo, and become aiga etc. throughout the present subjunctive and imperative forms (except for the imperative positive tu and vosotros forms)
2) The i in terminations beginning with ie or io changes to y when unaccented (following the unaccented i between two vowels rule, as in **8-O. Creer.**)

Note: a number of verbs with aer endings, apart from taking aigo, are irregular in the preterite and related imperfect subjunctive forms and in these cases the y rule is not relevant. For example Traer)

Stem/Stress Changing Verbs.

Stem or radical changing verbs.
Further types of irregular verbs are those which undergo some change in their root or stem vowel, but which otherwise follow the regular rules for the endings. Regretably there are very many such verbs and moreover there is no easy criteria for indicating whether a verb will be stem changing just from it's appearance. It is necessary to become acquainted with them by experience and usage. For this reason with these types of verbs, two examples of each have been provided.

With most of these stem changing verbs the changes will occur only in the present, the present subjunctive and the imperative forms. However there are also some which have stem changes in the preterite tense and consequently in the imperfect subjunctive forms which are drawn from the preterite. When you learnt the preterite you will easily know the imperfect subjunctive forms. In short: pay special attention to the present (which will generally give the key to the present subjunctive and the imperative) and the preterite (which always govern the imperfect subjunctive forms)

Examples of verbs with stem changes

24-S-Alentar-Acertar Verb ending in ar with stem vowel e.
Changes: to present, present subjunctive and imperative.
The e becomes ie when accented; but not where it is not accented.

25-S-Perder-Entender Verb ending in er with stem vowel e.
Changes: to present, present subjunctive and imperative.
The e becomes ie when accented; but not where it is not accented.

26-S-Aprobar-Acortar Verb ending in ar with stem vowel o.
Changes: to present, present subjunctive and imperative.
The stem vowel o becomes ue when accented; but not where it is not accented.

27-S-Morder-Remover Verb ending in er with stem vowel o.
Changes: to present, present subjunctive and imperative.
The stem vowel o becomes ue when accented; but not where it is not accented.

28-S-Oler Verb ending in er with stem vowel o. First letter is O.
Changes: to present, present subjunctive and imperative
1) O becomes ue when accented; but not where it is not accented.
2) H is inserted before the ue because Spanish words cannot begin with ue.

29-S-Discernir-Cernir Verb ending in ir with stem vowel e.
Changes: to present, present subjunctive and imperative
E becomes ie when accented; but not where it is not accented.
Compare with **30-S-Sentir**

30-S-Sentir-Advertir Verb ending in ir with stem vowel e.
Changes: to Present-Participle, present, preterite, present subjunctive, imperfect subjunctive and imperative.
1) E becomes ie when accented.
2) There is a further change in the preterite (and in the two imperfect subjunctive forms which are drawn from the preterite) and in the present subjunctive, the imperative and in the Present-Participle as follows. When the stem e is not accented, the e becomes i if the next

69

syllable contains a vowel other than just i on it's own (in other words if followed by two vowels or by a).
3) Compare with **29-S-Discernir**

31-S-Servir-Competir Verb ending in ir where the stem vowel is e.
Changes: to Present-Participle, present, present subjunctive, imperfect subjunctive and imperative.
1) In the present, the present subjunctive, and the imperative, the e becomes i when the i is accented, or when followed by a.
2) In the preterite (and in the two imperfect subjunctive forms which are drawn from the preterite) and the Present-Participle: the e becomes i when the stem e is not accented and the next syllable contains a vowel other than just i on it's own (ie: if followed by two vowels).

32-S-Adquirir-Inquirir Verb ending in ir with stem i
Changes: to present, present subjunctive and imperative
The i becomes ie when accented.

33-S-Dormir-Morir Verb ending in ir where the stem vowel is o.
Changes: to participles, present, preterite, present subjunctive, imperfect subjunctive and imperative.
1) In the present, the present subjunctive, and the imperative, the o becomes ue when the o is accented, or when followed by a.
2) In the preterite (and in the two imperfect subjunctive forms which are drawn from the preterite) and the Present-Participle: the o becomes u when the stem o is not accented and the next syllable contains a vowel other than just i on it's own (ie: if followed by two vowels).

34-S-Jugar Verb ending in gar where the stem vowel is u.
Changes: to present, preterite, present subjunctive and imperative
1) In the present, the present subjunctive, and the imperative, the u becomes ue when the u is accented, or when followed by a.
2) In the preterite: the present subjunctive, and the imperative, g becomes gu before e, following the rule in 7-O-Pagar.

35-S-Reir-Freir Verb ending in eir (nb the stem vowel is e).
Changes: to Present-Participle, the present, preterite, present subjunctive, imperfect subjunctive and imperative
1) As with 27-S-Servir, in the present, the present subjunctive, and the imperative, the e becomes i when the i is accented, or when followed by a.
2) As with 27-S-Servir, in the preterite (and in the two imperfect subjunctive forms which are drawn from the preterite) and the Present-Participle: the e becomes i when the stem e is not accented and the next syllable contains a vowel other than just i on it's own (ie: if followed by two vowels).
3) In both 1) and 2), when the stem vowel e changes to i, the i of the terminations beginning with ie and io lose the i (ie: not a double i). Hence the Present-Participle is riendo (not reiendo or riiendo)

36-S-Colegir-Elegir Verb ending in egir. (ie both gir and stem vowel e)
Changes: to Present-Participle, the present, preterite, present subjunctive, imperfect subjunctive and imperative
1) As with 10-O-Dirigir the g changes to j before a or o.
2) As with 27-S-Servir: in the present, the present subjunctive, and the imperative, the e becomes i when the i is accented, or when followed by a.
3) As with 27-S-Servir: in the preterite (and in the two imperfect subjunctive forms which are drawn from the preterite) and the Present-Participle: the e becomes i when the stem e is not accented and the next syllable contains a vowel other than just i on it's own (ie: if followed by two vowels.)

Verbs with stress changes. (Verbs ending in uar or iar or which have u or i in their stem)

Verbs which have two vowels next to one another, generally have the accent on the strong vowel; in other words on the a, e or o; the letters u and i being the weak vowels. However this is not invariable.

A number verbs with the endings uar and iar, or which have u or i in their stem, may place the stress on the u or on the i as follows: namely in the yo, tu, él, and ellos forms (ie all persons other than nosotros and vosotros) of the present indicative, the present subjunctive, and the imperative.

Typical verbs like this are:

90-Ú/Í-Evaluar, 91-Ú/Í-Ampliar, 92-Ú/Í-Aullar, 96-Ú/Í-Reunir, 94-Ú/Í-Rehusar (the h is silent so in effect eu), **93-Ú/Í-Airar, 95-Ú/Í-Prohibir** (silent h so in effect oi).

Verbs with mixed types of irregularities: ie those with conjugations derived from more than one of the variants described.

Several verbs with mixed types of irregularities are included with the full conjugations examples of verbs with orthographic or euphonic changes and verbs with Stem or radical changes. See: **6-O-Henchir, 21-O-Instruir, 22-O-Argüir, 23-O-Caer, 28-S-Oler, and 36-S-Colegir-Elegir.**

Other verbs with mixed irregularities include: **80-M-Agorar, 81-M-Almorzar, 82-M-Avergonzar, 83-M-Ceñir, 84-M-Colgar, 85-M-Empezar, 86-M-Forzar, 87-M-Regar, 88-M-Seguir, 89-M-Trocar,**

Part Two: Examples of Every Different Spanish Verb Type Fully Conjugated

Chapter 22.
104 Fully Conjugated Types of Spanish Verbs. All the model verbs you need to be able to conjugate any and every Spanish verb.

Key to abbreviations:
R= Regular
O= Changes mostly Orthographic/Euphonic
S= Stem changes
RF= Reflexive
I= Irregular
M= Mixed changes/irregularities
Ú/Í= Stem U or stem I verb with stress changes
DC= Conjugation derived from some other verb
Past-P= Past-Participle
Pres P= Present-Participle
O/W = Otherwise
D= Defective verb. Only available in some conjugations.

List of verbs for which fully conjugated models are provided.

Models of fully conjugated Regular verbs	
1-R-Hablar	2-R-Beber
3-R-Discutir	

Models of fully conjugated verbs with changes mostly Orthographic and/or Euphonic	
4-O-Bullir-Empeller	5-O-Bruñir-Tañer
6-O-Henchir	7-O-Rezar
8-O-Creer	9-O-Tocar
10-O-Pagar	11-O-Averiguar

12-O-Escoger	13-O-Dirigir
14-O-Distinguir	15-O-Delinquir
16-O-Vencer	17-O-Esparcir
18-O-Conocer	19-O-Lucir
20-M-Producir	21-O-Instruir
22-O-Argüir	23-O-Caer

Models of fully conjugated examples verbs with Stem changes

24-S-Alentar-Acertar	25-S-Perder-Entender
26-S-Aprobar-Acortar	27-S-Morder-Remover
28-S-Oler	29-S-Discernir-Cernir
30-S-Sentir-Advertir	31-S-Servir-Competir
32-S-Adquirir-Inquirir	33-S-Dormir-Morir
34-S-Jugar	35-S-Reir-Freir
36-S-Colegir-Elegir	

Models of fully conjugated Reflexive Verbs

37-R-RF-Abrirse	38-R-RF-Alejarse
39-I-RF-Caerse	40-S-RF-Convertirse
41-S-RF-Defenderse	42-S-RF-Despedirse
43-S-RF-Desvestirse	44-I-RF-Detenerse
45-O-RF-Dirigirse	46-S-RF-Divertirse
47-R-RF-Inscribirse	48-I-RF-Irse
49-R-RF-Levantarse	50-S-RF-Morderse
51-I-RF-Ponerse	52-S-RF-Reírse
53-S-RF-Sentarse	54-S-RF-Sentirse

Models of fully conjugated completely Irregular Verbs

55-I-Andar	56-I-Asir
57-I-Caber	58-I-Cocer
59-I-Dar	60-I-Decir
61-I-Errar	62-I-Estar
63-I-Haber_and 63-I-RF-Haber	64-I-Hacer
65-I-Ir	66-I-Oir
67-I-Poder	68-I-Poner
69-I-Querer	70-I-Roer
71-I-Saber	72-I-Salir
73-I-Satisfacer	74-I-Ser
75-I-Tener	76-I-Traer
77-I-Valer	78-I-Venir
79-I-Ver	

Models of fully conjugated verbs with mixed irregularities

80-M-Agorar	81-M-Almorzar
82-M-Avergonzar	83-M-Ceñir
84-M-Colgar	85-M-Empezar
86-M-Forzar	87-M-Regar
88-M-Seguir	89-M-Trocar

Models of fully conjugated Uar, Iar, and stem U and stem I verbs with stress changes

90-Ú/Í-Evaluar	91-Ú/Í-Ampliar
92-Ú/Í-Aullar	93-Ú/Í-Airar
94-Ú/Í-Rehusar	95-Ú/Í-Prohibir
96-Ú/Í-Reunir	97-Ú/Í-Atraillar

Models of fully conjugated verbs with conjugation derived from some other irregular verb

98-DC-Deshacer	conjugated same way as Hacer
99-DC-Componer	conjugated same way as Poner
100-DC-Sobresalir	conjugated same way as Salir
104-DC-Equivaler	conjugated same way as Valer
102-DC-Retraer	conjugated same way as Retraer
103-DC-Convenir	conjugated same way as Venir
104-DC-Prever	conjugated same way as Ver

Regular AR verbs
1-R-Hablar

Verb infinitive	Participles	Imperfect-subjunctive 1
Hablar, to talk	hablado: hablando	yo hablara
		tú hablaras
Present	**Future**	él hablara
yo hablo	yo hablaré	nos'os habláramos
tú hablas	tú hablarás	vos'os hablarais
él habla	él hablará	ellos hablaran
nos'os hablamos	nos'os hablaremos	
vos'os habláis	vos'os hablaréis	**Imp'fect-sub've 2**
ellos hablan	ellos hablarán	yo hablase
		tú hablases
Imperfect	**Conditional**	él hablase
yo hablaba	yo hablaría	nos'os hablásemos
tú hablabas	tú hablarías	vos'os hablaseis
él hablaba	él hablaría	ellos hablasen
nos'os hablábamos	nos'os hablaríamos	
vos'os hablabais	vos'os hablaríais	**Imperative -Do**
ellos hablaban	ellos hablarían	(tú) habla
		(él) hable
Preterite	**Present subj've**	(nos'os) hablemos
yo hablé	yo hable	(vos'os) hablad
tú hablaste	tú hables	(ellos) hablen
él habló	él hable	
nos'os hablamos	nos'os hablemos	**Imperative-Don't**
vos'os hablasteis	vos'os habléis	no hables
ellos hablaron	ellos hablen	no hable
		no hablemos
Comp'nd tenses- 63-I-Haber +Past-P		no habléis
		no hablen

77

Regular ER verbs
2-R-Beber

Verb infinitive	Participles	Imperfect-subjunctive 1
Beber, to drink	bebido: bebiendo	yo bebiera
		tú bebieras
Present	**Future**	él bebiera
yo bebo	yo beberé	nos'os bebiéramos
tú bebes	tú beberás	vos'os bebierais
él bebe	él beberá	ellos bebieran
nos'os bebemos	nos'os beberemos	
vos'os bebéis	vos'os beberéis	**Imp'fect-sub've 2**
ellos beben	ellos beberán	yo bebiese
		tú bebieses
Imperfect	**Conditional**	él bebiese
yo bebía	yo bebería	nos'os bebiésemos
tú bebías	tú beberías	vos'os bebieseis
él bebía	él bebería	ellos bebiesen
nos'os bebíamos	nos'os beberíamos	
vos'os bebíais	vos'os beberíais	**Imperative-Do**
ellos bebían	ellos beberían	(tú) bebe
		(él) beba
Preterite	**Present subj've**	(nos'os) bebamos
yo bebí	yo beba	(vos'os) bebed
tú bebiste	tú bebas	(ellos) beban
él bebió	él beba	
nos'os bebimos	nos'os bebamos	**Imperative-Don't**
vos'os bebisteis	vos'os bebáis	no bebas
ellos bebieron	ellos beban	no beba
		no bebamos
Comp'nd tenses- 63-I-Haber +Past-P		no bebáis
		no beban

78

Regular IR verbs
3-R-Discutir

Verb infinitive	Participles	Imperfect-subjunctive 1
Discutir, to discuss, to argue	discutido: discutiendo	yo discutiera
		tú discutieras
Present	**Future**	él discutiera
yo discuto	yo discutiré	nos'os discutiéramos
tú discutes	tú discutirás	vos'os discutierais
él discute	él discutirá	ellos discutieran
nos'os discutimos	nos'os discutiremos	
vos'os discutís	vos'os discutiréis	**Imp'fect-sub've 2**
ellos discuten	ellos discutirán	yo discutiese
		tú discutieses
Imperfect	**Conditional**	él discutiese
yo discutía	yo discutiría	nos'os discutiésemos
tú discutías	tú discutirías	vos'os discutieseis
él discutía	él discutiría	ellos discutiesen
nos'os discutíamos	nos'os discutiríamos	
vos'os discutíais	vos'os discutiríais	**Imperative-Do**
ellos discutían	ellos discutirían	(tú) discute
		(él) discuta
Preterite	**Present subj've**	(nos'os) discutamos
yo discutí	yo discuta	(vos'os) discutid
tú discutiste	tú discutas	(ellos) discutan
él discutió	él discuta	
nos'os discutimos	nos'os discutamos	**Imperative-Don't**
vos'os discutisteis	vos'os discutáis	no discutas
ellos discutieron	ellos discutan	no discuta
		no discutamos
Comp'nd tenses- 63-I-Haber +Past-P		no discutáis
		no discutan

4(a)-O-Bullir Comment/explanation: See Chapter 21

Verb infinitive	Participles	Imperfect-subjunctive 1
Bullir: to boil, to stir	bullido: bullendo	yo bullera
		tú bulleras
Present	**Future**	él bullera
yo bullo	yo bulliré	nos'os bulléramos
tú bulles	tú bullirás	vos'os bullerais
él bulle	él bullirá	ellos bulleran
nos'os bullimos	nos'os bulliremos	
vos'os bullís	vos'os bulliréis	**Imp'fect-sub've 2**
ellos bullen	ellos bullirán	yo bullese
		tú bulleses
Imperfect	**Conditional**	él bullese
yo bullía	yo bulliría	nos'os bullésemos
tú bullías	tú bullirías	vos'os bulleseis
él bullía	él bulliría	ellos bullesen
nos'os bullíamos	nos'os bulliríamos	
vos'os bullíais	vos'os bulliríais	**Imperative-Do**
ellos bullían	ellos bullirían	(tú) bulle
		(él) bulla
Preterite	**Present subj've**	(nos'os) bullamos
yo bullí	yo bulla	(vos'os) bullid
tú bulliste	tú bullas	(ellos) bullan
él bulló	él bulla	
nos'os bullimos	nos'os bullamos	**Imperative-Don't**
vos'os bullisteis	vos'os bulláis	no bullas
ellos bulleron	ellos bullan	no bulla
		no bullamos
Comp'nd tenses- 63-I-Haber +Past-P		no bulláis
		no bullan

4(b)-O-Empeller Comment/explanation: See Chapter 21

Verb infinitive	Participles	Imperfect-subjunctive 1
Empeller, (o/w empellar) to push, to shove	empellido: empellendo	yo empellera
		tú empelleras
Present	**Future**	él empellera
yo empello	yo empelleré	nos'os empelléramos
tú empelles	tú empellerás	vos'os empellerais
él empelle	él empellerá	ellos empelleran
nos'os empellemos	nos'os empelleremos	
vos'os empelléis	vos'os empelleréis	**Imp'fect-sub've 2**
ellos empellen	ellos empellerán	yo empellese
		tú empelleses
Imperfect	**Conditional**	él empellese
yo empellía	yo empellería	nos'os empellésemos
tú empellías	tú empellerías	vos'os empelleseis
él empellía	él empellería	ellos empellesen
nos'os empelliamos	nos'os empelleríamos	
vos'os empellíais	vos'os empelleríais	**Imperative-Do**
ellos empellían	ellos empellerían	(tú) empelle
		(él) empella
Preterite	**Present subj've**	(nos'os) empellamos
yo empellí	yo empella	(vos'os) empelled
tú empellíste	tú empellas	(ellos) empellan
él empelló	él empella	
nos'os empellimos	nos'os empellamos	**Imperative-Don't**
vos'os empellísteis	vos'os empelláis	no empellas
ellos empelleron	ellos empellan	no empella
		no empellamos
Comp'nd tenses- 63-I-Haber +Past-P		no empelláis
		no empellan

81

5(a)-O-Bruñir Comment/explanation: See Chapter 21

Verb infinitive	Participles	Imperfect-subjunctive 1
Bruñir: to burnish	bruñido, bruñendo	yo bruñera
		tú bruñeras
Present	**Future**	él bruñera
yo bruño	yo bruñiré	nos'os bruñéramos
tú bruñes	tú bruñirás	vos'os bruñerais
él bruñe	él bruñirá	ellos bruñeran
nos'os bruñimos	nos'os bruñiremos	
vos'os bruñís	vos'os bruñiréis	**Imp'fect-sub've 2**
ellos bruñen	ellos bruñirán	yo bruñese
		tú bruñeses
Imperfect	**Conditional**	él bruñese
yo bruñía	yo bruñiría	nos'os bruñésemos
tú bruñías	tú bruñirías	vos'os bruñeseis
él bruñía	él bruñiría	ellos bruñesen
nos'os bruñíamos	nos'os bruñiríamos	
vos'os bruñíais	vos'os bruñiríais	**Imperative-Do**
ellos bruñían	ellos bruñirían	(tú) bruñe
		(él) bruña
Preterite	**Present subj've**	(nos'os)bruñamos
yo bruñí	yo bruña	(vos'os) bruñid
tú bruñiste	tú bruñas	(ellos) bruñan
él bruñó	él bruña	
nos'os bruñimos	nos'os bruñamos	**Imperative-Don't**
vos'os bruñisteis	vos'os bruñáis	no bruñas
ellos bruñeron	ellos bruñan	no bruña
		no bruñamos
Comp'nd tenses-63-I-Haber +Past-P		no bruñáis
		no bruñan

5(b)-O-Tañer Comment/explanation: See Chapter 21

Verb infinitive	Participles	Imperfect-subjunctive 1
Tañer, to play (ie music/sound)	tañido: tañendo	yo tañera
		tú tañeras
Present	**Future**	él tañera
yo taño	yo tañeré	nos'os tañéramos
tú tañes	tú tañerás	vos'os tañerais
él tañe	él tañerá	ellos tañeran
nos'os tañemos	nos'os tañeremos	
vos'os tañéis	vos'os tañeréis	**Imp'fect-sub've 2**
ellos tañen	ellos tañerán	yo tañese
		tú tañeses
Imperfect	**Conditional**	él tañese
yo tañía	yo tañería	nos'os tañésemos
tú tañías	tú tañerías	vos'os tañeseis
él tañía	él tañería	ellos tañesen
nos'os tañíamos	nos'os tañeríamos	
vos'os tañíais	vos'os tañeríais	**Imperative-Do**
ellos tañían	ellos tañerían	(tú) tañe
		(él) taña
Preterite	**Present subj've**	(nos'os) tañamos
yo tañí	yo taña	(vos'os) tañed
tú tañiste	tú tañas	(ellos) tañan
él tañó	él taña	
nos'os tañimos	nos'os tañamos	**Imperative-Don't**
vos'os tañisteis	vos'os tañáis	no tañas
ellos tañeron	ellos tañan	no taña
		no tañamos
Comp'nd tenses-63-I-Haber +Past-P		no tañáis
		no tañan

83

6-O-Henchir Comment/explanation: See Chapter 21

Verb infinitive	Participles	Imperfect-subjunctive 1
Henchir: to fill	henchido: hinchendo	yo hinchera
		tú hincheras
Present	**Future**	él hinchera
yo hincho	yo henchiré	nos'os hinchéramos
tú hinches	tú henchirás	vos'os hincherais
él hinche	él henchirá	ellos hincheran
nos'os henchimos	nos'os henchiremos	
vos'os henchís	vos'os henchiréis	**Imp'fect-sub've 2**
ellos hinchen	ellos henchirán	yo hinchese
		tú hincheses
Imperfect	**Conditional**	él hinchese
yo henchía	yo henchiría	nos'os hinchésemos
tú henchías	tú henchirías	vos'os hincheseis
él henchía	él henchiría	ellos hinchesen
nos'os henchíamos	nos'os henchiríamos	
vos'os henchíais	vos'os henchiríais	**Imperative-Do**
ellos henchían	ellos henchirían	(tú) hinche
		(él) hincha
Preterite	**Present subj've**	(nos'os) hinchamos
yo henchí	yo hincha	(vos'os) henchid
tú henchiste	tú hinchas	(ellos) hinchan
él hinchó	él hincha	
nos'os henchimos	nos'os hinchamos	**Imperative-Don't**
vos'os henchisteis	vos'os hincháis	no hinchas
ellos hincheron	ellos hinchan	no hincha
		no hinchamos
Comp'nd tenses- 63-I-Haber +Past-P		no hincháis
		no hinchan

7-O-Rezar Comment/explanation: See Chapter 21

Verb infinitive	Participles	Imperfect-subjunctive 1
Rezar: to pray	rezado: rezando	yo rezara
		tú rezaras
Present	**Future**	él rezara
yo rezo	yo rezaré	nos'os rezáramos
tú rezas	tú rezarás	vos'os rezarais
él reza	él rezará	ellos rezaran
nos'os rezamos	nos'os rezaremos	
vos'os rezáis	vos'os rezaréis	**Imp'fect-sub've 2**
ellos rezan	ellos rezarán	yo rezase
		tú rezases
Imperfect	**Conditional**	él rezase
yo rezaba	yo rezaría	nos'os rezásemos
tú rezabas	tú rezarías	vos'os rezaseis
él rezaba	él rezaría	ellos rezasen
nos'os rezábamos	nos'os rezaríamos	
vos'os rezabais	vos'os rezaríais	**Imperative-Do**
ellos rezaban	ellos rezarían	(tú) reza
		(él) rece
Preterite	**Present subj've**	(nos'os) recemos
yo recé	yo rece	(vos'os) rezad
tú rezaste	tú reces	(ellos) recen
él rezó	él rece	
nos'os rezamos	nos'os recemos	**Imperative-Don't**
vos'os rezasteis	vos'os recéis	no reces
ellos rezaron	ellos recen	no rece
		no recemos
Comp'nd tenses- 63-I-Haber +Past-P		no recéis
		no recen

85

8-O-Creer Comment/explanation: See Chapter 21

Verb infinitive	Participles	Imperfect-subjunctive 1
Creer: to believe.	creído: creyendo	yo creyera
		tú creyeras
Present	**Future**	él creyera
yo creo	yo creeré	nos'os creyéramos
tú crees	tú creerás	vos'os creyerais
él cree	él creerá	ellos creyeran
nos'os creemos	nos'os creeremos	
vos'os creéis	vos'os creeréis	**Imp'fect-sub've 2**
ellos creen	ellos creerán	yo creyese
		tú creyeses
Imperfect	**Conditional**	él creyese
yo creía	yo creería	nos'os creyésemos
tú creías	tú creerías	vos'os creyeseis
él creía	él creería	ellos creyesen
nos'os creíamos	nos'os creeríamos	
vos'os creíais	vos'os creeríais	**Imperative-Do**
ellos creían	ellos creerían	(tú) cree
		(él) crea
Preterite	**Present subj've**	(nos'os) creamos
yo creí	yo crea	(vos'os) creed
tú creíste	tú creas	(ellos) crean
él creyó	él crea	
nos'os creímos	nos'os creamos	**Imperative-Don't**
vos'os creísteis	vos'os creáis	no creas
ellos creyeron	ellos crean	no crea
		no creamos
Comp'nd tenses- 63-I-Haber +Past-P		no creáis
		no crean

9-O-Tocar Comment/explanation: See Chapter 21

Verb infinitive	Participles	Imperfect-subjunctive 1
Tocar: to touch, to play	tocado: tocando	yo tocara
		tú tocaras
Present	**Future**	él tocara
yo toco	yo tocaré	nos'os tocáramos
tú tocas	tú tocarás	vos'os tocarais
él toca	él tocará	ellos tocaran
nos'os tocamos	nos'os tocaremos	
vos'os tocáis	vos'os tocaréis	**Imp'fect-sub've 2**
ellos tocan	ellos tocarán	yo tocase
		tú tocases
Imperfect	**Conditional**	él tocase
yo tocaba	yo tocaría	nos'os tocásemos
tú tocabas	tú tocarías	vos'os tocaseis
él tocaba	él tocaría	ellos tocasen
nos'os tocábamos	nos'os tocaríamos	
vos'os tocabais	vos'os tocaríais	**Imperative-Do**
ellos tocaban	ellos tocarían	(tú) toca
		(él) toque
Preterite	**Present subj've**	(nos'os) toquemos
yo toqué	yo toque	(vos'os) tocad
tú tocaste	tú toques	(ellos) toquen
él tocó	él toque	
nos'os tocamos	nos'os toquemos	**Imperative-Don't**
vos'os tocasteis	vos'os toquéis	no toques
ellos tocaron	ellos toquen	no toque
		no toquemos
Comp'nd tenses- 63-I-Haber +Past-P		no toquéis
		no toquen

10-O-Pagar Comment/explanation: See Chapter 21

Verb infinitive	Participles	Imperfect-subjunctive 1
Pagar: to pay	pagado: pagando	yo pagara
		tú pagaras
Present	**Future**	él pagara
yo pago	yo pagaré	nos'os pagáramos
tú pagas	tú pagarás	vos'os pagarais
él paga	él pagará	ellos pagaran
nos'os pagamos	nos'os pagaremos	
vos'os pagáis	vos'os pagaréis	**Imp'fect-sub've 2**
ellos pagan	ellos pagarán	yo pagase
		tú pagases
Imperfect	**Conditional**	él pagase
yo pagaba	yo pagaría	nos'os pagásemos
tú pagabas	tú pagarías	vos'os pagaseis
él pagaba	él pagaría	ellos pagasen
nos'os pagábamos	nos'os pagaríamos	
vos'os pagabais	vos'os pagaríais	**Imperative-Do**
ellos pagaban	ellos pagarían	(tú) paga
		(él) pague
Preterite	**Present subj've**	(nos'os) paguemos
yo pagué	yo pague	(vos'os) pagad
tú pagaste	tú pagues	(ellos) paguen
él pagó	él pague	
nos'os pagamos	nos'os paguemos	**Imperative-Don't**
vos'os pagasteis	vos'os paguéis	no pagues
ellos pagaron	ellos paguen	no pague
		no paguemos
Comp'nd tenses- 63-I-Haber +Past-P		no paguéis
		no paguen

88

11-O-Averiguar Comment/explanation: See Chapter 21

Verb infinitive	Participles	Imperfect-subjunctive 1
Averiguar: to ascertain	averiguado: averiguando	yo averiguara
		tú averiguaras
Present	**Future**	él averiguara
yo averiguo	yo averiguaré	nos'os averiguáramos
tú averiguas	tú averiguarás	vos'os averiguarais
él averigua	él averiguará	ellos averiguaran
nos'os averiguamos	nos'os averiguaremos	
vos'os averiguáis	vos'os averiguaréis	**Imp'fect-sub'ive2**
ellos averiguan	ellos averiguarán	yo averiguase
		tú averiguases
Imperfect	**Conditional**	él averiguase
yo averiguaba	yo averiguaría	nos'os averiguásemos
tú averiguabas	tú averiguarías	vos'os averiguaseis
él averiguaba	él averiguaría	ellos averiguasen
nos'os averiguábamos	nos'os averiguaríamos	
vos'os averiguabais	vos'os averiguaríais	**Imperative-Do**
ellos averiguaban	ellos averiguarían	(tú) averigua
		(él) averigüe
Preterite	**Present subj've**	(nos'os) averigüemos
yo averigüé	yo averigüe	(vos'os) averiguad
tú averiguaste	tú averigües	(ellos) averigüen
él averiguó	él averigüe	
nos'os averiguamos	nos'os averigüemos	**Imperative-Don't**
vos'os averiguasteis	vos'os averigüéis	no averigües
ellos averiguaron	ellos averigüen	no averigüe
		no averigüemos
Comp'nd tenses- 63-I-Haber +Past-P		no averigüéis
		no averigüen

89

12-O-Escoger Comment/explanation: See Chapter 21

Verb infinitive	Participles	Imperfect-subjunctive 1
Escoger: to choose	escogido: escogiendo	yo escogiera
		tú escogieras
Present	**Future**	él escogiera
yo escojo	yo escogeré	nos'os escogiéramos
tú escoges	tú escogerás	vos'os escogierais
él escoge	él escogerá	ellos escogieran
nos'os escogemos	nos'os escogeremos	
vos'os escogéis	vos'os escogeréis	**Imp'fect-sub've 2**
ellos escogen	ellos escogerán	yo escogiese
		tú escogieses
Imperfect	**Conditional**	él escogiese
yo escogía	yo escogería	nos'os escogiésemos
tú escogías	tú escogerías	vos'os escogieseis
él escogía	él escogería	ellos escogiesen
nos'os escogíamos	nos'os escogeríamos	
vos'os escogíais	vos'os escogeríais	**Imperative-Do**
ellos escogían	ellos escogerían	(tú) escoge
		(él) escoja
Preterite	**Present subj've**	(nos'os) escojamos
yo escogí	yo escoja	(vos'os) escoged
tú escogiste	tú escojas	(ellos) escojan
él escogió	él escoja	
nos'os escogimos	nos'os escojamos	**Imperative-Don't**
vos'os escogisteis	vos'os escojáis	no escojas
ellos escogieron	ellos escojan	no escoja
		no escojamos
Comp'nd tenses- 63-I-Haber +Past-P		no escojáis
		no escojan

13-O-Dirigir Comment/explanation: See Chapter 21

Verb infinitive	Participles	Imperfect-subjunctive 1
Dirigir: to guide	dirigido: dirigiendo	yo dirigiera
		tú dirigieras
Present	**Future**	él dirigiera
yo dirijo	yo dirigiré	nos'os dirigiéramos
tú diriges	tú dirigirás	vos'os dirigierais
él dirige	él dirigirá	ellos dirigieran
nos'os dirigimos	nos'os dirigiremos	
vos'os dirigís	vos'os dirigiréis	**Imp'fect-sub've 2**
ellos dirigen	ellos dirigirán	yo dirigiese
		tú dirigieses
Imperfect	**Conditional**	él dirigiese
yo dirigía	yo dirigiría	nos'os dirigiésemos
tú dirigías	tú dirigirías	vos'os dirigieseis
él dirigía	él dirigiría	ellos dirigiesen
nos'os dirigíamos	nos'os dirigiríamos	
vos'os dirigíais	vos'os dirigiríais	**Imperative-Do**
ellos dirigían	ellos dirigirían	(tú) dirige
		(él) dirija
Preterite	**Present subj've**	(nos'os) dirijamos
yo dirigí	yo dirija	(vos'os) dirigid
tú dirigiste	tú dirijas	(ellos) dirijan
él dirigió	él dirija	
nos'os dirigimos	nos'os dirijamos	**Imperative-Don't**
vos'os dirigisteis	vos'os dirijáis	no dirijas
ellos dirigieron	ellos dirijan	no dirija
		no dirijamos
Comp'nd tenses- 63-I-Haber +Past-P		no dirijáis
		no dirijan

14-O-Distinguir Comment/explanation: See Chapter 21

Verb infinitive	Participles	Imperfect-subjunctive 1
Distinguir:	distinguido, distinguiendo	yo distinguiera
		tú distinguieras
Present	**Future**	él distinguiera
yo distingo	yo distinguiré	nos'os distinguiéramos
tú distingues	tú distinguirás	vos'os distinguierais
él distingue	él distinguirá	ellos distinguieran
nos'os distinguimos	nos'os distinguiremos	
vos'os distinguís	vos'os distinguiréis	**Imp'fect-sub've 2**
ellos distinguen	ellos distinguirán	yo distinguiese
		tú distinguieses
Imperfect	**Conditional**	él distinguiese
yo distinguía	yo distinguiría	nos'os distinguiésemos
tú distinguías	tú distinguirías	vos'os distinguieseis
él distinguía	él distinguiría	ellos distinguiesen
nos'os distinguíamos	nos'os distinguiríamos	
vos'os distinguíais	vos'os distinguiríais	**Imperative-Do**
ellos distinguían	ellos distinguirían	(tú) distingue
		(él) distinga
Preterite	**Present subj've**	(nos'os) distingamos
yo distinguí	yo distinga	(vos'os) distinguid
tú distinguiste	tú distingas	(ellos) distingan
él distinguió	él distinga	
nos'os distinguimos	nos'os distingamos	**Imperative-Don't**
vos'os distinguisteis	vos'os distingáis	no distingas
ellos distinguieron	ellos distingan	no distinga
		no distingamos
Comp'nd tenses- 63-I-Haber +Past-P		no distingáis
		no distingan

15-O-Delinquir Comment/explanation: See Chapter 21

Verb infinitive	Participles	Imperfect-subjunctive 1
delinquir to transgress, to sin	delinquido: delinquiendo	yo delinquiera
		tú delinquieras
Present	**Future**	él delinquiera
yo delinco	yo delinquiré	nos'os delinquiéramos
tú delinques	tú delinquirás	vos'os delinquierais
él delinque	él delinquirá	ellos delinquieran
nos'os delinquimos	nos'os delinquiremos	
vos'os delinquís	vos'os delinquiréis	**Imp'fect-sub've 2**
ellos delinquen	ellos delinquirán	yo delinquiese
		tú delinquieses
Imperfect	**Conditional**	él delinquiese
yo delinquía	yo delinquiría	nos'os delinquiésemos
tú delinquías	tú delinquirías	vos'os delinquieseis
él delinquía	él delinquiría	ellos delinquiesen
nos'os delinquíamos	nos'os delinquiríamos	
vos'os delinquíais	vos'os delinquiríais	**Imperative-Do**
ellos delinquían	ellos delinquirían	(tú) delinque
		(él) delinca
Preterite	**Present subj've**	(nos'os) delincamos
yo delinquí	yo delinca	(vos'os) delinquid
tú delinquiste	tú delincas	(ellos) delincan
él delinquió	él delinca	
nos'os delinquimos	nos'os delincamos	**Imperative-Don't**
vos'os delinquisteis	vos'os delincáis	no delincas
ellos delinquieron	ellos delincan	no delinca
		no delincamos
Comp'nd tenses- 63-I-Haber +Past-P		no delincáis
		no delincan

93

16-O-Vencer Comment/explanation: See Chapter 21

Verb infinitive	Participles	Imperfect-subjunctive 1
Vencer, to conquer	vencido: venciendo	yo venciera
		tú vencieras
Present	**Future**	él venciera
yo venzo	yo venceré	nos'os venciéramos
tú vences	tú vencerás	vos'os vencierais
él vence	él vencerá	ellos vencieran
nos'os vencemos	nos'os venceremos	
vos'os vencéis	vos'os venceréis	**Imp'fect-sub've 2**
ellos vencen	ellos vencerán	yo venciese
		tú vencieses
Imperfect	**Conditional**	él venciese
yo vencía	yo vencería	nos'os venciésemos
tú vencías	tú vencerías	vos'os vencieseis
él vencía	él vencería	ellos venciesen
nos'os vencíamos	nos'os venceríamos	
vos'os vencíais	vos'os venceríais	**Imperative-Do**
ellos vencían	ellos vencerían	(tú) vence
		(él) venza
Preterite	**Present subj've**	(nos'os) venzamos
yo vencí	yo venza	(vos'os) venced
tú venciste	tú venzas	(ellos) venzan
él venció	él venza	
nos'os vencimos	nos'os venzamos	**Imperative-Don't**
vos'os vencisteis	vos'os venzáis	no venzas
ellos vencieron	ellos venzan	no venza
		no venzamos
Comp'nd tenses- 63-I-Haber +Past-P		no venzáis
		no venzan

17-O-Esparcir Comment/explanation: See Chapter 21

Verb infinitive	Participles	Imperfect-subjunctive 1
Esparcir, to scatter	esparcido: esparciendo	yo esparciera
		tú esparcieras
Present	**Future**	él esparciera
yo esparzo	yo esparciré	nos'os esparciéramos
tú esparces	tú esparcirás	vos'os esparcierais
él esparce	él esparcirá	ellos esparcieran
nos'os esparcimos	nos'os esparciremos	
vos'os esparcís	vos'os esparciréis	**Imp'fect-sub've 2**
ellos esparzen	ellos esparcirán	yo esparciese
		tú esparcieses
Imperfect	**Conditional**	él esparciese
yo esparcía	yo esparciría	nos'os esparciésemos
tú esparcías	tú esparcirías	vos'os esparcieseis
él esparcía	él esparciría	ellos esparciesen
nos'os esparcíamos	nos'os esparciríamos	
vos'os esparcíais	vos'os esparciríais	**Imperative-Do**
ellos esparcían	ellos esparcirían	(tú) esparce
		(él) esparza
Preterite	**Present subj've**	(nos'os) esparzamos
yo esparcí	yo esparza	(vos'os) esparcid
tú esparciste	tú esparzas	(ellos) esparzan
él esparció	él esparza	
nos'os esparcimos	nos'os esparzamos	**Imperative-Don't**
vos'os esparcisteis	vos'os esparzáis	no esparzas
ellos esparcieron	ellos esparzan	no esparza
		no esparzamos
Comp'nd tenses- 63-I-Haber +Past-P		no esparzáis
		no esparzan

95

18-O-Conocer Comment/explanation: See Chapter 21

Verb infinitive	Participles	Imperfect-subjunctive 1
Conocer, to know	conocido: conociendo	yo conociera
		tú conocieras
Present	**Future**	él conociera
yo conozco	yo conoceré	nos'os conociéramos
tú conoces	tú conocerás	vos'os conocierais
él conoce	él conocerá	ellos conocieran
nos'os conocemos	nos'os conoceremos	
vos'os conocéis	vos'os conoceréis	**Imp'fect-sub've 2**
ellos conocen	ellos conocerán	yo conociese
		tú conocieses
Imperfect	**Conditional**	él conociese
yo conocía	yo conocería	nos'os conociésemos
tú conocías	tú conocerías	vos'os conocieseis
él conocía	él conocería	ellos conociesen
nos'os conocíamos	nos'os conoceríamos	
vos'os conocíais	vos'os conoceríais	**Imperative-Do**
ellos conocían	ellos conocerían	(tú) conoce
		(él) conozca
Preterite	**Present subj've**	(nos'os) conozcamos
yo conocí	yo conozca	(vos'os) conoced
tú conociste	tú conozcas	(ellos) conozcan
él conoció	él conozca	
nos'os conocimos	nos'os conozcamos	**Imperative-Don't**
vos'os conocisteis	vos'os conozcáis	no conozcas
ellos conocieron	ellos conozcan	no conozca
		no conozcamos
Comp'nd tenses- 63-I-Haber +Past-P		no conozcáis
		no conozcan

19-O-Lucir Comment/explanation: See Chapter 21

Verb infinitive	Participles	Imperfect-subjunctive 1
Lucir, to shine	lucido: luciendo	yo luciera
		tú lucieras
Present	**Future**	él luciera
yo luzco	yo luciré	nos'os luciéramos
tú luces	tú lucirás	vos'os lucierais
él luce	él lucirá	ellos lucieran
nos'os lucimos	nos'os luciremos	
vos'os lucís	vos'os luciréis	**Imp'fect-sub've 2**
ellos lucen	ellos lucirán	yo luciese
		tú lucieses
Imperfect	**Conditional**	él luciese
yo lucía	yo luciría	nos'os luciésemos
tú lucías	tú lucirías	vos'os lucieseis
él lucía	él luciría	ellos luciesen
nos'os lucíamos	nos'os luciríamos	
vos'os lucíais	vos'os luciríais	**Imperative-Do**
ellos lucían	ellos lucirían	**Imperative-Do**
		(tú) luce
Preterite	**Present subj've**	(él) luzca
yo lucí	yo luzca	(nos'os) luzcamos
tú luciste	tú luzcas	(vos'os) lucid
él lució	él luzca	(ellos) luzcan
nos'os lucimos	nos'os luzcamos	**Imperative-Don't**
vos'os lucisteis	vos'os luzcáis	no luzcas
ellos lucieron	ellos luzcan	no luzca
		no luzcamos
Comp'nd tenses- 63-I-Haber +Past-P		no luzcáis
		no luzcan

97

20-M-Producir Comment/explanation: See Chapter 21

Verb infinitive	Participles	Imperfect-subjunctive 1
Producir, to produce	producido: produciendo	yo produjera
		tú produjeras
Present	**Future**	él produjera
yo produzco	yo produciré	nos'os produjéramos
tú produces	tú producirás	vos'os produjerais
él produce	él producirá	ellos produjeran
nos'os producimos	nos'os produciremos	
vos'os producís	vos'os produciréis	**Imp'fect-sub've 2**
ellos producen	ellos producirán	yo produjese
		tú produjeses
Imperfect	**Conditional**	él produjese
yo producía	yo produciría	nos'os produjésemos
tú producías	tú producirías	vos'os produjeseis
él producía	él produciría	ellos produjesen
nos'os producíamos	nos'os produciríamos	
vos'os producíais	vos'os produciríais	**Imperative-Do**
ellos producían	ellos producirían	(tú) produce
		(él) produzca
Preterite	**Present subj've**	(nos'os) produzcamos
yo produje	yo produzca	(vos'os) producid
tú produjiste	tú produzcas	(ellos) produzcan
él produjo	él produzca	
nos'os produjimos	nos'os produzcamos	**Imperative-Don't**
vos'os produjisteis	vos'os produzcáis	no produzcas
ellos produjeron	ellos produzcan	no produzca
		no produzcamos
Comp'nd tenses- 63-I-Haber +Past-P		no produzcáis
		no produzcan

21-O-Instruir Comment/explanation: See Chapter 24

Verb infinitive	Participles	Imperfect-subjunctive 1
Instruir, to instruct	instruido: instruyendo	yo instruyera
		tú instruyeras
Present	**Future**	él instruyera
yo instruyo	yo instruiré	nos'os instruyéramos
tú instruyes	tú instruirás	vos'os instruyerais
él instruye	él instruirá	ellos instruyeran
nos'os instruimos	nos'os instruiremos	
vos'os instruís	vos'os instruiréis	**Imp'fect-sub've 2**
ellos instruyen	ellos instruirán	yo instruyese
		tú instruyeses
Imperfect	**Conditional**	él instruyese
yo instruía	yo instruiría	nos'os instruyésemos
tú instruías	tú instruirías	vos'os instruyeseis
él instruía	él instruiría	ellos instruyesen
nos'os instruíamos	nos'os instruiríamos	
vos'os instruíais	vos'os instruiríais	**Imperative-Do**
ellos instruían	ellos instruirían	(tú) instruye
		(él) instruya
Preterite	**Present subj've**	(nos'os) instruyamos
yo instruí	yo instruya	(vos'os) instruid
tú instruiste	tú instruyas	(ellos) instruyan
él instruyó	él instruya	
nos'os instruimos	nos'os instruyamos	**Imperative-Don't**
vos'os instruisteis	vos'os instruyáis	no instruyas
ellos instruyeron	ellos instruyan	no instruya
		no instruyamos
Comp'nd tenses- 63-I-Haber +Past-P		no instruyáis
		no instruyan

22-O-Argüir Comment/explanation: See Chapter 24

Verb infinitive	Participles	Imperfect-subjunctive 1
Argüir, to argue	argüido: arguyendo	yo arguyera
		tú arguyeras
Present	**Future**	él arguyera
yo arguyo	yo argüiré	nos'os arguyéramos
tú arguyes	tú argüirás	vos'os arguyerais
él arguye	él argüirá	ellos arguyeran
nos'os argüimos	nos'os argüiremos	
vos'os argüís	vos'os argüiréis	**Imp'fect-sub've 2**
ellos arguyen	ellos argüirán	yo arguyese
		tú arguyeses
Imperfect	**Conditional**	él arguyese
yo argüía	yo argüiría	nos'os arguyésemos
tú argüías	tú argüirías	vos'os arguyeseis
él argüía	él argüiría	ellos arguyesen
nos'os argüíamos	nos'os argüiríamos	
vos'os argüíais	vos'os argüiríais	**Imperative-Do**
ellos argüían	ellos argüirían	(tú) arguye
		(él) arguya
Preterite	**Present subj've**	(nos'os) arguyamos
yo argüí	yo arguya	(vos'os) argüid
tú argüiste	tú arguyas	(ellos) arguyan
él arguyó	él arguya	
nos'os argüimos	nos'os arguyamos	**Imperative-Don't**
vos'os argüisteis	vos'os arguyáis	no arguyas
ellos arguyeron	ellos arguyan	no arguya
		no arguyamos
Comp'nd tenses- 63-I-Haber +Past-P		no arguyáis
		no arguyan

23-O-Caer Comment/explanation: See Chapter 24

Verb infinitive	Participles	Imperfect-subjunctive 1
Caer, to fall	caído: cayendo	yo cayera
		tú cayeras
Present	**Future**	él cayera
yo caigo	yo caeré	nos'os cayéramos
tú caes	tú caerás	vos'os cayerais
él cae	él caerá	ellos cayeran
nos'os caemos	nos'os caeremos	
vos'os caéis	vos'os caeréis	**Imp'fect-sub've 2**
ellos caen	ellos caerán	yo cayese
		tú cayeses
Imperfect	**Conditional**	él cayese
yo caía	yo caería	nos'os cayésemos
tú caías	tú caerías	vos'os cayeseis
él caía	él caería	ellos cayesen
nos'os caíamos	nos'os caeríamos	
vos'os caíais	vos'os caeríais	**Imperative-Do**
ellos caían	ellos caerían	(tú) cae
		(él) caiga
Preterite	**Present subj've**	(nos'os) caigamos
yo caí	yo caiga	(vos'os) caed
tú caíste	tú caigas	(ellos) caigan
él cayó	él caiga	
nos'os caímos	nos'os caigamos	**Imperative-Don't**
vos'os caísteis	vos'os caigáis	no caigas
ellos cayeron	ellos caigan	no caiga
		no caigamos
Comp'nd tenses- 63-I-Haber +Past-P		no caigáis
		no caigan

24(a)-S-Alentar Comment/explanation: See Chapter 24

Verb infinitive	Participles	Imperfect-subjunctive 1
Alentar, to to encourage, to give heart to	alentado: alentando	yo alentara
		tú alentaras
Present	**Future**	él alentara
yo aliento	yo alentaré	nos'os alentáramos
tú alientas	tú alentarás	vos'os alentarais
él alienta	él alentará	ellos alentaran
nos'os alentamos	nos'os alentaremos	
vos'os alentáis	vos'os alentaréis	**Imp'fect-sub've 2**
ellos alientan	ellos alentarán	yo alentase
		tú alentases
Imperfect	**Conditional**	él alentase
yo alentaba	yo alentaría	nos'os alentásemos
tú alentabas	tú alentarías	vos'os alentaseis
él alentaba	él alentaría	ellos alentasen
nos'os alentábamos	nos'os alentaríamos	
vos'os alentabais	vos'os alentaríais	**Imperative-Do**
ellos alentaban	ellos alentarían	(tú) alienta
		(él) aliente
Preterite	**Present subj've**	(nos'os) alentemos
yo alenté	yo aliente	(vos'os) alentad
tú alentaste	tú alientes	(ellos) alienten
él alentó	él aliente	
nos'os alentamos	nos'os alentemos	**Imperative-Don't**
vos'os alentasteis	vos'os alentéis	no alientes
ellos alentaron	ellos alienten	no aliente
		no alentemos
Comp'nd tenses- 63-I-Haber +Past-P		no alentéis
		no alienten

24(b)-S -Acertar

Verb infinitive	Participles	Imperfect-subjunctive 1
Acertar, to get right, to hit the target	acertado: acertando	yo acertara
		tú acertaras
Present	**Future**	él acertara
yo acierto	yo acertaré	nos'os acertáramos
tú aciertas	tú acertarás	vos'os acertarais
él acierta	él acertará	ellos acertaran
nos'os acertamos	nos'os acertaremos	
vos'os acertáis	vos'os acertaréis	**Imp'fect-sub've 2**
ellos aciertan	ellos acertarán	yo acertase
		tú acertases
Imperfect	**Conditional**	él acertase
yo acertaba	yo acertaría	nos'os acertásemos
tú acertabas	tú acertarías	vos'os acertaseis
él acertaba	él acertaría	ellos acertasen
nos'os acertábamos	nos'os acertaríamos	
vos'os acertabais	vos'os acertaríais	**Imperative-Do**
ellos acertaban	ellos acertarían	(tú) acierta
		(él) acierte
Preterite	**Present subj've**	(nos'os) acertemos
yo acerté	yo acierte	(vos'os) acertad
tú acertaste	tú aciertes	(ellos) acierten
él acertó	él acierte	
nos'os acertamos	nos'os acertemos	**Imperative-Don't**
vos'os acertasteis	vos'os acertéis	no aciertes
ellos acertaron	ellos acierten	no acierte
		no acertemos
Comp'nd tenses- 63-I-Haber +Past-P		no acertéis
		no acierten

25(a)-S-Perder Comment/explanation: See Chapter 24

Verb infinitive	Participles	Imperfect-subjunctive 1
Perder, to lose	perdido: perdiendo	yo perdiera
		tú perdieras
Present	**Future**	él perdiera
yo pierdo	yo perderé	nos'os perdiéramos
tú pierdes	tú perderás	vos'os perdierais
él pierde	él perderá	ellos perdieran
nos'os perdemos	nos'os perderemos	
vos'os perdéis	vos'os perderéis	**Imp'fect-sub've 2**
ellos pierden	ellos perderán	yo perdiese
		tú perdieses
Imperfect	**Conditional**	él perdiese
yo perdía	yo perdería	nos'os perdiésemos
tú perdías	tú perderías	vos'os perdieseis
él perdía	él perdería	ellos perdiesen
nos'os perdíamos	nos'os perderíamos	
vos'os perdíais	vos'os perderíais	**Imperative-Do**
ellos perdían	ellos perderían	tú) pierde
		(él) pierda
Preterite	**Present subj've**	(nos'os) perdamos
yo perdí	yo pierda	(vos'os) perded
tú perdiste	tú pierdas	(ellos) pierdan
él perdió	él pierda	
nos'os perdimos	nos'os perdamos	**Imperative-Don't**
vos'os perdisteis	vos'os perdáis	no pierdas
ellos perdieron	ellos pierdan	no pierda
		no perdamos
Comp'nd tenses- 63-I-Haber +Past-P		no perdáis
		no pierdan

104

25(b)-S-Entender Comment/explanation: See Chapter 24

Verb infinitive	Participles	Imperfect-subjunctive 1
Entender, to understand	entendido: entendiendo	yo entendiera
		tú entendieras
Present	**Future**	él entendiera
yo entiendo	yo entenderé	nos'os entendiéramos
tú entiendes	tú entenderás	vos'os entendierais
él entiende	él entenderá	ellos entendieran
nos'os entendemos	nos'os entenderemos	
vos'os entendéis	vos'os entenderéis	**Imp'fect-sub've 2**
ellos entienden	ellos entenderán	yo entendiese
		tú entendieses
Imperfect	**Conditional**	él entendiese
yo entendía	yo entendería	nos'os entendiésemos
tú entendías	tú entenderías	vos'os entendieseis
él entendía	él entendería	ellos entendiesen
nos'os entendíamos	nos'os entenderíamos	
vos'os entendíais	vos'os entenderíais	**Imperative-Do**
ellos entendían	ellos entenderían	(tú) entiende
		(él) entienda
Preterite	**Present subj've**	(nos'os) entendamos
yo entendí	yo entienda	(vos'os) entended
tú entendiste	tú entiendas	(ellos) entiendan
él entendió	él entienda	
nos'os entendimos	nos'os entendamos	**Imperative-Don't**
vos'os entendisteis	vos'os entendáis	no entiendas
ellos entendieron	ellos entiendan	no entienda
		no entendamos
Comp'nd tenses- 63-I-Haber +Past-P		no entendáis
		no entiendan

26(a)-S-Aprobar Comment/explanation: See Chapter 24

Verb infinitive	Participles	Imperfect-subjunctive 1
Aprobar, to approve, to consent to	aprobado: aprobando	yo aprobara
		tú aprobaras
Present	**Future**	él aprobara
yo apruebo	yo aprobaré	nos'os aprobáramos
tú apruebas	tú aprobarás	vos'os aprobarais
él aprueba	él aprobará	ellos aprobaran
nos'os aprobamos	nos'os aprobaremos	
vos'os aprobáis	vos'os aprobaréis	**Imp'fect-sub've 2**
ellos aprueban	ellos aprobarán	yo aprobase
		tú aprobases
Imperfect	**Conditional**	él aprobase
yo aprobaba	yo aprobaría	nos'os aprobásemos
tú aprobabas	tú aprobarías	vos'os aprobaseis
él aprobaba	él aprobaría	ellos aprobasen
nos'os aprobábamos	nos'os aprobaríamos	
vos'os aprobabais	vos'os aprobaríais	**Imperative-Do**
ellos aprobaban	ellos aprobarían	(tú) aprueba
		(él) apruebe
Preterite	**Present subj've**	(nos'os) aprobemos
yo aprobé	yo apruebe	(vos'os) aprobad
tú aprobaste	tú apruebes	(ellos) aprueben
él aprobó	él apruebe	
nos'os aprobamos	nos'os aprobemos	**Imperative-Don't**
vos'os aprobasteis	vos'os aprobéis	no apruebes
ellos aprobaron	ellos aprueben	no apruebe
		no aprobemos
Comp'nd tenses- 63-I-Haber +Past-P		no aprobéis
		no aprueben

106

26(b)-S-Acortar Comment/explanation: See Chapter 24

Verb infinitive	Participles	Imperfect-subjunctive 1
Acortar, to shorten, to reduce	acortado: acortando	yo acortara
		tú acortaras
Present	**Future**	él acortara
yo acuerto	yo acortaré	nos'os acortáramos
tú acuertas	tú acortarás	vos'os acortarais
él acuerta	él acortará	ellos acortaran
nos'os acortamos	nos'os acortaremos	
vos'os acortáis	vos'os acortaréis	**Imp'fect-sub've 2**
ellos acuertan	ellos acortarán	yo acortase
		tú acortases
Imperfect	**Conditional**	él acortase
yo acortaba	yo acortaría	nos'os acortásemos
tú acortabas	tú acortarías	vos'os acortaseis
él acortaba	él acortaría	ellos acortasen
nos'os acortábamos	nos'os acortaríamos	
vos'os acortabais	vos'os acortaríais	**Imperative-Do**
ellos acortaban	ellos acortarían	(tú) acuerta
		(él) acuerte
Preterite	**Present subj've**	(nos'os) acortemos
yo acorté	yo acuerte	(vos'os) acortad
tú acortaste	tú acuertes	(ellos) acuerten
él acortó	él acuerte	
nos'os acortamos	nos'os acortemos	**Imperative-Don't**
vos'os acortasteis	vos'os acortéis	no acuertes
ellos acortaron	ellos acuerten	no acuerte
		no acortemos
Comp'nd tenses- 63-I-Haber +Past-P		no acortéis
		no acuerten

107

27(a)-S-Morder Comment/explanation: See Chapter 24

Verb infinitive	Participles	Imperfect-subjunctive 1
Morder, to bite	mordido: mordiendo	yo mordiera
		tú mordieras
Present	**Future**	él mordiera
yo muerdo	yo morderé	nos'os mordiéramos
tú muerdes	tú morderás	vos'os mordierais
él muerde	él morderá	ellos mordieran
nos'os mordemos	nos'os morderemos	
vos'os mordéis	vos'os morderéis	**Imp'fect-sub've 2**
ellos muerden	ellos morderán	yo mordiese
		tú mordieses
Imperfect	**Conditional**	él mordiese
yo mordía	yo mordería	nos'os mordiésemos
tú mordías	tú morderías	vos'os mordieseis
él mordía	él mordería	ellos mordiesen
nos'os mordíamos	nos'os morderíamos	
vos'os mordíais	vos'os morderíais	**Imperative-Do**
ellos mordían	ellos morderían	(tú) muerde
		(él) muerda
Preterite	**Present subj've**	(nos'os) mordamos
yo mordí	yo muerda	(vos'os) morded
tú mordiste	tú muerdas	(ellos) muerdan
él mordió	él muerda	
nos'os mordimos	nos'os mordamos	**Imperative-Don't**
vos'os mordisteis	vos'os mordáis	no muerdas
ellos mordieron	ellos muerdan	no muerda
		no mordamos
Comp'nd tenses- 63-I-Haber +Past-P		no mordáis
		no muerdan

27(b)-S-Remover Comment/explanation: See Chapter 24

Verb infinitive	Participles	Imperfect-subjunctive 1
Remover, to stir, to turn over	removido: removiendo	yo removiera
		tú removieras
Present	**Future**	él removiera
yo remuevo	yo removeré	nos'os removiéramos
tú remueves	tú removerás	vos'os removierais
él remueve	él removerá	ellos removieran
nos'os removemos	nos'os removeremos	
vos'os removéis	vos'os removeréis	**Imp'fect-sub've 2**
ellos remueven	ellos removerán	yo removiese
		tú removieses
Imperfect	**Conditional**	él removiese
yo removía	yo removería	nos'os removiésemos
tú removías	tú removerías	vos'os removieseis
él removía	él removería	ellos removiesen
nos'os removíamos	nos'os removeríamos	
vos'os removíais	vos'os removeríais	**Imperative-Do**
ellos removían	ellos removerían	(tú) remueve
		(él) remueva
Preterite	**Present subj've**	(nos'os) removamos
yo removí	yo remueva	(vos'os) removed
tú removiste	tú remuevas	(ellos) remuevan
él removió	él remueva	
nos'os removimos	nos'os removamos	**Imperative-Don't**
vos'os removisteis	vos'os remováis	no remuevas
ellos removieron	ellos remuevan	no remueva
		no removamos
Comp'nd tenses- 63-I-Haber +Past-P		no remováis
		no remuevan

109

28-S-Oler Comment/explanation: See Chapter 24

Verb infinitive	Participles	Imperfect-subjunctive 1
Oler, to smell.	olido: oliendo	yo oliera
		tú olieras
Present	**Future**	él oliera
yo huelo	yo oleré	nos'os oliéramos
tú hueles	tú olerás	vos'os olierais
él huele	él olerá	ellos olieran
nos'os olemos	nos'os oleremos	
vos'os oléis	vos'os oleréis	**Imp'fect-sub've 2**
ellos huelen	ellos olerán	yo oliese
		tú olieses
Imperfect	**Conditional**	él oliese
yo olía	yo olería	nos'os oliésemos
tú olías	tú olerías	vos'os olieseis
él olía	él olería	ellos oliesen
nos'os olíamos	nos'os oleríamos	
vos'os olíais	vos'os oleríais	**Imperative-Do**
ellos olían	ellos olerían	(tú) huele
		(él) huela
Preterite	**Present subj've**	(nos'os) olamos
yo olí	yo huela	(vos'os) oled
tú oliste	tú huelas	(ellos) huelan
él olió	él huela	
nos'os olimos	nos'os olamos	**Imperative-Don't**
vos'os olisteis	vos'os oláis	no huelas
ellos olieron	ellos huelan	no huela
		no olamos
Comp'nd tenses- 63-I-Haber +Past-P		no oláis
		no huelan

29(a)-S-Discernir Comment/explanation: See Chapter 24

Verb infinitive	Participles	Imperfect-subjunctive 1
Discernir, to discern	discernido: discerniendo	yo discerniera
		tú discernieras
Present	**Future**	él discerniera
yo discierno	yo discerniré	nos'os discerniéramos
tú disciernes	tú discernirás	vos'os discernierais
él discierne	él discernirá	ellos discernieran
nos'os discernimos	nos'os discerniremos	
vos'os discernís	vos'os discerniréis	**Imp'fect-sub've 2**
ellos disciernen	ellos discernirán	yo discerniese
		tú discernieses
Imperfect	**Conditional**	él discerniese
yo discernía	yo discerniría	nos'os discerniésemos
tú discernías	tú discernirías	vos'os discernieseis
él discernía	él discerniría	ellos discerniesen
nos'os discerníamos	nos'os discerniríamos	
vos'os discerníais	vos'os discerniríais	**Imperative-Do**
ellos discernían	ellos discernirían	(tú) discierne
		(él) discierna
Preterite	**Present subj've**	(nos'os) discernamos
yo discerní	yo discierna	(vos'os) discernid
tú discerniste	tú disciernas	(ellos) disciernan
él discernió	él discierna	
nos'os discernimos	nos'os discernamos	**Imperative-Don't**
vos'os discernisteis	vos'os discernáis	no disciernas
ellos discernieron	ellos disciernan	no discierna
		no discernamos
Comp'nd tenses- 63-I-Haber +Past-P		no discernáis
		no disciernan

111

29(b)-S-Cernir Comment/explanation: See Chapter 24

Verb infinitive	Participles	Imperfect-subjunctive 1
Cernir, to sift, to sieve	cernido: cerniendo	yo cerniera
		tú cernieras
Present	**Future**	él cerniera
yo cierno	yo cerniré	nos'os cerniéramos
tú ciernes	tú cernirás	vos'os cernierais
él cierne	él cernirá	ellos cernieran
nos'os cernimos	nos'os cerniremos	
vos'os cernís	vos'os cerniréis	**Imp'fect-sub've 2**
ellos ciernen	ellos cernirán	yo cerniese
		tú cernieses
Imperfect	**Conditional**	él cerniese
yo cernía	yo cerniría	nos'os cerniésemos
tú cernías	tú cernirías	vos'os cernieseis
él cernía	él cerniría	ellos cerniesen
nos'os cerníamos	nos'os cerniríamos	
vos'os cerníais	vos'os cerniríais	**Imperative-Do**
ellos cernían	ellos cernirían	(tú) cierne
		(él) cierna
Preterite	**Present subj've**	(nos'os) cernamos
yo cerní	yo cierna	(vos'os) cernid
tú cerniste	tú ciernas	(ellos) ciernan
él cernió	él cierna	
nos'os cernimos	nos'os cernamos	**Imperative-Don't**
vos'os cernisteis	vos'os cernáis	no ciernas
ellos cernieron	ellos ciernan	no cierna
		no cernamos
Comp'nd tenses- 63-I-Haber +Past-P		no cernáis
		no ciernan

30(a)-S-Sentir Comment/explanation: See Chapter 24

Verb infinitive	Participles	Imperfect-subjunctive 1
Sentir, to feel	sentido: sintiendo	yo sintiera
		tú sintieras
Present	**Future**	él sintiera
yo siento	yo sentiré	nos'os sintiéramos
tú sientes	tú sentirás	vos'os sintierais
él siente	él sentirá	ellos sintieran
nos'os sentimos	nos'os sentiremos	
vos'os sentís	vos'os sentiréis	**Imp'fect-sub've 2**
ellos sienten	ellos sentirán	yo sintiese
		tú sintieses
Imperfect	**Conditional**	él sintiese
yo sentía	yo sentiría	nos'os sintiésemos
tú sentías	tú sentirías	vos'os sintieseis
él sentía	él sentiría	ellos sintiesen
nos'os sentíamos	nos'os sentiríamos	
vos'os sentíais	vos'os sentiríais	**Imperative-Do**
ellos sentían	ellos sentirían	(tú) siente
		(él) sienta
Preterite	**Present subj've**	(nos'os) sintamos
yo sentí	yo sienta	(vos'os) sentid
tú sentiste	tú sientas	(ellos) sientan
él sintió	él sienta	
nos'os sentimos	nos'os sintamos	**Imperative-Don't**
vos'os sentisteis	vos'os sintáis	no sientas
ellos sintieron	ellos sientan	no sienta
		no sintamos
Comp'nd tenses- 63-I-Haber +Past-P		no sintáis
		no sientan

113

30(b)-S-Advertir Comment/explanation: See Chapter 24

Verb infinitive	Participles	Imperfect-subjunctive 1
Advertir, to give notice, to give warning	advertido: advirtiendo	yo advirtiera
		tú advirtieras
Present	**Future**	él advirtiera
yo advierto	yo advertiré	nos'os advirtiéramos
tú adviertes	tú advertirás	vos'os advirtierais
él advierte	él advertirá	ellos advirtieran
nos'os advertimos	nos'os advertiremos	
vos'os advertís	vos'os advertiréis	**Imp'fect-sub've 2**
ellos advierten	ellos advertirán	yo advirtiese
		tú advirtieses
Imperfect	**Conditional**	él advirtiese
yo advertía	yo advertiría	nos'os advirtiésemos
tú advertías	tú advertirías	vos'os advirtieseis
él advertía	él advertiría	ellos advirtiesen
nos'os advertíamos	nos'os advertiríamos	
vos'os advertíais	vos'os advertiríais	**Imperative-Do**
ellos advertían	ellos advertirían	(tú) advierte
		(él) advierta
Preterite	**Present subj've**	(nos'os) advirtamos
yo advertí	yo advierta	(vos'os) advertid
tú advertiste	tú adviertas	(ellos) adviertan
él advirtió	él advierta	
nos'os advertimos	nos'os advirtamos	**Imperative-Don't**
vos'os advertisteis	vos'os advirtáis	no adviertas
ellos advirtieron	ellos adviertan	no advierta
		no advirtamos
Comp'nd tenses- 63-I-Haber +Past-P		no advirtáis
		no adviertan

31(a)-S-Servir Comment/explanation: See Chapter 24

Verb infinitive	Participles	Imperfect-subjunctive 1
Servir, to serve	servido: sirviendo	yo sirviera
		tú sirvieras
Present	**Future**	él sirviera
yo sirvo	yo serviré	nos'os sirviéramos
tú sirves	tú servirás	vos'os sirvierais
él sirve	él servirá	ellos sirvieran
nos'os servimos	nos'os serviremos	
vos'os servís	vos'os serviréis	**Imp'fect-sub've 2**
ellos sirven	ellos servirán	yo sirviese
		tú sirvieses
Imperfect	**Conditional**	él sirviese
yo servía	yo serviría	nos'os sirviésemos
tú servías	tú servirías	vos'os sirvieseis
él servía	él serviría	ellos sirviesen
nos'os servíamos	nos'os serviríamos	
vos'os servíais	vos'os serviríais	**Imperative-Do**
ellos servían	ellos servirían	(tú) sirve
		(él) sirva
Preterite	**Present subj've**	(nos'os) sirvamos
yo serví	yo sirva	(vos'os) servid
tú serviste	tú sirvas	(ellos) sirvan
él sirvió	él sirva	
nos'os servimos	nos'os sirvamos	**Imperative-Don't**
vos'os servisteis	vos'os sirváis	no sirvas
ellos sirvieron	ellos sirvan	no sirva
		no sirvamos
Comp'nd tenses-63-I-Haber +Past-P		no sirváis
		no sirvan

31(b)-S-Competir Comment/explanation: See Chapter 24

Verb infinitive	Participles	Imperfect-subjunctive 1
Competir, to compete	competido: compitiendo	yo compitiera
		tú compitieras
Present	**Future**	él compitiera
yo compito	yo competiré	nos'os compitiéramos
tú compites	tú competirás	vos'os compitierais
él compite	él competirá	ellos compitieran
nos'os competimos	nos'os competiremos	
vos'os competís	vos'os competiréis	**Imp'fect-sub've 2**
ellos compiten	ellos competirán	yo compitiese
		tú compitieses
Imperfect	**Conditional**	él compitiese
yo competía	yo competiría	nos'os compitiésemos
tú competías	tú competirías	vos'os compitieseis
él competía	él competiría	ellos compitiesen
nos'os competíamos	nos'os competiríamos	
vos'os competíais	vos'os competiríais	**Imperative-Do**
ellos competían	ellos competirían	(tú) compite
		(él) compita
Preterite	**Present subj've**	(nos'os) compitamos
yo competí	yo compita	(vos'os) competid
tú competiste	tú compitas	(ellos) compitan
él compitió	él compita	
nos'os competimos	nos'os compitamos	**Imperative-Don't**
vos'os competisteis	vos'os compitáis	no compitas
ellos compitieron	ellos compitan	no compita
		no compitamos
Comp'nd tenses- 63-I-Haber +Past-P		no compitáis
		no compitan

116

32(a)-S-Adquirir Comment/explanation: See Chapter 24

Verb infinitive	Participles	Imperfect-subjunctive 1
Adquirir, to acquire	adquirido: adquiriendo	yo adquiriera
		tú adquirieras
Present	**Future**	él adquiriera
yo adquiero	yo adquiriré	nos'os adquiriéramos
tú adquieres	tú adquirirás	vos'os adquirierais
él adquiere	él adquirirá	ellos adquirieran
nos'os adquirimos	nos'os adquiriremos	
vos'os adquirís	vos'os adquiriréis	**Imp'fect-sub've 2**
ellos adquieren	ellos adquirirán	yo adquiriese
		tú adquirieses
Imperfect	**Conditional**	él adquiriese
yo adquiría	yo adquiriría	nos'os adquiriésemos
tú adquirías	tú adquirirías	vos'os adquirieseis
él adquiría	él adquiriría	ellos adquiriesen
nos'os adquiríamos	nos'os adquiriríamos	
vos'os adquiríais	vos'os adquiriríais	**Imperative-Do**
ellos adquirían	ellos adquirirían	(tú) adquiere
		(él) adquiera
Preterite	**Present subj've**	(nos'os) adquiramos
yo adquirí	yo adquiera	(vos'os) adquirid
tú adquiriste	tú adquieras	(ellos) adquieran
él adquirió	él adquiera	
nos'os adquirimos	nos'os adquiramos	**Imperative-Don't**
vos'os adquiristeis	vos'os adquiráis	no adquieras
ellos adquirieron	ellos adquieran	no adquiera
		no adquiramos
Comp'nd tenses- 63-I-Haber +Past-P		no adquiráis
		no adquieran

117

32(b)-S-Inquirir Comment/explanation: See Chapter 24

Verb infinitive	Participles	Imperfect-subjunctive 1
Inquirir, to enquire, to investigate	inquirido: inquiriendo	yo inquiriera
		tú inquirieras
Present	**Future**	él inquiriera
yo inquiero	yo inquiriré	nos'os inquiriéramos
tú inquieres	tú inquirirás	vos'os inquirierais
él inquiere	él inquirirá	ellos inquirieran
nos'os inquirimos	nos'os inquiriremos	
vos'os inquirís	vos'os inquiriréis	**Imp'fect-sub've 2**
ellos inquieren	ellos inquirirán	yo inquiriese
		tú inquirieses
Imperfect	**Conditional**	él inquiriese
yo inquiría	yo inquiriría	nos'os inquiriésemos
tú inquirías	tú inquirirías	vos'os inquirieseis
él inquiría	él inquiriría	ellos inquiriesen
nos'os inquiríamos	nos'os inquiriríamos	
vos'os inquiríais	vos'os inquiriríais	**Imperative-Do**
ellos inquirían	ellos inquirirían	(tú) inquiere
		(él) inquiera
Preterite	**Present subj've**	(nos'os) inquiramos
yo inquirí	yo inquiera	(vos'os) inquirid
tú inquiriste	tú inquieras	(ellos) inquieran
él inquirió	él inquiera	
nos'os inquirimos	nos'os inquiramos	**Imperative-Don't**
vos'os inquiristeis	vos'os inquiráis	no inquieras
ellos inquirieron	ellos inquieran	no inquiera
		no inquiramos
Comp'nd tenses- 63-I-Haber +Past-P		no inquiráis
		no inquieran

118

33(a)-S-Dormir Comment/explanation: See Chapter 24

Verb infinitive	Participles	Imperfect-subjunctive 1
Dormir, to sleep	dormido: durmiendo	yo durmiera
		tú durmieras
Present	**Future**	él durmiera
yo duermo	yo dormiré	nos'os durmiéramos
tú duermes	tú dormirás	vos'os durmierais
él duerme	él dormirá	ellos durmieran
nos'os dormimos	nos'os dormiremos	
vos'os dormís	vos'os dormiréis	**Imp'fect-sub've 2**
ellos duermen	ellos dormirán	yo durmiese
		tú durmieses
Imperfect	**Conditional**	él durmiese
yo dormía	yo dormiría	nos'os durmiésemos
tú dormías	tú dormirías	vos'os durmieseis
él dormía	él dormiría	ellos durmiesen
nos'os dormíamos	nos'os dormiríamos	
vos'os dormíais	vos'os dormiríais	**Imperative-Do**
ellos dormían	ellos dormirían	(tú) duerme
		(él) duerma
Preterite	**Present subj've**	(nos'os) durmamos
yo dormí	yo duerma	(vos'os) dormid
tú dormiste	tú duermas	(ellos) duerman
él durmió	él duerma	
nos'os dormimos	nos'os durmamos	**Imperative-Don't**
vos'os dormisteis	vos'os durmáis	no duermas
ellos durmieron	ellos duerman	no duerma
		no durmamos
Comp'nd tenses- 63-I-Haber +Past-P		no durmáis
		no duerman

119

33(b)-S-Morir Comment/explanation: See Chapter 24

Verb infinitive	Participles	Imperfect-subjunctive 1
Morir, to die	muerto: muriendo	yo muriera
		tú murieras
Present	**Future**	él muriera
yo muero	yo moriré	nos'os muriéramos
tú mueres	tú morirás	vos'os murierais
él muere	él morirá	ellos murieran
nos'os morimos	nos'os moriremos	
vos'os morís	vos'os moriréis	**Imp'fect-sub've 2**
ellos mueren	ellos morirán	yo muriese
		tú murieses
Imperfect	**Conditional**	él muriese
yo moría	yo moriría	nos'os muriésemos
tú morías	tú morirías	vos'os murieseis
él moría	él moriría	ellos muriesen
nos'os moríamos	nos'os moriríamos	
vos'os moríais	vos'os moriríais	**Imperative-Do**
ellos morían	ellos morirían	(tú) muere
		(él) muera
Preterite	**Present subj've**	(nos'os) muramos
yo morí	yo muera	(vos'os) morid
tú moriste	tú mueras	(ellos) mueran
él murió	él muera	
nos'os morimos	nos'os muramos	**Imperative-Don't**
vos'os moristeis	vos'os muráis	no mueras
ellos murieron	ellos mueran	no muera
		no muramos
Comp'nd tenses- 63-I-Haber +Past-P		no muráis
		no mueran

120

34-S-Jugar Comment/explanation: See Chapter 24

Verb infinitive	Participles	Imperfect-subjunctive 1
Jugar, to	jugado: jugando	yo jugara
		tú jugaras
Present	**Future**	él jugara
yo juego	yo jugaré	nos'os jugáramos
tú juegas	tú jugarás	vos'os jugarais
él juega	él jugará	ellos jugaran
nos'os jugamos	nos'os jugaremos	
vos'os jugáis	vos'os jugaréis	**Imp'fect-sub've 2**
ellos juegan	ellos jugarán	yo jugase
		tú jugases
Imperfect	**Conditional**	él jugase
yo jugaba	yo jugaría	nos'os jugásemos
tú jugabas	tú jugarías	vos'os jugaseis
él jugaba	él jugaría	ellos jugasen
nos'os jugábamos	nos'os jugaríamos	
vos'os jugabais	vos'os jugaríais	**Imperative-Do**
ellos jugaban	ellos jugarían	(tú) juega
		(él) juegue
Preterite	**Present subj've**	(nos'os) juguemos
yo jugué	yo juegue	(vos'os) jugad
tú jugaste	tú juegues	(ellos) jueguen
él jugó	él juegue	
nos'os jugamos	nos'os juguemos	**Imperative-Don't**
vos'os jugasteis	vos'os juguéis	no juegues
ellos jugaron	ellos jueguen	no juegue
		no juguemos
Comp'nd tenses- 63-I-Haber +Past-P		no juguéis
		no jueguen

121

35(a)-S-Reír Comment/explanation: See Chapter 24

Verb infinitive	Participles	Imperfect-subjunctive 1
Reír, to laugh	reído: riendo	yo riera
		tú rieras
Present	**Future**	él riera
yo río	yo reiré	nos'os riéramos
tú ríes	tú reirás	vos'os rierais
él ríe	él reirá	ellos rieran
nos'os reímos	nos'os reiremos	
vos'os reís	vos'os reiréis	**Imp'fect-sub've 2**
ellos ríen	ellos reirán	yo riese
		tú rieses
Imperfect	**Conditional**	él riese
yo reía	yo reiría	nos'os riésemos
tú reías	tú reirías	vos'os rieseis
él reía	él reiría	ellos riesen
nos'os reíamos	nos'os reiríamos	
vos'os reíais	vos'os reiríais	**Imperative-Do**
ellos reían	ellos reirían	(tú) ríe
		(él) ría
Preterite	**Present subj've**	(nos'os) riamos
yo reí	yo ría	(vos'os) reíd
tú reíste	tú rías	(ellos) rían
él rió	él ría	
nos'os reímos	nos'os riamos	**Imperative-Don't**
vos'os reísteis	vos'os riáis	no rías
ellos rieron	ellos rían	no ría
		no riamos
Comp'nd tenses- 63-I-Haber +Past-P		no riáis
		no rían

35(b)-S-Freír Comment/explanation: See Chapter 24

Verb infinitive	Participles	Imperfect-subjunctive 1
Freír, to fry	freído; frito: friendo	yo friera
		tú frieras
Present	**Future**	él friera
yo frío	yo freiré	nos'os friéramos
tú fríes	tú freirás	vos'os frierais
él fríe	él freirá	ellos frieran
nos'os freímos	nos'os freiremos	
vos'os freís	vos'os freiréis	**Imp'fect-sub've 2**
ellos fríen	ellos freirán	yo friese
		tú frieses
Imperfect	**Conditional**	él friese
yo freía	yo freiría	nos'os friésemos
tú freías	tú freirías	vos'os frieseis
él freía	él freiría	ellos friesen
nos'os freíamos	nos'os freiríamos	
vos'os freíais	vos'os freiríais	**Imperative-Do**
ellos freían	ellos freirían	(tú) fríe
		(él) fría
Preterite	**Present subj've**	(nos'os) friamos
yo freí	yo fría	(vos'os) freíd
tú freíste	tú frías	(ellos) frían
él frió	él fría	
nos'os freímos	nos'os friamos	**Imperative-Don't**
vos'os freísteis	vos'os friáis	no frías
ellos frieron	ellos frían	no fría
		no friamos
Comp'nd tenses- 63-I-Haber +Past-P		no friáis
		no frían

123

36(a)-S-Colegir Comment/explanation: See Chapter 24

Verb infinitive	Participles	Imperfect-subjunctive 1
Colegir, to gather	colegido: coligiendo	yo coligiera
		tú coligieras
Present	**Future**	él coligiera
yo colijo	yo colegiré	nos'os coligiéramos
tú coliges	tú colegirás	vos'os coligierais
él colige	él colegirá	ellos coligieran
nos'os colegimos	nos'os colegiremos	
vos'os colegís	vos'os colegiréis	**Imp'fect-sub've 2**
ellos coligen	ellos colegirán	yo coligiese
		tú coligieses
Imperfect	**Conditional**	él coligiese
yo colegía	yo colegiría	nos'os coligiésemos
tú colegías	tú colegirías	vos'os coligieseis
él colegía	él colegiría	ellos coligiesen
nos'os colegíamos	nos'os colegiríamos	
vos'os colegíais	vos'os colegiríais	**Imperative-Do**
ellos colegían	ellos colegirían	(tú) colige
		(él) colija
Preterite	**Present subj've**	(nos'os) colijamos
yo colegí	yo colija	(vos'os) colegid
tú colegiste	tú colijas	(ellos) colijan
él coligió	él colija	
nos'os colegimos	nos'os colijamos	**Imperative-Don't**
vos'os colegisteis	vos'os colijáis	no colijas
ellos coligieron	ellos colijan	no colija
		no colijamos
Comp'nd tenses- 63-I-Haber +Past-P		no colijáis
		no colijan

36(b)-S-Elegir Comment/explanation: See Chapter 24

Verb infinitive	Participles	Imperfect-subjunctive 1
Elegir, to select, to choose	elegido: eligiendo	yo eligiera
		tú eligieras
Present	**Future**	él eligiera
yo elijo	yo elegiré	nos'os eligiéramos
tú eliges	tú elegirás	vos'os eligierais
él elige	él elegirá	ellos eligieran
nos'os elegimos	nos'os elegiremos	
vos'os elegís	vos'os elegiréis	**Imp'fect-sub've 2**
ellos eligen	ellos elegirán	yo eligiese
		tú eligieses
Imperfect	**Conditional**	él eligiese
yo elegía	yo elegiría	nos'os eligiésemos
tú elegías	tú elegirías	vos'os eligieseis
él elegía	él elegiría	ellos eligiesen
nos'os elegíamos	nos'os elegiríamos	
vos'os elegíais	vos'os elegiríais	**Imperative-Do**
ellos elegían	ellos elegirían	(tú) elige
		(él) elija
Preterite	**Present subj've**	(nos'os) elijamos
yo elegí	yo elija	(vos'os) elegid
tú elegiste	tú elijas	(ellos) elijan
él eligió	él elija	
nos'os elegimos	nos'os elijamos	**Imperative-Don't**
vos'os elegisteis	vos'os elijáis	no elijas
ellos eligieron	ellos elijan	no elija
		no elijamos
Comp'nd tenses- 63-I-Haber +Past-P		no elijáis
		no elijan

125

37-R-RF-Abrirse   Note: participles.

Verb infinitive	Participles	Imperfect-subjunctive 1
Abrirse, to open our	abierto: abriéndose	me abriera
		te abrieras
Present	**Future**	se abriera
me abro	me abriré	nos abriéramos
te abres	te abrirás	os abrierais
se abre	se abrirá	se abrieran
nos abrimos	nos abriremos	
os abrís	os abriréis	**Imp'fect-sub've 2**
se abren	se abrirán	me abriese
		te abrieses
Imperfect	**Conditional**	se abriese
me abría	me abriría	nos abriésemos
te abrías	te abrirías	os abrieseis
se abría	se abriría	se abriesen
nos abríamos	nos abriríamos	
os abríais	os abriríais	**Imperative-Do**
se abrían	se abrirían	(tú) ábrete
		(él) ábrase
Preterite	**Present subj've**	(nos'os) abrámonos
me abrí	me abra	(vos'os) abríos
te abriste	te abras	(ellos) ábranse
se abrió	se abra	
nos abrimos	nos abramos	**Imperative-Don't**
os abristeis	os abráis	no te abras
se abrieron	se abran	no se abra
		no nos abramos
Comp'nd tenses- 63-I-Haber +Past-P		no os abráis
		no se abran

126

38-R-RF-Alejarse

Verb infinitive	Participles	Imperfect-subjunctive 1
Alejarse, to draw further off	alejado: alejándose	me alejara
		te alejaras
Present	**Future**	se alejara
me alejo	me alejaré	nos alejáramos
te alejas	te alejarás	os alejarais
se aleja	se alejará	se alejaran
nos alejamos	nos alejaremos	
os alejáis	os alejaréis	**Imp'fect-sub've 2**
se alejan	se alejarán	me alejase
		te alejases
Imperfect	**Conditional**	se alejase
me alejaba	me alejaría	nos alejásemos
te alejabas	te alejarías	os alejaseis
se alejaba	se alejaría	se alejasen
nos alejábamos	nos alejaríamos	
os alejabais	os alejaríais	**Imperative-Do**
se alejaban	se alejarían	(tú) aléjate
		(él) aléjese
Preterite	**Present subj've**	(nos'os) alejémonos
me alejé	me aleje	(vos'os) alejaos
te alejaste	te alejes	(ellos) aléjense
se alejó	se aleje	
nos alejamos	nos alejemos	**Imperative-Don't**
os alejasteis	os alejéis	no te alejes
se alejaron	se alejen	no se aleje
		no nos alejemos
Comp'nd tenses- 63-I-Haber +Past-P		no os alejéis
		no se alejen

39-I-RF-Caerse

Note: participles. present. preterite. present subjunctive. imperfect-subjunctive. imperative.

Verb infinitive	Participles	Imperfect-subjunctive 1
Caerse, to fall down	caído: cayéndose	me cayera
		te cayeras
Present	**Future**	se cayera
me caigo	me caeré	nos cayéramos
te caes	te caerás	os cayerais
se cae	se caerá	se cayeran
nos caemos	nos caeremos	
os caéis	os caeréis	**Imp'fect-sub've 2**
se caen	se caerán	me cayese
		te cayeses
Imperfect	**Conditional**	se cayese
me caía	me caería	nos cayésemos
te caías	te caerías	os cayeseis
se caía	se caería	se cayesen
nos caíamos	nos caeríamos	
os caíais	os caeríais	**Imperative-Do**
se caían	se caerían	(tú) cáete
		(él) cáigase
Preterite	**Present subj've**	(nos'os) caigámonos
me caí	me caiga	(vos'os) caeos
te caíste	te caigas	(ellos) cáiganse
se cayó	se caiga	
nos caímos	nos caigamos	**Imperative-Don't**
os caísteis	os caigáis	no te caigas
se cayeron	se caigan	no se caiga
		no nos caigamos
Comp'nd tenses- 63-I-Haber +Past-P		no os caigáis
		no se caigan

128

40-I-RF-Convertirse

Note: participles. present. preterite. present subjunctive. imperfect-subjunctive. imperative.

Verb infinitive	Participles	Imperfect-subjunctive 1
Convertirse, to be transformed, to be converted	convertido: convirtiéndose	me convirtiera
		te convirtieras
Present	**Future**	se convirtiera
me convierto	me convertiré	nos convirtiéramos
te conviertes	te convertirás	os convirtierais
se convierte	se convertirá	se convirtieran
nos convertimos	nos convertiremos	
os convertís	os convertiréis	**Imp'fect-sub've 2**
se convierten	se convertirán	me convirtiese
		te convirtieses
Imperfect	**Conditional**	se convirtiese
me convertía	me convertiría	nos convirtiésemos
te convertías	te convertirías	os convirtieseis
se convertía	se convertiría	se convirtiesen
nos convertíamos	nos convertiríamos	
os convertíais	os convertiríais	**Imperative-Do**
se convertían	se convertirían	(tú) conviértete
		(él) conviértase
Preterite	**Present subj've**	(nos'os) convirtámonos
me convertí	me convierta	(vos'os) convertíos
te convertiste	te conviertas	(ellos) conviértanse
se convirtió	se convierta	
nos convertimos	nos convirtamos	**Imperative-Don't**
os convertisteis	os convirtáis	no te conviertas
se convirtieron	se conviertan	no se convierta
		no nos convirtamos
Comp'nd tenses- 63-I-Haber +Past-P		no os convirtáis
		no se conviertan

129

41-S-RF-Defenderse

Note: present. present subjunctive. imperative.

Verb infinitive	Participles	Imperfect-subjunctive 1
Defenderse, to defend oneself	defendido: defendiéndose	me defendiera
		te defendieras
Present	**Future**	se defendiera
me defiendo	me defenderé	nos defendiéramos
te defiendes	te defenderás	os defendierais
se defiende	se defenderá	se defendieran
nos defendemos	nos defenderemos	
os defendéis	os defenderéis	**Imp'fect-sub've 2**
se defienden	se defenderán	me defendiese
		te defendieses
Imperfect	**Conditional**	se defendiese
me defendía	me defendería	nos defendiésemos
te defendías	te defenderías	os defendieseis
se defendía	se defendería	se defendiesen
nos defendíamos	nos defenderíamos	
os defendíais	os defenderíais	**Imperative-Do**
se defendían	se defenderían	(tú) defiéndete
		(él) defiéndase
Preterite	**Present subj've**	(nos'os) defendámonos
me defendí	me defienda	(vos'os) defendeos
te defendiste	te defiendas	(ellos) defiéndanse
se defendió	se defienda	
nos defendimos	nos defendamos	**Imperative-Don't**
os defendisteis	os defendáis	no te defiendas
se defendieron	se defiendan	no se defienda
		no nos defendamos
Comp'nd tenses- 63-I-Haber +Past-P		no os defendáis
		no se defiendan

130

42-S-RF-Despedirse

Note: participles. present. preterite. present subjunctive. imperfect-subjunctive. imperative.

Verb infinitive	Participles	Imperfect-subjunctive 1
Despedirse, to say goodbye to	despedido: despidiéndose	me despidiera
		te despidieras
Present	**Future**	se despidiera
me despido	me despediré	nos despidiéramos
te despides	te despedirás	os despidierais
se despide	se despedirá	se despidieran
nos despedimos	nos despediremos	
os despedís	os despediréis	**Imp'fect-sub've 2**
se despiden	se despedirán	me despidiese
		te despidieses
Imperfect	**Conditional**	se despidiese
me despedía	me despediría	nos despidiésemos
te despedías	te despedirías	os despidieseis
se despedía	se despediría	se despidiesen
nos despedíamos	nos despediríamos	
os despedíais	os despediríais	**Imperative-Do**
se despedían	se despedirían	(tú) despídete
		(él) despídase
Preterite	**Present subj've**	(nos'os) despidámonos
me despedí	me despida	(vos'os) despedíos
te despediste	te despidas	(ellos) despídanse
se despidió	se despida	
nos despedimos	nos despidamos	**Imperative-Don't**
os despedisteis	os despidáis	no te despidas
se despidieron	se despidan	no se despida
		no nos despidamos
Comp'nd tenses- 63-I-Haber +Past-P		no os despidáis
		no se despidan

131

43-I-RF-Desvestirse

Note: participles. present. preterite. present subjunctive. imperfect-subjunctive. imperative.

Verb infinitive	Participles	Imperfect-subjunctive 1
Desvestirse, to undress oneself	desvestido: desvistiéndose	me desvistiera
		te desvistieras
Present	**Future**	se desvistiera
me desvisto	me desvestiré	nos desvistiéramos
te desvistes	te desvestirás	os desvistierais
se desviste	se desvestirá	se desvistieran
nos desvestimos	nos desvestiremos	
os desvestís	os desvestiréis	**Imp'fect-sub've 2**
se desvisten	se desvestirán	me desvistiese
		te desvistieses
Imperfect	**Conditional**	se desvistiese
me desvestía	me desvestiría	nos desvistiésemos
te desvestías	te desvestirías	os desvistieseis
se desvestía	se desvestiría	se desvistiesen
nos desvestíamos	nos desvestiríamos	
os desvestíais	os desvestiríais	**Imperative-Do**
se desvestían	se desvestirían	(tú) desvístete
		(él) desvístase
Preterite	**Present subj've**	(nos'os) desvistámonos
me desvestí	me desvista	(vos'os) desvestíos
te desvestiste	te desvistas	(ellos) desvístanse
se desvistió	se desvista	
nos desvestimos	nos desvistamos	**Imperative-Don't**
os desvestisteis	os desvistáis	no te desvistas
se desvistieron	se desvistan	no se desvista
		no nos desvistamos
Comp'nd tenses- 63-I-Haber +Past-P		no os desvistáis
		no se desvistan

132

44-I-RF-Detenerse

Note: present. preterite. future. conditional. present subjunctive. imperfect-subjunctive. imperative.

Verb infinitive	Participles	Imperfect-subjunctive 1
Detenerse, to stop oneself	detenido: deteniéndose	me detuviera
		te detuvieras
Present	**Future**	se detuviera
me detengo	me detendré	nos detuviéramos
te detienes	te detendrás	os detuvierais
se detiene	se detendrá	se detuvieran
nos detenemos	nos detendremos	
os detenéis	os detendréis	**Imp'fect-sub've 2**
se detienen	se detendrán	me detuviese
		te detuvieses
Imperfect	**Conditional**	se detuviese
me detenía	me detendría	nos detuviésemos
te detenías	te detendrías	os detuvieseis
se detenía	se detendría	se detuviesen
nos deteníamos	nos detendríamos	
os deteníais	os detendríais	**Imperative-Do**
se detenían	se detendrían	(tú) detente
		(él) deténgase
Preterite	**Present subj've**	(nos'os) detengámonos
me detuve	me detenga	(vos'os) deteneos
te detuviste	te detengas	(ellos deténganse
se detuvo	se detenga	
nos detuvimos	nos detengamos	**Imperative-Don't**
os detuvisteis	os detengáis	no te detengas
se detuvieron	se detengan	no se detenga
		no nos detengamos
Comp'nd tenses- 63-I-Haber +Past-P		no os detengáis
		no se detengan

133

45-I-RF-Dirigirse

Note: participles. present. present subjunctive. imperative.

Verb infinitive	Participles	Imperfect-subjunctive 1
Dirigirse, to direct oneself, to make one's way	dirigido: dirigiéndose	me dirigiera
		te dirigieras
Present	**Future**	se dirigiera
me dirijo	me dirigiré	nos dirigiéramos
te diriges	te dirigirás	os dirigierais
se dirige	se dirigirá	se dirigieran
nos dirigimos	nos dirigiremos	
os dirigís	os dirigiréis	**Imp'fect-sub've 2**
se dirigen	se dirigirán	me dirigiese
		te dirigieses
Imperfect	**Conditional**	se dirigiese
me dirigía	me dirigiría	nos dirigiésemos
te dirigías	te dirigirías	os dirigieseis
se dirigía	se dirigiría	se dirigiesen
nos dirigíamos	nos dirigiríamos	
os dirigíais	os dirigiríais	**Imperative-Do**
se dirigían	se dirigirían	(tú) dirígete
		(él) diríjase
Preterite	**Present subj've**	(nos'os) dirijámonos
me dirigí	me dirija	(vos'os) dirigíos
te dirigiste	te dirijas	(ellos) diríjanse
se dirigió	se dirija	
nos dirigimos	nos dirijamos	**Imperative-Don't**
os dirigisteis	os dirijáis	no te dirijas
se dirigieron	se dirijan	no se dirija
		no nos dirijamos
Comp'nd tenses- 63-I-Haber +Past-P		no os dirijáis
		no se dirijan

46-I-RF-Divertirse

Note: participles. present. preterite. present subjunctive. imperfect-subjunctive. imperative.

Verb infinitive	Participles	Imperfect-subjunctive 1
Divertirse, to amuse oneself	divertido: divirtiéndose	me divirtiera
		te divirtieras
Present	**Future**	se divirtiera
me divierto	me divertiré	nos divirtiéramos
te diviertes	te divertirás	os divirtierais
se divierte	se divertirá	se divirtieran
nos divertimos	nos divertiremos	
os divertís	os divertiréis	**Imp'fect-sub've 2**
se divierten	se divertirán	me divirtiese
		te divirtieses
Imperfect	**Conditional**	se divirtiese
me divertía	me divertiría	nos divirtiésemos
te divertías	te divertirías	os divirtieseis
se divertía	se divertiría	se divirtiesen
nos divertíamos	nos divertiríamos	
os divertíais	os divertiríais	**Imperative-Do**
se divertían	se divertirían	(tú) diviértete
		(él) diviértase
Preterite	**Present subj've**	(nos'os) divirtámonos
me divertí	me divierta	(vos'os) divertíos
te divertiste	te diviertas	(ellos) diviértanse
se divirtió	se divierta	
nos divertimos	nos divirtamos	**Imperative-Don't**
os divertisteis	os divirtáis	no te diviertas
se divirtieron	se diviertan	no se divierta
		no nos divirtamos
Comp'nd tenses- 63-I-Haber +Past-P		no os divirtáis
		no se diviertan

135

47-R-RF-Inscribirse
Note: participles

Verb infinitive	Participles	Imperfect-subjunctive 1
Inscribirse, to sign up to	inscrito: inscribiéndose	me inscribiera
		te inscribieras
Present	**Future**	se inscribiera
me inscribo	me inscribiré	nos inscribiéramos
te inscribes	te inscribirás	os inscribierais
se inscribe	se inscribirá	se inscribieran
nos inscribimos	nos inscribiremos	
os inscribís	os inscribiréis	**Imp'fect-sub've 2**
se inscriben	se inscribirán	me inscribiese
		te inscribieses
Imperfect	**Conditional**	se inscribiese
me inscribía	me inscribiría	nos inscribiésemos
te inscribías	te inscribirías	os inscribieseis
se inscribía	se inscribiría	se inscribiesen
nos inscribíamos	nos inscribiríamos	
os inscribíais	os inscribiríais	**Imperative-Do**
se inscribían	se inscribirían	(tú) inscríbete
		(él) inscríbase
Preterite	**Present subj've**	(nos'os) inscribámonos
me inscribí	me inscriba	(vos'os) inscribíos
te inscribiste	te inscribas	(ellos) inscríbanse
se inscribió	se inscriba	
nos inscribimos	nos inscribamos	**Imperative-Don't**
os inscribisteis	os inscribáis	no te inscribas
se inscribieron	se inscriban	no se inscriba
		no nos inscribamos
Comp'nd tenses- 63-I-Haber +Past-P		no os inscribáis
		no se inscriban

136

48-I-RF-Irse

Note: participles. present. preterite. imperfect. present subjunctive. imperfect-subjunctive. imperative.

Verb infinitive	Participles	Imperfect-subjunctive 1
Irse, to go away	ido: yéndose	me fuera
		te fueras
Present	**Future**	se fuera
me voy	me iré	nos fuéramos
te vas	te irás	os fuerais
se va	se irá	se fueran
nos vamos	nos iremos	
os vais	os iréis	**Imp'fect-sub've 2**
se van	se irán	me fuese
		te fueses
Imperfect	**Conditional**	se fuese
me iba	me iría	nos fuésemos
te ibas	te irías	os fueseis
se iba	se iría	se fuesen
nos íbamos	nos iríamos	
os ibais	os iríais	**Imperative-Do**
se iban	se irían	(tú) vete
		(él) váyase
Preterite	**Present subj've**	(nos'os) vámonos
me fui	me vaya	(vos'os) idos
te fuiste	te vayas	(ellos) váyanse
se fue	se vaya	
nos fuimos	nos vayamos	**Imperative-Don't**
os fuisteis	os vayáis	no te vayas
se fueron	se vayan	no se vaya
		no nos vayamos
Comp'nd tenses- 63-I-Haber +Past-P		no os vayáis
		no se vayan

137

49-R-RF-Levantarse

Verb infinitive	Participles	Imperfect-subjunctive 1
Levantarse, to get up, to arise	levantado: levantándose	me levantara
		te levantaras
Present	me levantaré	se levantara
me levanto	te levantarás	nos levantáramos
te levantas	se levantará	os levantarais
se levanta	nos levantaremos	se levantaran
nos levantamos	os levantaréis	
os levantáis	se levantarán	**Imp'fect-sub've 2**
se levantan		me levantase
	Conditional	te levantases
Imperfect	me levantaría	se levantase
me levantaba	te levantarías	nos levantásemos
te levantabas	se levantaría	os levantaseis
se levantaba	nos levantaríamos	se levantasen
nos levantábamos	os levantaríais	
os levantabais	se levantarían	**Imperative-Do**
se levantaban		(tú) levántate
		(él) levántese
Preterite	**Present subj've**	(nos'os) levantémonos
me levanté	me levante	(vos'os) levantaos
te levantaste	te levantes	(ellos) levántense
se levantó	se levante	
nos levantamos	nos levantemos	**Imperative-Don't**
os levantasteis	os levantéis	no te levantes
se levantaron	se levanten	no se levante
		no nos levantemos
Comp'nd tenses- 63-I-Haber +Past-P		no os levantéis
		no se levanten

138

50-I-RF-Morderse

Note: present. present subjunctive. imperative.

Verb infinitive	Participles	Imperfect-subjunctive 1
Morderse, to bite oneself	mordido: mordiéndose	me mordiera
		te mordieras
Present	**Future**	se mordiera
me muerdo	me morderé	nos mordiéramos
te muerdes	te morderás	os mordierais
se muerde	se morderá	se mordieran
nos mordemos	nos morderemos	
os mordéis	os morderéis	**Imp'fect-sub've 2**
se muerden	se morderán	me mordiese
		te mordieses
Imperfect	**Conditional**	se mordiese
me mordía	me mordería	nos mordiésemos
te mordías	te morderías	os mordieseis
se mordía	se mordería	se mordiesen
nos mordíamos	nos morderíamos	
os mordíais	os morderíais	**Imperative-Do**
se mordían	se morderían	((tú) muérdete
		(él) muérdase
Preterite	**Present subj've**	(nos'os) mordámonos
me mordí	me muerda	(vos'os) mordeos
te mordiste	te muerdas	(ellos) muérdanse
se mordió	se muerda	
nos mordimos	nos mordamos	**Imperative-Don't**
os mordisteis	os mordáis	no te muerdas
se mordieron	se muerdan	no se muerda
		no nos mordamos
Comp'nd tenses- 63-I-Haber +Past-P		no os mordáis
		no se muerdan

139

51-I-RF-Ponerse

Note: present. preterite. future. conditional. present subjunctive. imperfect-subjunctive. imperative.

Verb infinitive	Participles	Imperfect-subjunctive 1
Ponerse, to put on, to become	puesto: poniéndose	me pusiera
		te pusieras
Present	**Future**	se pusiera
me pongo	me pondré	nos pusiéramos
te pones	te pondrás	os pusierais
se pone	se pondrá	se pusieran
nos ponemos	nos pondremos	
os ponéis	os pondréis	**Imp'fect-sub've 2**
se ponen	se pondrán	me pusiese
		te pusieses
Imperfect	**Conditional**	se pusiese
me ponía	me pondría	nos pusiésemos
te ponías	te pondrías	os pusieseis
se ponía	se pondría	se pusiesen
nos poníamos	nos pondríamos	
os poníais	os pondríais	**Imperative-Do**
se ponían	se pondrían	(tú) ponte
		(él) póngase
Preterite	**Present subj've**	(nos'os) pongámonos
me puse	me ponga	(vos'os) poneos
te pusiste	te pongas	(ellos) pónganse
se puso	se ponga	
nos pusimos	nos pongamos	**Imperative-Don't**
os pusisteis	os pongáis	no te pongas
se pusieron	se pongan	no se ponga
		no nos pongamos
Comp'nd tenses- 63-I-Haber +Past-P		no os pongáis
		no se pongan

52-S-RF-Reírse

Note: participles. present. preterite. present subjunctive. imperfect-subjunctive. imperative.

Verb infinitive	Participles	Imperfect-subjunctive 1
Reírse, to laugh at	reído: riéndose	me riera
		te rieras
Present	**Future**	se riera
me río	me reiré	nos riéramos
te ríes	te reirás	os rierais
se ríe	se reirá	se rieran
nos reímos	nos reiremos	
os reís	os reiréis	**Imp'fect-sub've 2**
se ríen	se reirán	me riese
		te rieses
Imperfect	**Conditional**	se riese
me reía	me reiría	nos riésemos
te reías	te reirías	os rieseis
se reía	se reiría	se riesen
nos reíamos	nos reiríamos	
os reíais	os reiríais	**Imperative-Do**
se reían	se reirían	(tú) ríete
		(él) ríase
Preterite	**Present subj've**	(nos'os) riámonos
me reí	me ría	(vos'os) reíos
te reíste	te rías	(ellos) ríanse
se rió	se ría	
nos reímos	nos riamos	**Imperative-Don't**
os reísteis	os riáis	no te rías
se rieron	se rían	no se ría
		no nos riamos
Comp'nd tenses- 63-I-Haber +Past-P		no os riáis
		no se rían

53-I-RF-Sentarse
Note:. present. preterite. present subjunctive. imperative.

Verb infinitive	Participles	Imperfect-subjunctive 1
Sentarse, to sit down	sentado: sentándose	me sentara
		te sentaras
Present	**Future**	se sentara
me siento	me sentaré	nos sentáramos
te sientas	te sentarás	os sentarais
se sienta	se sentará	se sentaran
nos sentamos	nos sentaremos	
os sentáis	os sentaréis	**Imp'fect-sub've 2**
se sientan	se sentarán	me sentase
		te sentases
Imperfect	**Conditional**	se sentase
me sentaba	me sentaría	nos sentásemos
te sentabas	te sentarías	os sentaseis
se sentaba	se sentaría	se sentasen
nos sentábamos	nos sentaríamos	
os sentabais	os sentaríais	**Imperative-Do**
se sentaban	se sentarían	(tú) siéntate
		(él) siéntese
Preterite	**Present subj've**	(nos'os) sentémonos
me senté	me siente	(vos'os) sentaos
te sentaste	te sientes	(ellos) siéntense
se sentó	se siente	
nos sentamos	nos sentemos	**Imperative-Don't**
os sentasteis	os sentéis	no te sientes
se sentaron	se sienten	no se siente
		no nos sentemos
Comp'nd tenses- 63-I-Haber +Past-P		no os sentéis
		no se sienten

142

54-S-RF-Sentirse

Note: participles. present. preterite. present subjunctive. imperfect-subjunctive. imperative.

Verb infinitive	Participles	Imperfect-subjunctive 1
Sentirse, to feel	sentido: sintiéndose	me sintiera
		te sintieras
Present	**Future**	se sintiera
me siento	me sentiré	nos sintiéramos
te sientes	te sentirás	os sintierais
se siente	se sentirá	se sintieran
nos sentimos	nos sentiremos	
os sentís	os sentiréis	**Imp'fect-sub've 2**
se sienten	se sentirán	me sintiese
		te sintieses
Imperfect	**Conditional**	se sintiese
me sentía	me sentiría	nos sintiésemos
te sentías	te sentirías	os sintieseis
se sentía	se sentiría	se sintiesen
nos sentíamos	nos sentiríamos	
os sentíais	os sentiríais	**Imperative-Do**
se sentían	se sentirían	(tú) siéntete
		(él) siéntase
Preterite	**Present subj've**	(nos'os) sintámonos
me sentí	me sienta	(vos'os) sentíos
te sentiste	te sientas	(ellos) siéntanse
se sintió	se sienta	
nos sentimos	nos sintamos	**Imperative-Don't**
os sentisteis	os sintáis	no te sientas
se sintieron	se sientan	no se sienta
		no nos sintamos
Comp'nd tenses- 63-I-Haber +Past-P		no os sintáis
		no se sientan

143

55-I-Andar

Note: preterite. imperfect-subjunctive.

Verb infinitive	Participles	Imperfect-subjunctive 1
Andar, to walk	andado: andando	yo anduviera
		tú anduvieras
Present	**Future**	él anduviera
yo ando	yo andaré	nos'os anduviéramos
tú andas	tú andarás	vos'os anduvierais
él anda	él andará	ellos anduvieran
nos'os andamos	nos'os andaremos	
vos'os andáis	vos'os andaréis	**Imp'fect-sub've 2**
ellos andan	ellos andarán	yo anduviese
		tú anduvieses
Imperfect	**Conditional**	él anduviese
yo andaba	yo andaría	nos'os anduviésemos
tú andabas	tú andarías	vos'os anduvieseis
él andaba	él andaría	ellos anduviesen
nos'os andábamos	nos'os andaríamos	
vos'os andabais	vos'os andaríais	**Imperative-Do**
ellos andaban	ellos andarían	(tú) anda
		(él) ande
Preterite	**Present subj've**	(nos'os) andemos
yo anduve	yo ande	(vos'os) andad
tú anduviste	tú andes	(ellos) anden
él anduvo	él ande	
nos'os anduvimos	nos'os andemos	**Imperative-Don't**
vos'os anduvisteis	vos'os andéis	no andes
ellos anduvieron	ellos anden	no ande
		no andemos
Comp'nd tenses- 63-I-Haber +Past-P		no andéis
		no anden

144

56-I-Asir

Note: present. preterite. present subjunctive. imperative.

Verb infinitive	Participles	Imperfect-subjunctive 1
Asir, to seize	asido: asiendo	yo asiera
		tú asieras
Present	**Future**	él asiera
yo asgo	yo asiré	nos'os asiéramos
tú ases	tú asirás	vos'os asierais
él ase	él asirá	ellos asieran
nos'os asimos	nos'os asiremos	
vos'os asís	vos'os asiréis	**Imp'fect-sub've 2**
ellos asen	ellos asirán	yo asiese
		tú asieses
Imperfect	**Conditional**	él asiese
yo asía	yo asiría	nos'os asiésemos
tú asías	tú asirías	vos'os asieseis
él asía	él asiría	ellos asiesen
nos'os asíamos	nos'os asiríamos	
vos'os asíais	vos'os asiríais	**Imperative-Do**
ellos asían	ellos asirían	(tú) ase
		(él) asga
Preterite	**Present subj've**	(nos'os) asgamos
yo así	yo asga	(vos'os) asid
tú asiste	tú asgas	(ellos) asgan
él asió	él asga	
nos'os asimos	nos'os asgamos	**Imperative-Don't**
vos'os asisteis	vos'os asgáis	no asgas
ellos asieron	ellos asgan	no asga
		no asgamos
Comp'nd tenses- 63-I-Haber +Past-P		no asgáis
		no asgan

57-I-Caber

Note: present. preterite. future. conditional. present subjunctive. imperfect-subjunctive. imperative.

Verb infinitive	Participles	Imperfect-subjunctive 1
Caber, to fit, to accommodate	cabido: cabiendo	yo cupiera
		tú cupieras
Present	**Future**	él cupiera
yo quepo	yo cabré	nos'os cupiéramos
tú cabes	tú cabrás	vos'os cupierais
él cabe	él cabrá	ellos cupieran
nos'os cabemos	nos'os cabremos	
vos'os cabéis	vos'os cabréis	**Imp'fect-sub've 2**
ellos caben	ellos cabrán	yo cupiese
		tú cupieses
Imperfect	**Conditional**	él cupiese
yo cabía	yo cabría	nos'os cupiésemos
tú cabías	tú cabrías	vos'os cupieseis
él cabía	él cabría	ellos cupiesen
nos'os cabíamos	nos'os cabríamos	
vos'os cabíais	vos'os cabríais	**Imperative-Do**
ellos cabían	ellos cabrían	(tú) cabe
		(él) quepa
Preterite	**Present subj've**	(nos'os) quepamos
yo cupe	yo quepa	(vos'os) cabed
tú cupiste	tú quepas	(ellos) quepan
él cupo	él quepa	
nos'os cupimos	nos'os quepamos	**Imperative-Don't**
vos'os cupisteis	vos'os quepáis	no quepas
ellos cupieron	ellos quepan	no quepa
		no quepamos
Comp'nd tenses- 63-I-Haber +Past-P		no quepáis
		no quepan

146

58-I-Cocer

Note: present. present subjunctive. imperative.

Verb infinitive	Participles	Imperfect-subjunctive 1
Cocer, to cook	cocido: cociendo	yo cociera
		tú cocieras
Present	**Future**	él cociera
yo cuezo	yo coceré	nos'os cociéramos
tú cueces	tú cocerás	vos'os cocierais
él cuece	él cocerá	ellos cocieran
nos'os cocemos	nos'os coceremos	
vos'os cocéis	vos'os coceréis	**Imp'fect-sub've 2**
ellos cuecen	ellos cocerán	yo cociese
		tú cocieses
Imperfect	**Conditional**	él cociese
yo cocía	yo cocería	nos'os cociésemos
tú cocías	tú cocerías	vos'os cocieseis
él cocía	él cocería	ellos cociesen
nos'os cocíamos	nos'os coceríamos	
vos'os cocíais	vos'os coceríais	**Imperative-Do**
ellos cocían	ellos cocerían	(tú) cuece
		(él) cueza
Preterite	**Present subj've**	(nos'os) cozamos
yo cocí	**Present**	(vos'os) coced
tú cociste	yo cueza	(ellos) cuezan
él coció	tú cuezas	
nos'os cocimos	él cueza	**Imperative-Don't**
vos'os cocisteis	nos'os cozamos	no cuezas
ellos cocieron	vos'os cozáis	no cueza
	ellos cuezan	no cozamos
Comp'nd tenses- 63-I-Haber +Past-P		no cozáis
		no cuezan

147

59-I-Dar

Note: present. preterite. present subjunctive. imperfect-subjunctive. imperative.

Verb infinitive	Participles	Imperfect-subjunctive 1
Dar, to give	dado: dando	yo diera
		tú dieras
Present	**Future**	él diera
yo doy	yo daré	nos'os diéramos
tú das	tú darás	vos'os dierais
él da	él dará	ellos dieran
nos'os damos	nos'os daremos	
vos'os dais	vos'os daréis	**Imp'fect-sub've 2**
ellos dan	ellos darán	yo diese
		tú dieses
Imperfect	**Conditional**	él diese
yo daba	yo daría	nos'os diésemos
tú dabas	tú darías	vos'os dieseis
él daba	él daría	ellos diesen
nos'os dábamos	nos'os daríamos	
vos'os dabais	vos'os daríais	**Imperative-Do**
ellos daban	ellos darían	(tú) da
		(él) dé
Preterite	**Present subj've**	(nos'os) demos
yo di	yo dé	(vos'os) dad
tú diste	tú des	(ellos) den
él dio	él dé	
nos'os dimos	nos'os demos	**Imperative-Don't**
vos'os disteis	vos'os deis	no des
ellos dieron	ellos den	no dé
		no demos
Comp'nd tenses- 63-I-Haber +Past-P		no deis
		no den

60-I-Decir

Note: present. preterite. future. conditional. present subjunctive. imperfect-subjunctive. imperative.

Verb infinitive	Participles	Imperfect-subjunctive 1
Decir, to say	dicho: diciendo	yo dijera
		tú dijeras
Present	**Future**	él dijera
yo digo	yo diré	nos'os dijéramos
tú dices	tú dirás	vos'os dijerais
él dice	él dirá	ellos dijeran
nos'os decimos	nos'os diremos	
vos'os decís	vos'os diréis	**Imp'fect-sub've 2**
ellos dicen	ellos dirán	yo dijese
		tú dijeses
Imperfect	**Conditional**	él dijese
yo decía	yo diría	nos'os dijésemos
tú decías	tú dirías	vos'os dijeseis
él decía	él diría	ellos dijesen
nos'os decíamos	nos'os diríamos	
vos'os decíais	vos'os diríais	**Imperative-Do**
ellos decían	ellos dirían	(tú) di
		(él) diga
Preterite	**Present subj've**	(nos'os) digamos
yo dije	yo diga	(vos'os) decid
tú dijiste	tú digas	(ellos) digan
él dijo	él diga	
nos'os dijimos	nos'os digamos	**Imperative-Don't**
vos'os dijisteis	vos'os digáis	no digas
ellos dijeron	ellos digan	no diga
		no digamos
Comp'nd tenses- 63-I-Haber +Past-P		no digáis
		no digan

149

61-I-Errar

Verb infinitive	Participles	Imperfect-subjunctive 1
Errar, to miss, to fail, to get wrong	errado: errando	yo errara
		tú erraras
Present	**Future**	él errara
yo yerro	yo erraré	nos'os erráramos
tú yerras	tú errarás	vos'os errarais
él yerra	él errará	ellos erraran
nos'os erramos	nos'os erraremos	
vos'os erráis	vos'os erraréis	**Imp'fect-sub've 2**
ellos yerran	ellos errarán	yo errase
		tú errases
Imperfect	**Conditional**	él errase
yo erraba	yo erraría	nos'os errásemos
tú errabas	tú errarías	vos'os erraseis
él erraba	él erraría	ellos errasen
nos'os errábamos	nos'os erraríamos	
vos'os errabais	vos'os erraríais	**Imperative-Do**
ellos erraban	ellos errarían	(tú) yerra
		(él) yerre
Preterite	**Present subj've**	(nos'os) erremos
yo erré	yo yerre	(vos'os) errad
tú erraste	tú yerres	(ellos) yerren
él erró	él yerre	
nos'os erramos	nos'os erremos	**Imperative-Don't**
vos'os errasteis	vos'os erréis	no yerres
ellos erraron	ellos yerren	no yerre
		no erremos
Comp'nd tenses- 63-I-Haber +Past-P		no erréis
		no yerren

150

62-I-Estar

Note: present. preterite. present subjunctive. imperfect-subjunctive. imperative.

Verb infinitive	Participles	Imperfect-subjunctive 1
Estar, to be	estado: estando	yo estuviera
		tú estuvieras
Present	**Future**	él estuviera
yo estoy	yo estaré	nos'os estuviéramos
tú estás	tú estarás	vos'os estuvierais
él está	él estará	ellos estuvieran
nos'os estamos	nos'os estaremos	
vos'os estáis	vos'os estaréis	**Imp'fect-sub've 2**
ellos están	ellos estarán	**Imperfect-subjunctive**
		yo estuviese
Imperfect	**Conditional**	tú estuvieses
yo estaba	yo estaría	él estuviese
tú estabas	tú estarías	nos'os estuviésemos
él estaba	él estaría	vos'os estuvieseis
nos'os estábamos	nos'os estaríamos	ellos estuviesen
vos'os estabais	vos'os estaríais	**Imperative-Do**
ellos estaban	ellos estarían	(tú) está
		(él) esté
Preterite	**Present subj've**	(nos'os) estemos
yo estuve	yo esté	(vos'os) estad
tú estuviste	tú estés	(ellos) estén
él estuvo	él esté	
nos'os estuvimos	nos'os estemos	**Imperative-Don't**
vos'os estuvisteis	vos'os estéis	no estés
ellos estuvieron	ellos estén	no esté
		no estemos
Comp'nd tenses- 63-I-Haber +Past-P		no estéis
		no estén

151

63(a)-I-Haber (auxillary verb) Note present. preterite. future. conditional. present subjunctive. imperfect-subjunctive. imperative.

Verb infinitive	Participles	
Haber, to have	habido: habiendo	
Present-Perfect	**Present-Perfect subjunctive**	**Future Perfect**
yo he+Past-P	yo haya+Past-P	yo habré+Past-P
tú has+Past-P	tú hayas+Past-P	tú habrás+Past-P
él ha+Past-P; hay	él haya+Past-P	él habrá+Past-P
nos'os hemos+Past-P	nos'os hayamos+Past-P	nos'os habremos+Past-P
vos'os habéis+Past-P	vos'os hayáis+Past-P	vos'os habréis+Past-P
ellos han+Past-P	ellos hayan+Past-P	ellos habrán+Past-P
Pluperfect	**Pluperfect subjunctive 1**	**Conditional Perfect**
yo había+Past-P	yo hubiera+Past-P	yo habría+Past-P
tú habías+Past-P	tú hubieras+Past-P	tú habrías+Past-P
él había+Past-P	él hubiera+Past-P	él habría+Past-P
nos'os habíamos+Past-P	nos'os hubiéramos+Past-P	nos'os habríamos+Past-P
vos'os habíais+Past-P	vos'os hubierais+Past-P	vos'os habríais+Past-P
ellos habían+Past-P	ellos hubieran+Past-P	ellos habrían+Past-P
Preterite Perfect	**Pluperfect-subjunctive 2**	
yo hube+Past-P	yo hubiese+Past-P	
tú hubiste+Past-P	tú hubieses+Past-P	
él hubo+Past-P	él hubiese+Past-P	
nos'os hubimos+Past-P	nos'os hubiésemos+Past-P	
vos'os hubisteis+Past-P	vos'os hubieseis+Past-P	
ellos hubieron+Past-P	ellos hubiesen+Past-P	

63(b)-I-RF-Haber(auxillary verb) used with reflexive verb
Note present. preterite. future. conditional. present subjunctive. imperfect-subjunctive. imperative

Verb infinitive	Participles	
Haber, to have: (reflexive form)	habido: habiendo	
Present-Perfect	**Present-Perfect subjunctive**	**Future Perfect**
me he+Past-P	me haya+Past-P	me habré+Past-P
te has+Past-P	te hayas+Past-P	te habrás+Past-P
se ha+Past-P	se haya+Past-P	se habrá+Past-P
nos hemos+Past-P	nos hayamos+Past-P	nos habremos+ Past-P
vos habéis+Past-P	vos hayáis+Past-P	vos habréis+Past-P
se han+Past-P	se hayan+Past-P	se habrán+Past-P
Pluperfect	**Pluperfect subjunctive 1**	**Conditional Perfect**
me había+Past-P	yo hubiera+Past-P	me habría+Past-P
te habías+Past-P	tú hubieras+Past-P	te habrías+Past-P
se había+Past-P	él hubiera+Past-P	se habría+Past-P
nos habíamos+Past-P	nos'os hubiéramos+Past-P	nos habríamos+ Past-P
vos habíais+Past-P	vos'os hubierais+Past-P	vos habríais+Past-P
se habían+Past-P	ellos hubieran+ Past-P	se habrían+Past-P
Preterite Perfect	**Pluperfect-subjunctive 2**	
me hube+Past-P	yo hubiese+Past-P	
te hubiste+Past-P	tú hubieses+Past-P	
se hubo+Past-P	él hubiese+Past-P	
nos hubimos+Past-P	nos'os hubiésemos+Past-P	
vos hubisteis+Past-P	vos'os hubieseis+Past-P	
se hubieron+Past-P	ellos hubiesen+ Past-P	

153

64-I-Hacer

Note: participles. present. preterite. future. conditional. present subjunctive. imperfect-subjunctive. imperative.

Verb infinitive	Participles	Imperfect-subjunctive 1
Hacer, to make, to do	hecho: haciendo	yo hiciera
		tú hicieras
Present	**Future**	él hiciera
yo hago	yo haré	nos'os hiciéramos
tú haces	tú harás	vos'os hicierais
él hace	él hará	ellos hicieran
nos'os hacemos	nos'os haremos	
vos'os hacéis	vos'os haréis	**Imp'fect-sub've 2**
ellos hacen	ellos harán	yo hiciese
		tú hicieses
Imperfect	**Conditional**	él hiciese
yo hacía	yo haría	nos'os hiciésemos
tú hacías	tú harías	vos'os hicieseis
él hacía	él haría	ellos hiciesen
nos'os hacíamos	nos'os haríamos	
vos'os hacíais	vos'os haríais	**Imperative-Do**
ellos hacían	ellos harían	(tú) haz
		(él) haga
Preterite	**Present subj've**	(nos'os) hagamos
yo hice	yo haga	(vos'os) haced
tú hiciste	tú hagas	(ellos) hagan
él hizo	él haga	
nos'os hicimos	nos'os hagamos	**Imperative-Don't**
vos'os hicisteis	vos'os hagáis	no hagas
ellos hicieron	ellos hagan	no haga
		no hagamos
Comp'nd tenses- 63-I-Haber +Past-P		no hagáis
		no hagan

154

65-I-Ir

Note: participles. present. preterite. imperfect. present subjunctive. imperfect-subjunctive. imperative.

Verb infinitive	Participles	Imperfect-subjunctive 1
Ir, to go	ido: yendo	yo fuera
		tú fueras
Present	**Future**	él fuera
yo voy	yo iré	nos'os fuéramos
tú vas	tú irás	vos'os fuerais
él va	él irá	ellos fueran
nos'os vamos	nos'os iremos	
vos'os vais	vos'os iréis	**Imp'fect-sub've 2**
ellos van	ellos irán	yo fuese
		tú fueses
Imperfect	**Conditional**	él fuese
yo iba	yo iría	nos'os fuésemos
tú ibas	tú irías	vos'os fueseis
él iba	él iría	ellos fuesen
nos'os íbamos	nos'os iríamos	
vos'os ibais	vos'os iríais	**Imperative-Do**
ellos iban	ellos irían	(tú) ve
		(él) vaya
Preterite	**Present subj've**	(nos'os) vamos;
yo fui	yo vaya	(vos'os) id
tú fuiste	tú vayas	(ellos) vayan
él fue	él vaya	
nos'os fuimos	nos'os vayamos	**Imperative-Don't**
vos'os fuisteis	vos'os vayáis	no vayas
ellos fueron	ellos vayan	no vaya
		no vayamos
Comp'nd tenses- 63-I-Haber +Past-P		no vayáis
		no vayan

155

66-I-Oir

Note: participles. present. preterite. present subjunctive. imperfect-subjunctive. imperative.

Verb infinitive	Participles	Imperfect-subjunctive 1
Oir, to hear	oído: oyendo	yo oyera
		tú oyeras
Present	**Future**	él oyera
yo oigo	yo oiré	nos'os oyéramos
tú oyes	tú oirás	vos'os oyerais
él oye	él oirá	ellos oyeran
nos'os oímos	nos'os oiremos	
vos'os oís	vos'os oiréis	**Imp'fect-sub've 2**
ellos oyen	ellos oirán	yo oyese
		tú oyeses
Imperfect	**Conditional**	él oyese
yo oía	yo oiría	nos'os oyésemos
tú oías	tú oirías	vos'os oyeseis
él oía	él oiría	ellos oyesen
nos'os oíamos	nos'os oiríamos	
vos'os oíais	vos'os oiríais	**Imperative-Do**
ellos oían	ellos oirían	(tú) oye
		(él) oiga
Preterite	**Present subj've**	(nos'os) oigamos
yo oí	yo oiga	(vos'os) oíd
tú oíste	tú oigas	(ellos) oigan
él oyó	él oiga	
nos'os oímos	nos'os oigamos	**Imperative-Don't**
vos'os oísteis	vos'os oigáis	no oigas
ellos oyeron	ellos oigan	no oiga
		no oigamos
Comp'nd tenses- 63-I-Haber +Past-P		no oigáis
		no oigan

156

67-I-Poder

Note: present. preterite. future. conditional. present subjunctive. imperfect-subjunctive. imperative.

Verb infinitive	Participles	Imperfect-subjunctive 1
Poder, to be able to	podido: podiendo	yo pudiera
		tú pudieras
Present	**Future**	él pudiera
yo puedo	yo podré	nos'os pudiéramos
tú puedes	tú podrás	vos'os pudierais
él puede	él podrá	ellos pudieran
nos'os podemos	nos'os podremos	
vos'os podéis	vos'os podréis	**Imp'fect-sub've 2**
ellos pueden	ellos podrán	yo pudiese
		tú pudieses
Imperfect	**Conditional**	él pudiese
yo podía	yo podría	nos'os pudiésemos
tú podías	tú podrías	vos'os pudieseis
él podía	él podría	ellos pudiesen
nos'os podíamos	nos'os podríamos	
vos'os podíais	vos'os podríais	**Imperative-Do**
ellos podían	ellos podrían	(tú) puede
		(él) pueda
Preterite	**Present subj've**	(nos'os) podamos
yo pude	yo pueda	(vos'os) poded
tú pudiste	tú puedas	(ellos) puedan
él pudo	él pueda	
nos'os pudimos	nos'os podamos	**Imperative-Don't**
vos'os pudisteis	vos'os podáis	no puedas
ellos pudieron	ellos puedan	no pueda
		no podamos
Comp'nd tenses- 63-I-Haber +Past-P		no podáis
		no puedan

157

68-I-Poner

Note: participles. present. preterite. future. conditional. present subjunctive imperfect-subjunctive. imperative.

Verb infinitive	Participles	Imperfect-subjunctive 1
Poner, to put, to place	puesto: poniendo	yo pusiera
		tú pusieras
Present	**Future**	él pusiera
yo pongo	yo pondré	nos'os pusiéramos
tú pones	tú pondrás	vos'os pusierais
él pone	él pondrá	ellos pusieran
nos'os ponemos	nos'os pondremos	
vos'os ponéis	vos'os pondréis	**Imp'fect-sub've 2**
ellos ponen	ellos pondrán	yo pusiese
		tú pusieses
Imperfect	**Conditional**	él pusiese
yo ponía	yo pondría	nos'os pusiésemos
tú ponías	tú pondrías	vos'os pusieseis
él ponía	él pondría	ellos pusiesen
nos'os poníamos	nos'os pondríamos	
vos'os poníais	vos'os pondríais	**Imperative-Do**
ellos ponían	ellos pondrían	(tú) pon
		(él) ponga
Preterite	**Present subj've**	(nos'os) pongamos
yo puse	yo ponga	(vos'os) poned
tú pusiste	tú pongas	(ellos) pongan
él puso	él ponga	
nos'os pusimos	nos'os pongamos	**Imperative-Don't**
vos'os pusisteis	vos'os pongáis	no pongas
ellos pusieron	ellos pongan	no ponga
		no pongamos
Comp'nd tenses- 63-I-Haber +Past-P		no pongáis
		no pongan

158

69-I-Querer

Note: present. preterite. future. conditional. present subjunctive. imperfect-subjunctive. imperative.

Verb infinitive	Participles	Imperfect-subjunctive 1
Querer, to want, to love	querido: queriendo	yo quisiera
		tú quisieras
Present	**Future**	él quisiera
yo quiero	yo querré	nos'os quisiéramos
tú quieres	tú querrás	vos'os quisierais
él quiere	él querrá	ellos quisieran
nos'os queremos	nos'os querremos	
vos'os queréis	vos'os querréis	**Imp'fect-sub've 2**
ellos quieren	ellos querrán	yo quisiere
		tú quisieres
Imperfect	**Conditional**	él quisiere
yo quería	yo querría	nos'os quisiéremos
tú querías	tú querrías	vos'os quisiereis
él quería	él querría	ellos quisieren
nos'os queríamos	nos'os querríamos	
vos'os queríais	vos'os querríais	**Imperative-Do**
ellos querían	ellos querrían	(tú) quiere
		(él) quiera
Preterite	**Present subj've**	(nos'os) queramos
yo quise	yo quiera	(vos'os) quered
tú quisiste	tú quieras	(ellos) quieran
él quiso	él quiera	
nos'os quisimos	nos'os queramos	**Imperative-Don't**
vos'os quisisteis	vos'os queráis	no quieras
ellos quisieron	ellos quieran	no quiera
		no queramos
Comp'nd tenses- 63-I-Haber +Past-P		no queráis
		no quieran

159

70-I-Roer

Verb infinitive	Participles	Imperfect-subjunctive 1
Roer, to gnaw, to nibble	roído: royendo	yo royera
		tú royeras
Present	**Future**	él royera
yo roigo	yo roeré	nos'os royéramos
tú roes	tú roerás	vos'os royerais
él roe	él roerá	ellos royeran
nos'os roemos	nos'os roeremos	
vos'os roéis	vos'os roeréis	**Imp'fect-sub've 2**
ellos roen	ellos roerán	yo royese
		tú royeses
Imperfect	**Conditional**	él royese
yo roía	yo roería	nos'os royésemos
tú roías	tú roerías	vos'os royeseis
él roía	é roería	ellos royesen
nos'os roíamos	nos'os roeríamos	
vos'os roíais	vos'os roeríais	**Imperative-Do**
ellos roían	ellos roerían	(tú) roe
		(él) roiga
Preterite	**Present subj've**	(nos'os) roigamos
yo roí	yo roiga	(vos'os) roed
tú roíste	tú roigas	(ellos) roigan
él royó	él roiga	
nos'os roímos	nos'os roigamos	**Imperative-Don't**
vos'os roísteis	vos'os roigáis	no roigas
ellos royeron	ellos roigan	no roiga
		no roigamos
Comp'nd tenses- 63-I-Haber +Past-P		no roigáis
		no roigan

71-I-Saber

Note: present. preterite. future. conditional. present subjunctive. imperfect-subjunctive. imperative.

Verb infinitive	Participles	Imperfect-subjunctive 1
Saber, to know	sabido: sabiendo	yo supiera
		tú supieras
Present	**Future**	él supiera
yo sé	yo sabré	nos'os supiéramos
tú sabes	tú sabrás	vos'os supierais
él sabe	él sabrá	ellos supieran
nos'os sabemos	nos'os sabremos	
vos'os sabéis	vos'os sabréis	**Imp'fect-sub've 2**
ellos saben	ellos sabrán	yo supiese
		tú supieses
Imperfect	**Conditional**	él supiese
yo sabía	yo sabría	nos'os supiésemos
tú sabías	tú sabrías	vos'os supieseis
él sabía	él sabría	ellos supiesen
nos'os sabíamos	nos'os sabríamos	
vos'os sabíais	vos'os sabríais	**Imperative-Do**
ellos sabían	ellos sabrían	(tú) sabe
		(él) sepa
Preterite	**Present subj've**	(nos'os) sepamos
yo supe	yo sepa	(vos'os) sabed
tú supiste	tú sepas	(ellos) sepan
él supo	él sepa	
nos'os supimos	nos'os sepamos	**Imperative-Don't**
vos'os supisteis	vos'os sepáis	no sepas
ellos supieron	ellos sepan	no sepa
		no sepamos
Comp'nd tenses- 63-I-Haber +Past-P		no sepáis
		no sepan

161

72-I-Salir

Note: present. future. conditional. present subjunctive. imperative.

Verb infinitive	Participles	Imperfect-subjunctive 1
Salir, to leave, to go out	salido: saliendo	yo saliera
		tú salieras
Present	**Future**	él saliera
yo salgo	yo saldré	nos'os saliéramos
tú sales	tú saldrás	vos'os salierais
él sale	él saldrá	ellos salieran
nos'os salimos	nos'os saldremos	
vos'os salís	vos'os saldréis	**Imp'fect-sub've 2**
ellos salen	ellos saldrán	yo saliese
		tú salieses
Imperfect	**Conditional**	él saliese
yo salía	yo saldría	nos'os saliésemos
tú salías	tú saldrías	vos'os salieseis
él salía	él saldría	ellos saliesen
nos'os salíamos	nos'os saldríamos	
vos'os salíais	vos'os saldríais	**Imperative-Do**
ellos salían	ellos saldrían	(tú) sal
		(él) salga
Preterite	**Present subj've**	(nos'os) salgamos
yo salí	yo salga	(vos'os) salid
tú saliste	tú salgas	(ellos) salgan
él salió	él salga	**Imperative-Don't**
nos'os salimos	nos'os salgamos	no salgas
vos'os salisteis	vos'os salgáis	no salga
ellos salieron	ellos salgan	no salgamos
		no salgáis
Comp'nd tenses- 63-I-Haber +Past-P		no salgan

162

73-I-Satisfacer

Note: participles. present. preterite. future. conditional. present subjunctive. imperfect-subjunctive. imperative.

Verb infinitive	Participles	Imperfect-subjunctive 1
Satisfacer, to satisfy	satisfecho: satisfaciendo	yo satisficiera
		tú satisficieras
Present	**Future**	él satisficiera
yo satisfago	yo satisfaré	nos'os satisficiéramos
tú satisfaces	tú satisfarás	vos'os satisficierais
él satisface	él satisfará	ellos satisficieran
nos'os satisfacemos	nos'os satisfaremos	
vos'os satisfacéis	vos'os satisfaréis	**Imp'fect-sub've 2**
ellos satisfacen	ellos satisfarán	yo satisficiese
		tú satisficieses
Imperfect	**Conditional**	él satisficiese
yo satisfacía	yo satisfaría	nos'os satisficiésemos
tú satisfacías	tú satisfarías	vos'os satisficieseis
él satisfacía	él satisfaría	ellos satisficiesen
nos'os satisfacíamos	nos'os satisfaríamos	
vos'os satisfacíais	vos'os satisfaríais	**Imperative-Do**
ellos satisfacían	ellos satisfarían	(tú) satisface;
		(él) satisfaga
Preterite	**Present subj've**	(nos'os) satisfagamos
yo satisfice	yo satisfaga	(vos'os) satisfaced
tú satisficiste	tú satisfagas	(ellos) satisfagan
él satisfizo	él satisfaga	
nos'os satisficimos	nos'os satisfagamos	**Imperative-Don't**
vos'os satisficisteis	vos'os satisfagáis	no satisfagas
ellos satisficieron	ellos satisfagan	no satisfaga
		no satisfagamos
Comp'nd tenses- 63-I-Haber +Past-P		no satisfagáis
		no satisfagan

163

74-I-Ser

Note: present. preterite. imperfect. present subjunctive. imperfect-subjunctive. imperative.

Verb infinitive	Participles	Imperfect-subjunctive 1
Ser, to be	sido: siendo	yo fuera
		tú fueras
Present	**Future**	él fuera
yo soy	yo seré	nos'os fuéramos
tú eres	tú serás	vos'os fuerais
él es	él será	ellos fueran
nos'os somos	nos'os seremos	
vos'os sois	vos'os seréis	**Imp'fect-sub've 2**
ellos son	ellos serán	yo fuese
		tú fueses
Imperfect	**Conditional**	él fuese
yo era	yo sería	nos'os fuésemos
tú eras	tú serías	vos'os fueseis
él era	él sería	ellos fuesen
nos'os éramos	nos'os seríamos	
vos'os erais	vos'os seríais	**Imperative-Do**
ellos eran	ellos serían	(tú) sé
		(él) sea
Preterite	**Present subj've**	(nos'os) seamos
yo fui	yo sea	(vos'os) sed
tú fuiste	tú seas	(ellos) sean
él fue	él sea	
nos'os fuimos	nos'os seamos	**Imperative-Don't**
vos'os fuisteis	vos'os seáis	no seas
ellos fueron	ellos sean	no sea
		no seamos
Comp'nd tenses- 63-I-Haber +Past-P		no seáis
		no sean

164

75-I-Tener

Note: present. preterite. future. conditional. present subjunctive.
imperfect-subjunctive. imperative.

Verb infinitive	Participles	Imperfect-subjunctive 1
Tener, to have	tenido: teniendo	yo tuviera
		tú tuvieras
Present	**Future**	él tuviera
yo tengo	yo tendré	nos'os tuviéramos
tú tienes	tú tendrás	vos'os tuvierais
él tiene	él tendrá	ellos tuvieran
nos'os tenemos	nos'os tendremos	
vos'os tenéis	vos'os tendréis	**Imp'fect-sub've 2**
ellos tienen	ellos tendrán	yo tuviese
		tú tuvieses
Imperfect	**Conditional**	él tuviese
yo tenía	yo tendría	nos'os tuviésemos
tú tenías	tú tendrías	vos'os tuvieseis
él tenía	él tendría	ellos tuviesen
nos'os teníamos	nos'os tendríamos	
vos'os teníais	vos'os tendríais	**Imperative-Do**
ellos tenían	ellos tendrían	(tú) ten
		(él) tenga
Preterite	**Present subj've**	(nos'os) tengamos
yo tuve	yo tenga	(vos'os) tened
tú tuviste	tú tengas	(ellos) tengan
él tuvo	él tenga	
nos'os tuvimos	nos'os tengamos	**Imperative-Don't**
vos'os tuvisteis	vos'os tengáis	no tengas
ellos tuvieron	ellos tengan	no tenga
		no tengamos
Comp'nd tenses- 63-I-Haber +Past-P		no tengáis
		no tengan

165

76-I-Traer

Note: participles. present. preterite. imperfect. future. conditional. present subjunctive. imperfect-subjunctive. imperative.

Verb infinitive	Participles	Imperfect-subjunctive 1
Traer, to bring	traído: trayendo	yo trajera
		tú trajeras
Present	**Future**	él trajera
yo traigo	yo traeré	nos'os trajéramos
tú traes	tú traerás	vos'os trajerais
él trae	él traerá	ellos trajeran
nos'os traemos	nos'os traeremos	
vos'os traéis	vos'os traeréis	**Imp'fect-sub've 2**
ellos traen	ellos traerán	yo trajese
		tú trajeses
Imperfect	**Conditional**	él trajese
yo traía	yo traería	nos'os trajésemos
tú traías	tú traerías	vos'os trajeseis
él traía	él traería	ellos trajesen
nos'os traíamos	nos'os traeríamos	
vos'os traíais	vos'os traeríais	**Imperative-Do**
ellos traían	ellos traerían	(tú) trae
		(él) traiga
Preterite	**Present subj've**	(nos'os) traigamos
yo traje	yo traiga	(vos'os) traed
tú trajiste	tú traigas	(ellos) traigan
él trajo	él traiga	
nos'os trajimos	nos'os traigamos	**Imperative-Don't**
vos'os trajisteis	vos'os traigáis	no traigas
ellos trajeron	ellos traigan	no traiga
		no traigamos
Comp'nd tenses- 63-I-Haber +Past-P		no traigáis
		no traigan

166

77-I-Valer

Note: present. future. conditional. present subjunctive. imperative.

Verb infinitive	Participles	Imperfect-subjunctive 1
Valer, to cost, to be worth	valido: valiendo	yo valiera
		tú valieras
Present	**Future**	él valiera
yo valgo	yo valdré	nos'os valiéramos
tú vales	tú valdrás	vos'os valierais
él vale	él valdrá	ellos valieran
nos'os valemos	nos'os valdremos	
vos'os valéis	vos'os valdréis	**Imp'fect-sub've 2**
ellos valen	ellos valdrán	yo valiese
		tú valieses
Imperfect	**Conditional**	él valiese
yo valía	yo valdría	nos'os valiésemos
tú valías	tú valdrías	vos'os valieseis
él valía	él valdría	ellos valiesen
nos'os valíamos	nos'os valdríamos	
vos'os valíais	vos'os valdríais	**Imperative-Do**
ellos valían	ellos valdrían	(tú) vale; val
		(él) valga
Preterite	**Present subj've**	(nos'os) valgamos
yo valí	yo valga	(vos'os) valed
tú valiste	tú valgas	(ellos) valgan
él valió	él valga	
nos'os valimos	nos'os valgamos	**Imperative-Don't**
vos'os valisteis	vos'os valgáis	no valgas
ellos valieron	ellos valgan	no valga
		no valgamos
Comp'nd tenses- 63-I-Haber +Past-P		no valgáis
		no valgan

167

78-I-Venir

Note: participles. present. preterite. future. conditional. present subjunctive. imperfect-subjunctive. imperative.

Verb infinitive	Participles	Imperfect-subjunctive 1
Venir, to come	venido: viniendo	yo viniera
		tú vinieras
Present	**Future**	él viniera
yo vengo	yo vendré	nos'os viniéramos
tú vienes	tú vendrás	vos'os vinierais
él viene	él vendrá	ellos vinieran
nos'os venimos	nos'os vendremos	
vos'os venís	vos'os vendréis	**Imp'fect-sub've 2**
ellos vienen	ellos vendrán	yo viniese
		tú vinieses
Imperfect	**Conditional**	él viniese
yo venía	yo vendría	nos'os viniésemos
tú venías	tú vendrías	vos'os vinieseis
él venía	él vendría	ellos viniesen
nos'os veníamos	nos'os vendríamos	
vos'os veníais	vos'os vendríais	**Imperative-Do**
ellos venían	ellos vendrían	(tú) ven
		(él) venga
Preterite	**Present subj've**	(nos'os) vengamos
yo vine	yo venga	(vos'os) venid
tú viniste	tú vengas	(ellos) vengan
él vino	él venga	
nos'os vinimos	nos'os vengamos	**Imperative-Don't**
vos'os vinisteis	vos'os vengáis	no vengas
ellos vinieron	ellos vengan	no venga
		no vengamos
Comp'nd tenses- 63-I-Haber +Past-P		no vengáis
		no vengan

79-I-Ver
Note: participles. present. preterite. present subjunctive. imperative.

Verb infinitive	Participles	Imperfect-subjunctive 1
Ver, to see	visto: viendo	yo viera
		tú vieras
Present	**Future**	él viera
yo veo	yo veré	nos'os viéramos
tú ves	tú verás	vos'os vierais
él ve	él verá	ellos vieran
nos'os vemos	nos'os veremos	
vos'os veis	vos'os veréis	**Imp'fect-sub've 2**
ellos ven	ellos verán	yo viese
		tú vieses
Imperfect	**Conditional**	él viese
yo veía	yo vería	nos'os viésemos
tú veías	tú verías	vos'os vieseis
él veía	él vería	ellos viesen
nos'os veíamos	nos'os veríamos	
vos'os veíais	vos'os veríais	**Imperative-Do**
ellos veían	ellos verían	(tú) ve
		(él) vea
Preterite	**Present subj've**	(nos'os) veamos
yo vi	yo vea	(vos'os) ved
tú viste	tú veas	(ellos) vean
él vio	él vea	
nos'os vimos	nos'os veamos	**Imperative-Don't**
vos'os visteis	vos'os veáis	no veas
ellos vieron	ellos vean	no vea
		no veamos
Comp'nd tenses- 63-I-Haber +Past-P		no veáis
		no vean

169

80-M-Agorar

Note: present. present subjunctive. imperative.

The o would become ue where it is accented, (as in **26-S-Aprobar-Acortar**) but with agorar the resulting gu becomes gü in front of e to preserve the correct sound.

Verb infinitive	Participles	Imperfect-subjunctive 1
Agorar, to bode, to be an omen of.	agorado: agorando	yo agorara
		tú agoraras
Present	**Future**	él agorara
yo agüero	yo agoraré	nos'os agoráramos
tú agüeras	tú agorarás	vos'os agorarais
él agüera	él agorará	ellos agoraran
nos'os agoramos	nos'os agoraremos	
vos'os agoráis	vos'os agoraréis	**Imp'fect-sub've 2**
ellos agüeran	ellos agorarán	yo agorase
		tú agorases
Imperfect	**Conditional**	él agorase
yo agoraba	yo agoraría	nos'os agorásemos
tú agorabas	tú agorarías	vos'os agoraseis
él agoraba	él agoraría	ellos agorasen
nos'os agorábamos	nos'os agoraríamos	
vos'os agorabais	vos'os agoraríais	**Imperative-Do**
ellos agoraban	ellos agorarían	(tú) agüera
		(él) agüere
Preterite	**Present subj've**	(nos'os) agoremos
yo agoré	yo agüere	(vos'os) agorad
tú agoraste	tú agüeres	(ellos) agüeren
él agoró	él agüere	
nos'os agoramos	nos'os agoremos	**Imperative-Don't**
vos'os agorasteis	vos'os agoréis	no agüeres
ellos agoraron	ellos agüeren	no agüere
		no agoremos
Comp'nd tenses- 63-I-Haber +Past-P		no agoréis
		no agüeren

170

81-M-Almorzar

Note: present. preterite. present subjunctive. imperative.
Combines verb types: **7-O-Rezar** and **26-S-Aprobar-Acortar**

Verb infinitive	Participles	Imperfect-subjunctive 1
Almorzar, to have lunch	almorzado: almorzando	yo almorzara
		tú almorzaras
Present	**Future**	él almorzara
yo almuerzo	yo almorzaré	nos'os almorzáramos
tú almuerzas	tú almorzarás	vos'os almorzarais
él almuerza	él almorzará	ellos almorzaran
nos'os almorzamos	nos'os almorzaremos	
vos'os almorzáis	vos'os almorzaréis	**Imp'fect-sub've 2**
ellos almuerzan	ellos almorzarán	yo almorzase
		tú almorzases
Imperfect	**Conditional**	él almorzase
yo almorzaba	yo almorzaría	nos'os almorzásemos
tú almorzabas	tú almorzarías	vos'os almorzaseis
él almorzaba	él almorzaría	ellos almorzasen
nos'os almorzábamos	nos'os almorzaríamos	
vos'os almorzabais	vos'os almorzaríais	**Imperative-Do**
ellos almorzaban	ellos almorzarían	(tú) almuerza
		(él) almuerce
Preterite	**Present subj've**	(nos'os) almorcemos
yo almorcé	yo almuerce	(vos'os) almorzad
tú almorzaste	tú almuerces	(ellos) almuercen
él almorzó	él almuerce	
nos'os almorzamos	nos'os almorcemos	**Imperative-Don't**
vos'os almorzasteis	vos'os almorcéis	no almuerces
ellos almorzaron	ellos almuercen	no almuerce
		no almorcemos
Comp'nd tenses- 63-I-Haber +Past-P		no almorcéis
		no almuercen

171

82-M-Avergonzar
Note: present. preterite. present subjunctive. imperative.

Verb infinitive	Participles	Imperfect-subjunctive 1
Avergonzar, to embarrass to shame	avergonzado: avergonzando	yo avergonzara
		tú avergonzaras
Present	**Future**	él avergonzara
yo avergüenzo	yo avergonzaré	nos'os avergonzáramos
tú avergüenzas	tú avergonzarás	vos'os avergonzarais
él avergüenza	él avergonzará	ellos avergonzaran
nos'os avergonzamos	nos'os avergonzaremos	
vos'os avergonzáis	vos'os avergonzaréis	**Imp'fect-sub've 2**
ellos avergüenzan	ellos avergonzarán	yo avergonzase
		tú avergonzases
Imperfect	**Conditional**	él avergonzase
yo avergonzaba	yo avergonzaría	nos'os avergonzásemos
tú avergonzabas	tú avergonzarías	vos'os avergonzaseis
él avergonzaba	él avergonzaría	ellos avergonzasen
nos'os avergonzábamos	nos'os avergonzaríamos	
vos'os avergonzabais	vos'os avergonzaríais	**Imperative-Do**
ellos avergonzaban	ellos avergonzarían	(tú) avergüenza
		(él) avergüence
Preterite	**Present subj've**	(nos'os) avergoncemos
yo avergoncé	yo avergüence	(vos'os) avergonzad
tú avergonzaste	tú avergüences	(ellos) avergüencen
él avergonzó	él avergüence	
nos'os avergonzamos	nos'os avergoncemos	**Imperative-Don't**
vos'os avergonzasteis	vos'os avergoncéis	no avergüences
ellos avergonzaron	ellos avergüencen	no avergüence
		no avergoncemos
Comp'nd tenses- 63-I-Haber +Past-P		no avergoncéis
		no avergüencen

172

83-M-Ceñir

Note: participles. present. preterite. present subjunctive. imperfect-subjunctive. imperative.

Combines verb types: **31-S-Servir-Competir** and **5-O-Bruñir-Tañer**

Verb infinitive	Participles	Imperfect-subjunctive 1
Ceñir, to encircle, to surround, to fit tightly	ceñido: ciñendo	yo ciñera
		tú ciñeras
Present	**Future**	él ciñera
yo ciño	yo ceñiré	nos'os ciñéramos
tú ciñes	tú ceñirás	vos'os ciñerais
él ciñe	él ceñirá	ellos ciñeran
nos'os ceñimos	nos'os ceñiremos	
vos'os ceñís	vos'os ceñiréis	**Imp'fect-sub've 2**
ellos ciñen	ellos ceñirán	yo ciñese
		tú ciñeses
Imperfect	**Conditional**	él ciñese
yo ceñía	yo ceñiría	nos'os ciñésemos
tú ceñías	tú ceñirías	vos'os ciñeseis
él ceñía	él ceñiría	ellos ciñesen
nos'os ceñíamos	nos'os ceñiríamos	
vos'os ceñíais	vos'os ceñiríais	**Imperative-Do**
ellos ceñían	ellos ceñirían	(tú) ciñe
		(él) ciña
Preterite	**Present subj've**	(nos'os) ciñamos
yo ceñí	yo ciña	(vos'os) ceñid
tú ceñiste	tú ciñas	(ellos) ciñan
él ciñó	él ciña	
nos'os ceñimos	nos'os ciñamos	**Imperative-Don't**
vos'os ceñisteis	vos'os ciñáis	no ciñas
ellos ciñeron	ellos ciñan	no ciña
		no ciñamos
Comp'nd tenses- 63-I-Haber +Past-P		no ciñáis
		no ciñan

173

84-M-Colgar

Note: present. preterite. present subjunctive. imperative.
Combines verb types **27-S-Morder-Remover** and **10-O-Pagar**

Verb infinitive	Participles	Imperfect-subjunctive 1
Colgar, to hang	colgado: colgando	yo colgara
		tú colgaras
Present	**Future**	él colgara
yo cuelgo	yo colgaré	nos'os colgáramos
tú cuelgas	tú colgarás	vos'os colgarais
él cuelga	él colgará	ellos colgaran
nos'os colgamos	nos'os colgaremos	
vos'os colgáis	vos'os colgaréis	**Imp'fect-sub've 2**
ellos cuelgan	ellos colgarán	yo colgase
		tú colgases
Imperfect	**Conditional**	él colgase
yo colgaba	yo colgaría	nos'os colgásemos
tú colgabas	tú colgarías	vos'os colgaseis
él colgaba	él colgaría	ellos colgasen
nos'os colgábamos	nos'os colgaríamos	
vos'os colgabais	vos'os colgaríais	**Imperative-Do**
ellos colgaban	ellos colgarían	(tú) cuelga
		(él) cuelgue
Preterite	**Present subj've**	(nos'os) colguemos
yo colgué	yo cuelgue	(vos'os) colgad
tú colgaste	tú cuelgues	(ellos) cuelguen
él colgó	él cuelgue	
nos'os colgamos	nos'os colguemos	**Imperative-Don't**
vos'os colgasteis	vos'os colguéis	no cuelgues
ellos colgaron	ellos cuelguen	no cuelgue
		no colguemos
Comp'nd tenses- 63-I-Haber +Past-P		no colguéis
		no cuelguen

174

85-M-Empezar

Note: present. preterite. present subjunctive. imperative.

See verb types **7-O-Rezar** and **24-S-Alentar-Acertar**

Verb infinitive	Participles	Imperfect-subjunctive 1
Empezar, to begin	empezado: empezando	yo empezara
		tú empezaras
Present	**Future**	él empezara
yo empiezo	yo empezaré	nos'os empezáramos
tú empiezas	tú empezarás	vos'os empezarais
él empieza	él empezará	ellos empezaran
nos'os empezamos	nos'os empezaremos	
vos'os empezáis	vos'os empezaréis	**Imp'fect-sub've 2**
ellos empiezan	ellos empezarán	yo empezase
		tú empezases
Imperfect	**Conditional**	él empezase
yo empezaba	yo empezaría	nos'os empezásemos
tú empezabas	tú empezarías	vos'os empezaseis
él empezaba	él empezaría	ellos empezasen
nos'os empezábamos	nos'os empezaríamos	
vos'os empezabais	vos'os empezaríais	**Imperative-Do**
ellos empezaban	ellos empezarían	(tú) empieza
		(él) empiece
Preterite	**Present subj've**	(nos'os) empecemos
yo empecé	yo empiece	(vos'os) empezad
tú empezaste	tú empieces	(ellos) empiecen
él empezó	él empiece	
nos'os empezamos	nos'os empecemos	**Imperative-Don't**
vos'os empezasteis	vos'os empecéis	no empieces
ellos empezaron	ellos empiecen	no empiece
		no empecemos
Comp'nd tenses- 63-I-Haber +Past-P		no empecéis
		no empiecen

175

86-M-Forzar

Note: present. preterite. present subjunctive. imperative.
See verb types **7-O-Rezar** and **26-S-Aprobar-Acortar**

Verb infinitive	Participles	Imperfect-subjunctive 1
Forzar, to force, to compel	forzado: forzando	yo forzara
		tú forzaras
Present	**Future**	él forzara
yo fuerzo	yo forzaré	nos'os forzáramos
tú fuerzas	tú forzarás	vos'os forzarais
él fuerza	él forzará	ellos forzaran
nos'os forzamos	nos'os forzaremos	
vos'os forzáis	vos'os forzaréis	**Imp'fect-sub've 2**
ellos fuerzan	ellos forzarán	yo forzase
		tú forzases
Imperfect	**Conditional**	él forzase
yo forzaba	yo forzaría	nos'os forzásemos
tú forzabas	tú forzarías	vos'os forzaseis
él forzaba	él forzaría	ellos forzasen
nos'os forzábamos	nos'os forzaríamos	
vos'os forzabais	vos'os forzaríais	**Imperative-Do**
ellos forzaban	ellos forzarían	(tú) fuerza
		(él) fuerce
Preterite	**Present subj've**	(nos'os) forcemos
yo forcé	yo fuerce	(vos'os) forzad
tú forzaste	tú fuerces	(ellos) fuercen
él forzó	él fuerce	
nos'os forzamos	nos'os forcemos	**Imperative-Don't**
vos'os forzasteis	vos'os forcéis	no fuerces
ellos forzaron	ellos fuercen	no fuerce
		no forcemos
Comp'nd tenses- 63-I-Haber +Past-P		no forcéis
		no fuercen

176

87-M-Regar

Note: present. preterite. present subjunctive. imperative.

See verb types **10-O-Pagar** and **24-S-Alentar-Acertar**

Verb infinitive	Participles	Imperfect-subjunctive 1
Regar, to water, to irrigate	regado: regando	yo regara
		tú regaras
Present	**Future**	él regara
yo riego	yo regaré	nos'os regáramos
tú riegas	tú regarás	vos'os regarais
él riega	él regará	ellos regaran
nos'os regamos	nos'os regaremos	
vos'os regáis	vos'os regaréis	**Imp'fect-sub've 2**
ellos riegan	ellos regarán	yo regase
		tú regases
Imperfect	**Conditional**	él regase
yo regaba	yo regaría	nos'os regásemos
tú regabas	tú regarías	vos'os regaseis
él regaba	él regaría	ellos regasen
nos'os regábamos	nos'os regaríamos	
vos'os regabais	vos'os regaríais	**Imperative-Do**
ellos regaban	ellos regarían	(tú) riega
		(él) riegue
Preterite	**Present subj've**	(nos'os) reguemos
yo regué	yo riegue	(vos'os) regad
tú regaste	tú riegues	(ellos) rieguen
él regó	él riegue	
nos'os regamos	nos'os reguemos	**Imperative-Don't**
vos'os regasteis	vos'os reguéis	no riegues
ellos regaron	ellos rieguen	no riegue
		no reguemos
Comp'nd tenses- 63-I-Haber +Past-P		no reguéis
		no rieguen

177

88-M-Seguir

Note: participles. present. preterite. present subjunctive. imperfect-subjunctive. imperative.

See verb types **31-S-Servir-Competir** and **14-O-Distinguir**

Verb infinitive	Participles	Imperfect-subjunctive 1
Seguir, to follow	seguido: siguiendo	yo siguiera
		tú siguieras
Present	**Future**	él siguiera
yo sigo	yo seguiré	nos'os siguiéramos
tú sigues	tú seguirás	vos'os siguierais
él sigue	él seguirá	ellos siguieran
nos'os seguimos	nos'os seguiremos	
vos'os seguís	vos'os seguiréis	**Imp'fect-sub've 2**
ellos siguen	ellos seguirán	yo siguiese
		tú siguieses
Imperfect	**Conditional**	él siguiese
yo seguía	yo seguiría	nos'os siguiésemos
tú seguías	tú seguirías	vos'os siguieseis
él seguía	él seguiría	ellos siguiesen
nos'os seguíamos	nos'os seguiríamos	
vos'os seguíais	vos'os seguiríais	**Imperative-Do**
ellos seguían	ellos seguirían	(tú) sigue
		(él) siga
Preterite	**Present subj've**	(nos'os) sigamos
yo seguí	yo siga	(vos'os) seguid
tú seguiste	tú sigas	(ellos) sigan
él siguió	él siga	
nos'os seguimos	nos'os sigamos	**Imperative-Don't**
vos'os seguisteis	vos'os sigáis	no sigas
ellos siguieron	ellos sigan	no siga
		no sigamos
Comp'nd tenses- 63-I-Haber +Past-P		no sigáis
		no sigan

178

89-M-Trocar

Note: present. preterite. present subjunctive. imperative.

See verb types **9-O-Tocar** and **26-S-Aprobar-Acortar**

Verb infinitive	Participles	Imperfect-subjunctive 1
Trocar, to exchange, to barter	trocado: trocando	yo trocara
		tú trocaras
Present	**Future**	él trocara
yo trueco	yo trocaré	nos'os trocáramos
tú truecas	tú trocarás	vos'os trocarais
él trueca	él trocará	ellos trocaran
nos'os trocamos	nos'os trocaremos	
vos'os trocáis	vos'os trocaréis	**Imp'fect-sub've 2**
ellos truecan	ellos trocarán	yo trocase
		tú trocases
Imperfect	**Conditional**	él trocase
yo trocaba	yo trocaría	nos'os trocásemos
tú trocabas	tú trocarías	vos'os trocaseis
él trocaba	él trocaría	ellos trocasen
nos'os trocábamos	nos'os trocaríamos	
vos'os trocabais	vos'os trocaríais	**Imperative-Do**
ellos trocaban	ellos trocarían	(tú) trueca
		(él) trueque
Preterite	**Present subj've**	(nos'os) troquemos
yo troqué	yo trueque	(vos'os) trocad
tú trocaste	tú trueques	(ellos) truequen
él trocó	él trueque	
nos'os trocamos	nos'os troquemos	**Imperative-Don't**
vos'os trocasteis	vos'os troquéis	no trueques
ellos trocaron	ellos truequen	no trueque
		no troquemos
Comp'nd tenses- 63-I-Haber +Past-P		no troquéis
		no truequen

179

90- Ú/Í -Evaluar

Note: present. present subjunctive. imperative.

Verb infinitive	Participles	Imperfect-subjunctive 1
Evaluar, to evaluate.	evaluado: evaluando	yo evaluara
		tú evaluaras
Present	**Future**	él evaluara
yo evalúo	yo evaluaré	nos'os evaluáramos
tú evalúas	tú evaluarás	vos'os evaluarais
él evalúa	él evaluará	ellos evaluaran
nos'os evaluamos	nos'os evaluaremos	
vos'os evaluáis	vos'os evaluaréis	**Imp'fect-sub've 2**
ellos evalúan	ellos evaluarán	yo evaluase
		tú evaluases
Imperfect	**Conditional**	él evaluase
yo evaluaba	yo evaluaría	nos'os evaluásemos
tú evaluabas	tú evaluarías	vos'os evaluaseis
él evaluaba	él evaluaría	ellos evaluasen
nos'os evaluábamos	nos'os evaluaríamos	
vos'os evaluabais	vos'os evaluaríais	**Imperative-Do**
ellos evaluaban	ellos evaluarían	(tú) evalúa
		(él) evalúe
Preterite	**Present subj've**	(nos'os) evaluemos
yo evalué	yo evalúe	(vos'os) evaluad
tú evaluaste	tú evalúes	(ellos) evalúen
él evaluó	él evalúe	
nos'os evaluamos	nos'os evaluemos	**Imperative-Don't**
vos'os evaluasteis	vos'os evaluéis	no evalúes
ellos evaluaron	ellos evalúen	no evalúe
		no evaluemos
Comp'nd tenses- 63-I-Haber +Past-P		no evaluéis
		no evalúen

91-Ú/Í-Ampliar

Note. present. present subjunctive. imperative.

Verb infinitive	Participles	Imperfect-subjunctive 1
Ampliar, to extend, to amplify	ampliado: ampliando	yo ampliara
		tú ampliaras
Present	**Future**	él ampliara
yo amplío	yo ampliaré	nos'os ampliáramos
tú amplías	tú ampliarás	vos'os ampliarais
él amplía	él ampliará	ellos ampliaran
nos'os ampliamos	nos'os ampliaremos	
vos'os ampliáis	vos'os ampliaréis	**Imp'fect-sub've 2**
ellos amplían	ellos ampliarán	yo ampliase
		tú ampliases
Imperfect	**Conditional**	él ampliase
yo ampliaba	yo ampliaría	nos'os ampliásemos
tú ampliabas	tú ampliarías	vos'os ampliaseis
él ampliaba	él ampliaría	ellos ampliasen
nos'os ampliábamos	nos'os ampliaríamos	
vos'os ampliabais	vos'os ampliaríais	**Imperative-Do**
ellos ampliaban	ellos ampliarían	(tú) amplía
		(él) amplíe
Preterite	**Present subj've**	(nos'os) ampliemos
yo amplié	yo amplíe	(vos'os) ampliad
tú ampliaste	tú amplíes	(ellos) amplíen
él amplió	él amplíe	
nos'os ampliamos	nos'os ampliemos	**Imperative-Don't**
vos'os ampliasteis	vos'os ampliéis	no amplíes
ellos ampliaron	ellos amplíen	no amplíe
		no ampliemos
Comp'nd tenses- 63-I-Haber +Past-P		no ampliéis
		no amplíen

181

92-Ú/Í-Aullar

Note: present. present subjunctive.. imperative.

Verb infinitive	Participles	Imperfect-subjunctive 1
Aullar, to howl, to yell	aullado: aullando	yo aullara
		tú aullaras
Present	**Future**	él aullara
yo aúllo	yo aullaré	nos'os aulláramos
tú aúllas	tú aullarás	vos'os aullarais
él aúlla	él aullará	ellos aullaran
nos'os aullamos	nos'os aullaremos	
vos'os aulláis	vos'os aullaréis	**Imp'fect-sub've 2**
ellos aúllan	ellos aullarán	yo aullase
		tú aullases
Imperfect	**Conditional**	él aullase
yo aullaba	yo aullaría	nos'os aullásemos
tú aullabas	tú aullarías	vos'os aullaseis
él aullaba	él aullaría	
nos'os aullábamos	nos'os aullaríamos	
vos'os aullabais	vos'os aullaríais	**Imperative-Do**
ellos aullaban	ellos aullarían	(tú) aúlla
		(él) aúlle
Preterite	**Present subj've**	(nos'os) aullemos
yo aullé	yo aúlle	(vos'os) aullad
tú aullaste	tú aúlles	(ellos) aúllen
él aulló	él aúlle	
nos'os aullamos	nos'os aullemos	**Imperative-Don't**
vos'os aullasteis	vos'os aulléis	no aúlles
ellos aullaron	ellos aúllen	no aúlle
		no aullemos
Comp'nd tenses- 63-I-Haber +Past-P		no aulléis
		no aúllen

182

93-Ú/Í-Airar

Note: present. present subjunctive. imperative

Verb infinitive	Participles	Imperfect-subjunctive 1
Airar, to annoy, to irritate	airado: airando	yo airara
		tú airaras
Present	**Future**	él airara
yo aíro	yo airaré	nos'os airáramos
tú aíras	tú airarás	vos'os airarais
él aíra	él airará	ellos airaran
nos'os airamos	nos'os airaremos	
vos'os airáis	vos'os airaréis	**Imp'fect-sub've 2**
ellos aíran	ellos airarán	yo airase
		tú airases
Imperfect	**Conditional**	él airase
yo airaba	yo airaría	nos'os airásemos
tú airabas	tú airarías	vos'os airaseis
él airaba	él airaría	ellos airasen
nos'os airábamos	nos'os airaríamos	
vos'os airabais	vos'os airaríais	**Imperative-Do**
ellos airaban	ellos airarían	(tú) aíra
		(él) aíre
Preterite	**Present subj've**	(nos'os) airemos
yo airé	yo aíre	(vos'os) airad
tú airaste	tú aíres	(ellos) aíren
él airó	él aíre	
nos'os airamos	nos'os airemos	**Imperative-Don't**
vos'os airasteis	vos'os airéis	no aíres
ellos airaron	ellos aíren	no aíre
		no airemos
Comp'nd tenses- 63-I-Haber +Past-P		no airéis
		no aíren

183

94-Ú/Í-Rehusar

Note: present. present subjunctive. imperative.

Verb infinitive	Participles	Imperfect-subjunctive 1
Rehusar, to decline, to refuse.	rehusado: rehusando	yo rehusara
		tú rehusaras
Present	**Future**	él rehusara
yo rehúso	yo rehusaré	nos'os rehusáramos
tú rehúsas	tú rehusarás	vos'os rehusarais
él rehúsa	él rehusará	ellos rehusaran
nos'os rehusamos	nos'os rehusaremos	
vos'os rehusáis	vos'os rehusaréis	**Imp'fect-sub've 2**
ellos rehúsan	ellos rehusarán	yo rehusase
		tú rehusases
Imperfect	**Conditional**	él rehusase
yo rehusaba	yo rehusaría	nos'os rehusásemos
tú rehusabas	tú rehusarías	vos'os rehusaseis
él rehusaba	él rehusaría	ellos rehusasen
nos'os rehusábamos	nos'os rehusaríamos	
vos'os rehusabais	vos'os rehusaríais	**Imperative-Do**
ellos rehusaban	ellos rehusarían	(tú) rehúsa
		(él) rehúse
Preterite	**Present subj've**	(nos'os) rehusemos
yo rehusé	yo rehúse	(vos'os) rehusad
tú rehusaste	tú rehúses	(ellos) rehúsen
él rehusó	él rehúse	
nos'os rehusamos	nos'os rehusemos	**Imperative-Don't**
vos'os rehusasteis	vos'os rehuséis	no rehúses
ellos rehusaron	ellos rehúsen	no rehúse
		no rehusemos
Comp'nd tenses- 63-I-Haber +Past-P		no rehuséis
		no rehúsen

184

95-Ú/Í-Prohibir

Note: present. present subjunctive. imperative

Verb infinitive	Participles	Imperfect-subjunctive 1
prohibir, to forbid, to prohibit	prohibido: prohibiendo	yo prohibiera
		tú prohibieras
Present	**Future**	él prohibiera
yo prohíbo	yo prohibiré	nos'os prohibiéramos
tú prohíbes	tú prohibirás	vos'os prohibierais
él prohíbe	él prohibirá	ellos prohibieran
nos'os prohibimos	nos'os prohibiremos	
vos'os prohibís	vos'os prohibiréis	**Imp'fect-sub've 2**
ellos prohíben	ellos prohibirán	yo prohibiese
		tú prohibieses
Imperfect	**Conditional**	él prohibiese
yo prohibía	yo prohibiría	nos'os prohibiésemos
tú prohibías	tú prohibirías	vos'os prohibieseis
él prohibía	él prohibiría	ellos prohibiesen
nos'os prohibíamos	nos'os prohibiríamos	
vos'os prohibíais	vos'os prohibiríais	**Imperative-Do**
ellos prohibían	ellos prohibirían	(tú) prohíbe
		(él) prohíba
Preterite	**Present subj've**	(nos'os) prohibamos
yo prohibí	yo prohíba	(vos'os) prohibid
tú prohibiste	tú prohíbas	(ellos) prohíban
él prohibió	él prohíba	
nos'os prohibimos	nos'os prohibamos	**Imperative-Don't**
vos'os prohibisteis	vos'os prohibáis	no prohíbas
ellos prohibieron	ellos prohíban	no prohíba
		no prohibamos
Comp'nd tenses- 63-I-Haber +Past-P		no prohibáis
		no prohíban

185

96-Ú/Í-Reunir

Note: present. present subjunctive. imperative

Verb infinitive	Participles	Imperfect-subjunctive 1
Reunir, to assemble, to gather	reunido reuniendo	yo reuniera
		tú reunieras
Present	**Future**	él reuniera
yo reúno	yo reuniré	nos'os reuniéramos
tú reúnes	tú reunirás	vos'os reunierais
él reúne	él reunirá	ellos reunieran
nos'os reunimos	nos'os reuniremos	
vos'os reunís	vos'os reuniréis	**Imp'fect-sub've 2**
ellos reúnen	ellos reunirán	yo reuniese
		tú reunieses
Imperfect	**Conditional**	él reuniese
yo reunía	yo reuniría	nos'os reuniésemos
tú reunías	tú reunirías	vos'os reunieseis
él reunía	él reuniría	ellos reuniesen
nos'os reuníamos	nos'os reuniríamos	
vos'os reuníais	vos'os reuniríais	**Imperative-Do**
ellos reunían	ellos reunirían	(tú) reúne
		(él) reúna
Preterite	**Present subj've**	(nos'os) reunamos
yo reuní	yo reúna	(vos'os) reunid
tú reuniste	tú reúnas	(ellos) reúnan
él reunió	él reúna	
nos'os reunimos	nos'os reunamos	**Imperative-Don't**
vos'os reunisteis	vos'os reunáis	no reúnas
ellos reunieron	ellos reúnan	no reúna
		no reunamos
Comp'nd tenses- 63-I-Haber +Past-P		no reunáis
		no reúnan

186

97-Ú/Í-Atraillar

Note: present. present subjunctive. imperative

Verb infinitive	Participles	Imperfect-subjunctive 1
atraillar, to put on a leash	atraillado atraillando	yo atraillara
		tú atraillaras
Present	**Future**	él atraillara
yo atraíllo	yo atraillaré	nos'os atrailláramos
tú atraíllas	tú atraillarás	vos'os atraillarais
él atraílla	él atraillará	ellos atraillaran
nos'os atraillamos	nos'os atraillaremos	
vos'os atrailláis	vos'os atraillaréis	**Imp'fect-sub've 2**
ellos atraíllan	ellos atraillarán	yo atraillase
		tú atraillases
Imperfect	**Conditional**	él atraillase
yo atraillaba	yo atraillaría	nos'os atraillásemos
tú atraillabas	tú atraillarías	vos'os atraillaseis
é atraillaba	é atraillaría	ellos atraillasen
nos'os atraillábamos	nos'os atraillaríamos	
vos'os atraillabais	vos'os atraillaríais	**Imperative-Do**
ellos atraillaban	ellos atraillarían	(tú) atraílla
		(él) atraílle
Preterite	**Present subj've**	(nos'os) atraillemos
yo atraillé	yo atraílle	(vos'os) atraillad
tú atraillaste	tú atraílles	(ellos) atraíllen
él atrailló	él atraílle	
nos'os atraillamos	nos'os atraillemos	**Imperative-Don't**
vos'os atraillasteis	vos'os atrailléis	no atraílles
ellos atraillaron	ellos atraíllen	no atraílle
		no atraillemos
Comp'nd tenses- 63-I-Haber +Past-P		no atrailléis
		no atraíllen

187

98-DC-Deshacer

Verb infinitive	Participles	Imperfect-subjunctive 1
deshacer, to undo	deshecho: deshaciendo	yo deshiciera
		tú deshicieras
Present	**Future**	él deshiciera
yo deshago	yo desharé	nos'os deshiciéramos
tú deshaces	tú desharás	vos'os deshicierais
él deshace	é deshará	ellos deshicieran
nos'os deshacemos	nos'os desharemos	
vos'os deshacéis	vos'os desharéis	**Imp'fect-sub've 2**
ellos deshacen	ellos desharán	yo deshiciese
		tú deshicieses
Imperfect	**Conditional**	él deshiciese
yo deshacía	yo desharía	nos'os deshiciésemos
tú deshacías	tú desharías	vos'os deshicieseis
él deshacía	él desharía	ellos deshiciesen
nos'os deshacíamos	nos'os desharíamos	
vos'os deshacíais	vos'os desharíais	**Imperative-Do**
ellos deshacían	ellos desharían	(tú) deshaz
		(él) deshaga
Preterite	**Present subj've**	(nos'os) deshagamos
yo deshice	yo deshaga	(vos'os) deshaced
tú deshiciste	tú deshagas	(ellos) deshagan
él deshizo	él deshaga	
nos'os deshicimos	nos'os deshagamos	**Imperative-Don't**
vos'os deshicisteis	vos'os deshagáis	no deshagas
ellos deshicieron	ellos deshagan	no deshaga
		no deshagamos
Comp'nd tenses- 63-I-Haber +Past-P		no deshagáis
		no deshagan

188

99-DC-Componer

Verb infinitive	Participles	Imperfect-subjunctive 1
componer to put together	compuesto: componiendo	yo compusiera
		tú compusieras
Present	**Future**	él compusiera
yo compongo	yo compondré	nos'os compusiéramos
tú compones	tú compondrás	vos'os compusierais
él compone	él compondrá	ellos compusieran
nos'os componemos	nos'os compondremos	
vos'os componéis	vos'os compondréis	**Imp'fect-sub've 2**
ellos componen	ellos compondrán	yo compusiese
		tú compusieses
Imperfect	**Conditional**	él compusiese
yo componía	yo compondría	nos'os compusiésemos
tú componías	tú compondrías	vos'os compusieseis
él componía	él compondría	ellos compusiesen
nos'os componíamos	nos'os compondríamos	
vos'os componíais	vos'os compondríais	**Imperative-Do**
ellos componían	ellos compondrían	(tú) compón
		(él) componga
Preterite	**Present subj've**	(nos'os) compongamos
yo compuse	yo componga	(vos'os) componed
tú compusiste	tú compongas	(ellos) compongan
él compuso	él componga	
nos'os compusimos	nos'os compongamos	**Imperative-Don't**
vos'os compusisteis	vos'os compongáis	no compongas
ellos compusieron	ellos compongan	no componga
		no compongamos
Comp'nd tenses- 63-I-Haber +Past-P		no compongáis
		no compongan

189

100-DC-Sobresalir

Verb infinitive	Participles	Imperfect-subjunctive 1
sobresalir, to project, to stand out	sobresalido: sobresaliendo	yo sobresaliera
		tú sobresalieras
Present	**Future**	él sobresaliera
yo sobresalgo	yo sobresaldré	nos'os sobresaliéramos
tú sobresales	tú sobresaldrás	vos'os sobresalierais
él sobresale	él sobresaldrá	ellos sobresalieran
nos'os sobresalimos	nos'os sobresaldremos	
vos'os sobresalís	vos'os sobresaldréis	**Imp'fect-sub've 2**
ellos sobresalen	ellos sobresaldrán	yo sobresaliese
		tú sobresalieses
Imperfect	**Conditional**	él sobresaliese
yo sobresalía	yo sobresaldría	nos'os sobresaliésemos
tú sobresalías	tú sobresaldrías	vos'os sobresalieseis
él sobresalía	él sobresaldría	ellos sobresaliesen
nos'os sobresalíamos	nos'os sobresaldríamos	
vos'os sobresalíais	vos'os sobresaldríais	**Imperative-Do**
ellos sobresalían	ellos sobresaldrían	(tú) sobresal
		(él) sobresalga
Preterite	**Present subj've**	(nos'os) sobresalgamos
yo sobresalí	yo sobresalga	(vos'os) sobresalid
tú sobresaliste	tú sobresalgas	(ellos) sobresalgan
él sobresalió	él sobresalga	
nos'os sobresalimos	nos'os sobresalgamos	**Imperative-Don't**
vos'os sobresalisteis	vos'os sobresalgáis	no sobresalgas
ellos sobresalieron	ellos sobresalgan	no sobresalga
		no sobresalgamos
Comp'nd tenses- 63-I-Haber +Past-P		no sobresalgáis
		no sobresalgan

101-DC-Equivaler

Verb infinitive	Participles	Imperfect-subjunctive 1
equivaler, to be equal to	equivalido: equivaliendo	yo equivaliera
		tú equivalieras
Present	**Future**	él equivaliera
yo equivalgo	yo equivaldré	nos'os equivaliéramos
tú equivales	tú equivaldrás	vos'os equivalierais
él equivale	él equivaldrá	ellos equivalieran
nos'os equivalemos	nos'os equivaldremos	
vos'os equivaléis	vos'os equivaldréis	**Imp'fect-sub've 2**
ellos equivalen	ellos equivaldrán	yo equivaliese
		tú equivalieses
Imperfect	**Conditional**	él equivaliese
yo equivalía	yo equivaldría	nos'os equivaliésemos
tú equivalías	tú equivaldrías	vos'os equivalieseis
él equivalía	él equivaldría	ellos equivaliesen
nos'os equivalíamos	nos'os equivaldríamos	
vos'os equivalíais	vos'os equivaldríais	**Imperative-Do**
ellos equivalían	ellos equivaldrían	(tú) equivale
		(él) equivalga
Preterite	**Present subj've**	(nos'os) equivalgamos
yo equivalí	yo equivalga	(vos'os) equivaled
tú equivaliste	tú equivalgas	(ellos) equivalgan
él equivalió	él equivalga	
nos'os equivalimos	nos'os equivalgamos	**Imperative-Don't**
vos'os equivalisteis	vos'os equivalgáis	no equivalgas
ellos equivalieron	ellos equivalgan	no equivalga
		no equivalgamos
Comp'nd tenses- 63-I-Haber +Past-P		no equivalgáis
		no equivalgan

102-DC-Retraer

Verb infinitive	Participles	Imperfect-subjunctive 1
retraer, to draw in, to retract	retraído: retrayendo	**yo retrajera**
		tú re**trajeras**
Present	**Future**	él re**trajera**
yo retraigo	yo retraeré	nos'os re**trajéramos**
tú retraes	tú retraerás	vos'os re**trajerais**
él retrae	él retraerá	ellos re**trajeran**
nos'os retraemos	nos'os retraeremos	
vos'os retraéis	vos'os retraeréis	**Imp'fect-sub've 2**
ellos retraen	ellos retraerán	yo retrajese
		tú retrajeses
Imperfect	**Conditional**	él retrajese
yo retraía	yo retraería	nos'os retrajésemos
tú retraías	tú retraerías	vos'os retrajeseis
él retraía	él retraería	ellos retrajesen
nos'os retraíamos	nos'os retraeríamos	
vos'os retraíais	vos'os retraeríais	**Imperative-Do**
ellos retraían	ellos retraerían	(tú) retrae
		(él) retraiga
Preterite	**Present subj've**	(nos'os) retraigamos
yo retraje	yo retraiga	(vos'os) retraed
tú retrajiste	tú retraigas	(ellos) retraigan
él retrajo	él retraiga	
nos'os retrajimos	nos'os retraigamos	**Imperative-Don't**
vos'os retrajisteis	vos'os retraigáis	no retraigas
ellos retrajeron	ellos retraigan	no retraiga
		no retraigamos
Comp'nd tenses- 63-I-Haber +Past-P		no retraigáis
		no retraigan

192

103-DC-Convenir

Verb infinitive	Participles	Imperfect-subjunctive 1
convenir, to agree, to suit	convenido: conviniendo	yo conviniera
		tú convinieras
Present	**Future**	él conviniera
yo convengo	yo convendré	nos'os conviniéramos
tú convienes	tú convendrás	vos'os convinierais
él conviene	él convendrá	ellos convinieran
nos'os convenimos	nos'os convendremos	
vos'os convenís	vos'os convendréis	**Imp'fect-sub've 2**
ellos convienen	ellos convendrán	yo conviniese
		tú convinieses
Imperfect	**Conditional**	él conviniese
yo convenía	yo convendría	nos'os conviniésemos
tú convenías	tú convendrías	vos'os convinieseis
él convenía	él convendría	ellos conviniesen
nos'os conveníamos	nos'os convendríamos	
vos'os conveníais	vos'os convendríais	**Imperative-Do**
ellos convenían	ellos convendrían	(tú) convén
		(él) convenga
Preterite	**Present subj've**	(nos'os) convengamos
yo convine	yo convenga	(vos'os) convenid
tú conviniste	tú convengas	(ellos) convengan
él convino	él convenga	
nos'os convinimos	nos'os convengamos	**Imperative-Don't**
vos'os convinisteis	vos'os convengáis	no convengas
ellos convinieron	ellos convengan	no convenga
		no convengamos
Comp'nd tenses- 63-I-Haber +Past-P		no convengáis
		no convengan

193

104-DC-Prever

Verb infinitive	Participles	Imperfect-subjunctive 1
prever, to foresee, to anticipate	previsto: previendo	yo previera
		tú previeras
Present	**Future**	él previera
yo preveo	yo preveré	nos'os previéramos
tú preves	tú preverás	vos'os previerais
él preve	él preverá	ellos previeran
nos'os prevemos	nos'os preveremos	
vos'os preveis	vos'os preveréis	**Imp'fect-sub've 2**
ellos preven	ellos preverán	yo previese
		tú previeses
Imperfect	**Conditional**	él previese
yo preveía	yo prevería	nos'os previésemos
tú preveías	tú preverías	vos'os previeseis
él preveía	él prevería	ellos previesen
nos'os preveíamos	nos'os preveríamos	
vos'os preveíais	vos'os preveríais	**Imperative-Do**
ellos preveían	ellos preverían	(tú) preve
		(él) prevea
Preterite	**Present subj've**	(nos'os) preveamos
yo preví	yo prevea	(vos'os) preved
tú previste	tú preveas	(ellos) prevean
él previó	él prevea	
nos'os previmos	nos'os preveamos	**Imperative-Don't**
vos'os previsteis	vos'os preveáis	no preveas
ellos previeron	ellos prevean	no prevea
		no preveamos
Comp'nd tenses- 63-I-Haber +Past-P		no preveáis
		no prevean

Part Three: The 1001 Essential Spanish Verbs

Chapter 23.
The 1001 Most Useful Spanish Verbs
each with conjugation guide to model verb.

Although there are many verbs in total in Spanish, the 1001 will be more than adequate for anyone wanting to understand and speak Spanish really competently and pleasantly. You may ask whether you would really not need much more. Well in Spanish (as with English) there are synonyms, and some Spanish verbs may be close in meaning to others. So, often even without having the exact verb, some thing suitable would be found in the selections provided. And when you can speak the language at even a modest level you will find that you naturally go on acquiring more verbs.

Key to abbreviations:
R= Regular
O= Changes mostly Orthographic/Euphonic
S= Stem changes
RF= Reflexive
I= Irregular
M= Mixed changes/irregularities
Ú/Í= Stem U or stem I verb with stress changes
DC= Conjugation derived from some other verb
Past-P= Past-Participle
Pres P= Present-Participle
O/W = Otherwise
D= Defective verb. Only available in some conjugations.

The number (1,2,3 etc) with the guide verb indicates the number of the verb in the list in **Chapter 22 - 104 Fully Conjugated Spanish Verbs.**

Verb Infinitive	Participles	Conjugation guide
abandonar: to leave to abandon	abandonando abandonado	1-R-Hablar
abanicar: to fan	abanicando abanicado	9-O-Tocar

abarcar: to include, to encompass	abarcando abarcado	9-O-Tocar
abatir: to demolish	abatiendo abatido	3-R-Discutir
abordar: to approach	abordado abordado	1-R-Hablar
abrazar: to embrace, to hug	abrazando abrazado	7-O-Rezar
abrir: to open	abriendo abierto	3-R-Discutir
abrirse: to open out	abriéndose abierto	37-R-RF-Abrirse
absorber: to absorb	absorbiendo absorbido	2-R-Beber
abstenerse de: to abstain	absteniéndose abstenido	44-I-RF-Detenerse
aburrir: to become bored	aburriendo aburrido	3-R-Discutir
acabar de: to finish, to end	acabando acabado	1-R-Hablar
acampar: to camp	acampando acampado	1-R-Hablar
acariciar: to caress	acariciando acariciado	1-R-Hablar
aceptar: to accept, to take	aceptando aceptado	1-R-Hablar
acercar: to bring closer, nearer	acercando acercado	9-O-Tocar
acercarse: to approach, to draw near	acercandose acercado	RF O/W 9-O-Tocar
acertar: to hit, to guess right	acertando acertado	24-S-Alentar-Acertar
aclarar: to explain/clarify	aclarando aclarado	1-R-Hablar
acoger: to receive, to welcome	acogiendo acogido	12-O-Escoger

196

acometer: to undertake, to attack	acometiendo acometido	2-R-Beber
acompañar: to accompany	acompañando acompañado	1-R-Hablar
aconsejar: to advise	aconsejando aconsejado	1-R-Hablar
acordarse: to remember	acordándose acordado	RF O/W 26-S-Aprobar-Acortar
acortar: to shorten, to reduce	acortando acortado	26-S-Aprobar-Acortar
acostarse: to go to bed	acostándose acostado	RF O/W 26-S-Aprobar-Acortar
acostumbrar: to be accustomed to	acostumbrando acostumbrado	1-R-Hablar
activar: to activate	activando activado	1-R-Hablar
actuar: to act (on stage)	actuando actuado	90-Ú/Í-Evaluar
acudir: to attend, to turn up	acudiendo acudido	3-R-Discutir
adaptarse: to adapt oneself	adaptándose adaptado	49-R-RF-Levantarse
adelantar: to advance, to bring forward	adelantando adelantado	1-R-Hablar
adivinar: to guess, to solve	adivinando adivinado	1-R-Hablar
admirar: to admire	admirando admirado	1-R-Hablar
admitir: to admit, to grant	admitiendo admitido	3-R-Discutir
adquirir: to obtain	adquiriendo adquirido	32-S-Adquirir-Inquirir
advertir: to advise, to warn	advirtiendo advertido	30-S-Sentir-Advertir
afeitarse: to shave oneself	afeitándose afeitado	49-R-RF-Levantarse
afirmar: to affirm, to assert	afirmando afirmado	1-R-Hablar

197

afligir: to afflict, to distress	afligiendo afligido	13-O-Dirigir
agarrar: to grab, to grasp	agarrando agarrado	1-R-Hablar
agitar: to shake, to stir	agitando agitado	1-R-Hablar
agorar: to predict	agorando agorado	80-M-Agorar
agradar: to please, to gratify	agradando agradado	1-R-Hablar
agradecer: to thank, to be grateful for	agradeciendo agradecido	18-O-Conocer
agrandar: to make bigger, to enlarge	agrandando agrandado	1-R-Hablar
agravar: to weigh down, to make heavier	agravando agravado	1-R-Hablar
agregar: to add, to collect	agregando agregado	10-O-Pagar
aguantar: to put up with, to endure	aguantando aguantado	1-R-Hablar
aguardar: to wait for	aguardando aguardado	1-R-Hablar
ahincar: to press, to hurry	ahincando ahincado	M 93-Ú/Í-Airar (NB the H is silent so ai) O/W 9-O-Tocar
ahogarse: to drown	ahogándose ahogado	RF O/W 10-O-Pagar
ahorrar: to save, to put aside	ahorrando ahorrado	1-R-Hablar
airar: to annoy	airando airado	93-Ú/Í-Airar
aislar: to isolate, to separate	aislando aislado	93-Ú/Í-Airar
alargarse : to stretch out	alegándose alegado	RF O/W 10-O-Pagar
albergar: to harbour, to shelter	aaa aaa	10-O-Pagar

alcanzar: to reach, to attain	alcanzando alcanzado	7-O-Rezar
alegrarse: to be glad, to rejoice	alegrándose alegrado	49-R-RF-Levantarse
alejarse: to draw further off	alejado alejándose	38-R-RF-Alejarse
alentar: to encourage, to hearten	alentando alentado	24-S-Alentar-Acertar
alimentar: to feed, to nourish	alimentando alimentado	1-R-Hablar
alinearse: to be aligned/arranged	alineándose alineado	49-R-RF-Levantarse
alisar:to smooth	alisando alisado	1-R-Hablar
almorzar: to lunch	almorzando almorzado	81-M-Almorzar
alojar: to accommodate, to lodge	alojando alojado	1-R-Hablar
alquilar: to rent	alquilando alquilado	1-R-Hablar
alterar: to alter, to change	alterando alterado	1-R-Hablar
alternar: to alternate, to rotate	alternando alternado	1-R-Hablar
alzarse: to rise up, to stand	alzándose alzado	RF O/W 7-O-Rezar
amanecer: to dawn	amaneciendo amanecido	D O/W 18-O-Conocer
amar: to love	amando amado	1-R-Hablar
amenazar: to threaten, to menace	amenazando amenazado	7-O-Rezar
ampliar: to extend, to enlarge	ampliando ampliado	91-Ú/Í-Ampliar
añadir: to add	añadiendo añadido	3-R-Discutir

199

analizar: to analyze	analizando analizado	7-O-Rezar
andar: to walk	andando andado	55-I-Andar
angustiarse: to be distressed	angustiándose angustiado	49-R-RF-Levantarse
animar: to animate, to give life to	animando animado	1-R-Hablar
anotar: to annotate, to note	anotando anotado	1-R-Hablar
ansiar: to be anxious, to be eager	ansiando ansiado	91-Ú/Í-Ampliar
anunciar: to announce, to advertize	anunciando anunciado	1-R-Hablar
apagar: to put out, to extinguish	apagando apagado	10-O-Pagar
aparcar: to park	aparcando aparcado	9-O-Tocar
aparecer: to appear, to show up	apareciendo aparecido	18-O-Conocer
apasionarse: to get excited	apasionándose apasionado	49-R-RF-Levantarse
apetecer: to fancy, to crave	apeteciendo apetecido	18-O-Conocer
aplastar: to crush	aplastando aplastado	1-R-Hablar
aplaudir: to applaud	aplaudiendo aplaudido	3-R-Discutir
aplazar: to postone, to defer	aplazando aplazado	7-O-Rezar
aplicar: to apply	aplicando aplicado	9-O-Tocar
aportar: to contribute, to furnish	aportando aportado	1-R-Hablar
apostar: to bet, to wager	apostando apostado	26-S-Aprobar-Acortar

apoyar: to support, to lean on	apoyando apoyado	1-R-Hablar
apreciar: to appreciate	apreciando apreciado	1-R-Hablar
aprender: to learn	aprendiendo aprendido	2-R-Beber
apretar: to tighten, to grip	apretando apretado	24-S-Alentar-Acertar
aprobar: to approve, to pass	aprobando aprobado	26-S-Aprobar-Acortar
aprovecharse : to take advantage	aprovechándose aprovechado	49-R-RF-Levantarse
apuntar: to aim, to point at	apuntando apuntado	1-R-Hablar
apurarse: to grieve, to worry	apurándose apurado	49-R-RF-Levantarse
arder: to burn	ardiendo ardido	2-R-Beber
armar: to arm, to prepare	armando armado	1-R-Hablar
arquear: to arch, to bow	arqueando arqueado	1-R-Hablar
arrancar: to pull out, to tear out	arrancando arrancado	9-O-Tocar
arreglar: to arrange, to fix	arreglando arreglado	1-R-Hablar
arriesgar: to risk	arriesgando arriesgado	10-O-Pagar
arrojar: to throw, to hurl	arrojando arrojado	1-R-Hablar
asar: to roast	asando asado	1-R-Hablar
ascender: to ascend, to rise	ascendiendo ascendido	25-S-Perder-Entender
asegurarse : to make sure, to ascertain	asegurándose asegurado	49-R-RF-Levantarse
asesinar: to murder	asesinando asesinado	1-R-Hablar

asentir: to assent	asintiendo asentido	30-S-Sentir-Advertir
aseverar: to assert	aseverando aseverado	1-R-Hablar
asir: to seize, to grasp	asiendo asido	56-I-Asir
asistir: to assist, to attend	asistiendo asistido	3-R-Discutir
asombrar: to astonish, to surprise	asombrando asombrado	1-R-Hablar
aspirar: to inhale, to suck in	aspirando aspirado	1-R-Hablar
asustarse: to be frightened	asustándose asustado	49-R-RF-Levantarse
atacar: to attack, to assault	atacando atacado	9-O-Tocar
atar: to tie	atando atado	1-R-Hablar
atardecer: to to get dark-become dark	atardeciendo atardecido	D O/W 18-O-Conocer
atender: to attend, to serve	atendiendo atendido	25-S-Perder-Entender
atenerse de: to abide by, to obey	ateniéndose atenido	RF O/W 75-I-Tener
aterrizar: to land	aterrizando aterrizado	7-O-Rezar
atracar: to hold up, to dock	atracando atracado	9-O-Tocar
atraer: to attract, to charm	atrayendo atraído	76-I-Traer
atraillar, to put on a leash	atraillando atraillado	97-Ú/Í-Atraillar
atravesar: to cross, to go over	atravesando atravesado	24-S-Alentar-Acertar
atropellar: to knock over, to trample	atropellando atropellado	1-R-Hablar
aullar: to howl, to yell	aullando aullado	92-Ú/Í-Aullar

aumentar: **to increase**	aumentando aumentado	1-R-Hablar
aunar: to unite, to join	aunando aunado	92-Ú/Í-Aullar
autorizar: **to authorize,** **to approve**	autorizando autorizado	7-O-Rezar
auxiliar: to help, to assist	auxiliando auxiliado	91-Ú/Í-Ampliar
avanzar: **to advance,** **to** **go forward**	avanzando avanzado	7-O-Rezar
avergonzar: to put to shame	avergonzando avergonzado	82-M-Avergonzar
avergonzarse: **to be ashamed**	avergonzándos e avergonzado	RF O/W 82-M-Avergonzar
averiguar: **to ascertain, to find out**	averiguando averiguado	11-O-Averiguar
ayudar: to assist to aid	ayudando ayudado	1-R-Hablar
bailar: to dance	bailando bailado	1-R-Hablar
bajar: to go down, to descend	bajando bajado	1-R-HablarAR
bajarse: **to** **bend down, to stoop**	bajándose bajado	49-R-RF-Levantarse
balbuccar: **to stammer**	balbuceando balbuceado	1-R-Hablar
bañarse: to take a bath, to bathe	bañándose bañado	49-R-RF-Levantarse
barrer: to sweep	barriendo barrido	2-R-Beber
basar: to base	basando basado	1-R-Hablar
bastar: **to** **be enough, to suffice**	bastando bastado	D O/W 1-R-Hablar
batir: to beat	batiendo batido	3-R-Discutir

beber: to drink	bebiendo bebido	2-R-Beber
bendecir: to bless	bendiciendo bendecido- bendito	NB. Participles O/W 60-I-Decir
besar: to kiss	besando besado	1-R-Hablar
blanquear: to whiten	blanqueando blanqueado	1-R-Hablar
bombardear: to bombard	bombardeando bombardeado	1-R-Hablar
borrar: to rub out	borrando borrado	1-R-Hablar
bostezar: to yawn	bostezando bostezado	7-O-Rezar
botar: to throw	botando botado	1-R-Hablar
brillar : to shine	brillando brillado	1-R-Hablar
brincar: to jump, to bounce	brincando brincado	9-O-Tocar
brindar: to offer, to present, to toast	brindando brindado	1-R-Hablar
broncear: to bronze	bronceando bronceado	1-R-Hablar
bruñir: to polish to burnish	bruñendo bruñido	5-O-Bruñir-Tañer
bucear: to dive/swim under water	buceando buceado	1-R-Hablar
bullir: to boil, to bubble up	bullendo bullido	4-O-Bullir-Empeller
burlar: to deceive, to trick	burlando burlado	1-R-Hablar
buscar: to look for	buscando buscado	9-O-Tocar
cabalgar: to ride	cabalgando cabalgado	10-O-Pagar
caber: to fit, to accommodate	cabiendo cabido	57-I-Caber

204

caer: to fall	cayendo caído	23-O-Caer
caerse: to fall	cayéndose caído	39-I-RF-Caerse
calentar: to warm up, to heat	calentando calentado	24-S-Alentar-Acertar
callarse: to shut up/ to be silent	callándose callado	49-R-RF-Levantarse
calmar: to calm, to soothe	calmando calmado	1-R-Hablar
calzar: to wear (shoes etc.)	calzando calzado	7-O-Rezar
cambiar : to change	cambiando cambiado	1-R-Hablar
caminar: to walk	caminando caminado	1-R-Hablar
cancelar: to cancel	cancelando cancelado	1-R-Hablar
cansarse: to become tired	cansándose cansado	49-R-RF-Levantarse
cantar: to sing	cantando cantado	1-R-Hablar
captar: to capture	captando captado	1-R-Hablar
carecer: to lack	careciendo carecido	18-O-Conocer
cargar: to load, to burden	cargando cargado	10-O-Pagar
cartearse: to correspond	carteándose carteado	49-R-RF-Levantarse
casarse: to marry	casándose casado	49-R-RF-Levantarse
castigar: to castigate, to punish	castigando castigado	10-O-Pagar
causar: to cause	causando causado	1-R-Hablar
cazar: to hunt	cazando cazado	7-O-Rezar

205

ceder: to hand over, to cede	cediendo cedido	2-R-Beber
celebrar: to celebrate	celebrando celebrado	1-R-Hablar
cenar: to dine, to have supper	cenando cenado	1-R-Hablar
ceñir: to encircle, to surround	ciñendo ceñido	83-M-Ceñir
cepillar: to brush	cepillando cepillado	1-R-Hablar
cercar: to surround	cercando cercado	9-O-Tocar
cernir: to sift	cerniendo cernido	29-S-Discernir-Cernir
cerrar: to close	cerrando cerrado	24-S-Alentar-Acertar
charlar: to chat	charlando charlado	1-R-Hablar
chismear: to gossip	chismeando chismeado	1-R-Hablar
chocar: to collide, to crash	chocando chocado	9-O-Tocar
chupar: to suck	chupando chupado	1-R-Hablar
cifrar: to encode	cifrando cifrado	1-R-Hablar
circular: to circulate	circulando circulado	1-R-Hablar
citar: to quote, to make a date	citando citando	1-R-Hablar
clarificar: to clarify, to make clear	clarificando clarificado	9-O-Tocar
clasificar: to classify, to rank	clasificando clasificado	9-O-Tocar
clausurar: to close down	clausurando clausurado	1-R-Hablar
clavar: to nail	clavando clavado	1-R-Hablar

cobijar: to shelter	cobijando cobijado	1-R-Hablar
cobrar: to charge, to collect	cobrando cobrado	1-R-Hablar
cocer: to cook	cociendo cocido	58-I-Cocer
cocinar: to cook	cocinando cocinado	1-R-Hablar
coger: to take, to catch, to seize	cogiendo cogido	12-O-Escoger
colaborar: to collaborate	colaborando colaborado	1-R-Hablar
colegir: to infer, to deduce	coligiendo colegido	36-S-Colegir-Elegir
colgar: to hang up	colgando colgado	84-M-Colgar
colocar: to place, to put	colocando colocado	9-O-Tocar
combatir: to attack, to fight	combatiendo combatido	3-R-Discutir
combinar: to combine, to match	combinado combinando	1-R-Hablar
comentar: to discuss, to comment	comentando comentado	1-R-Hablar
comenzar: to commence, to begin	comenzando comenzado	M 24-S-Alentar-Acertar+7-O-Rezar
comer: to eat	comiendo comido	2-R-Beber
cometer: to commit	cometiendo cometido	2-R-Beber
comparar: to compare	comparando comparado	1-R-Hablar
compartir: to share, to divide up	compartiendo compartido	3-R-Discutir
compensar: to compensate	compensando compensado	1-R-Hablar
competir: to compete	compitiendo competido	31-S-Servir-Competir

207

complacer: to please	complaciendo complaciendo	18-O-Conocer
completar: to complete	completando completado	1-R-Hablar
componer: to put together, to **constitute**	componiendo compuesto	99-DC-Componer
comprar: to buy	comprando comprado	1-R-Hablar
comprarse: to buy for oneself	comprándose comprado	49-R-RF-Levantarse
comprender: to **understand**	comprendiendo comprendido	2-R-Beber
comprobar: to **check, to verify**	comprobando comprobado	26-S-Aprobar-Acortar
concebir: to **conceive**	concibiendo concebido	31-S-Servir-Competir
conceder: to **concede**	concediendo concedido	2-R-Beber
concentrar: to **concentrate**	concentrando concentrado	1-R-Hablar
concertar: to **arrange,** to **coordinate**	concertando concertado	24-S-Alentar-Acertar
conciliar: to **reconcile,** to **conciliate**	conciliando conciliado	91-Ú/Í-Ampliar
concluir: to **conclude, to finish**	concluyendo concluido	21-O-Instruir
concretar: to **particularize,** to **pinpoint**	concretando concretado	1-R-Hablar
condenar: to **condemn, to find guilty**	condenando condenado	1-R-Hablar
condicionar: to **condition**	condicionando condicionado	1-R-Hablar
conducir: to lead, to conduct	conduciendo conducido	20-M-Producir

conectar: to **connect, to switch on**	conectando conectado	1-R-Hablar
confesar: to admit, to confess	confesando confesado	24-S-Alentar-Acertar
confiar: to trust, to confide	confiando confiado	91-Ú/Í-Ampliar
confirmar: to **confirm,** to **corroborate**	confirmando confirmado	1-R-Hablar
confiscar: to **confiscate**	confiscando confiscado	9-O-Tocar
conformar: to **shape, to agree with**	conformando conformado	1-R-Hablar
conformarse: to **conform,** to **observe**	conformándose conformado	49-R-RF-Levantarse
confundir: to blur, to confuse	confundiendo confundido	3-R-Discutir
congelar: to **freeze, to congeal**	congelando congelado	1-R-Hablar
conocer: to know, to meet	conociendo conocido	18-O-Conocer
conocerse: to **know oneself**	conociendo conocido	RF O/W 18-O-Conocer
conseguir : to **attain, to obtain**	consiguiendo conseguido	14-O-Distinguir
consentir: to **consent, to agree**	consintiendo consentido	30-S-Sentir-Advertir
conservar: to **preserve, to retain**	conservando conservado	1-R-Hablar
considerar: to **consider, to bear in mind**	considerando considerado	1-R-Hablar
consistir: to **consist of**	consistiendo consistido	3-R-Discutir
constiparse: to **catch a cold**	constipándose constipado	49-R-RF-Levantarse

constituir: **to constitute,** **to make up**	constituyendo constituido	21-O-Instruir
construir: to build, to construct	construyendo construido	21-O-Instruir
consultar: **to consult, to look up**	consultando consultado	1-R-Hablar
consumir: **to consume, to wear away**	consumiendo consumido	3-R-Discutir
contaminar: **to contaminate,** **to pollute**	contaminando contaminado	1-R-Hablar
contar: to tell, to relate	contando contado	26-S-Aprobar-Acortar
contener: **to contain, to contain**	conteniendo contenido	75-I-Tener
contestar **:** **to answer, to reply**	contestando contestado	1-R-Hablar
continuar: **to continue**	continuando continuado	90-Ú/Í-Evaluar
contraer: **to contract, to pick up**	contrayendo contraído	76-I-Traer
contrahacer,: **to copy,** **to counterfeit**	contrahaciendo contrahecho	64-I-Hacer
contratar: **to contract, to engage**	contratando contratado	1-R-Hablar
contribuir: **to contribute, to pay up**	contribuyendo contribuido	21-O-Instruir
controlar: **to controlar**	controlando controlado	1-R-Hablar
convencer: **to convince**	convenciendo convencido	16-O-Vencer
convenir: to agree with, to be fitting	conviniendo convenido	103-DC-Convenir
conversar: **to converse**	conversando conversado	1-R-Hablar

convertir: to **convert,** to **transform**	convirtiendo convertido	30-S-Sentir-Advertir
convertirse: to **change oneself, to convert**	convirtiendo convertido	RF O/W 30-S-Sentir-Advertir
convidar : to invite	convidando convidado	1-R-Hablar
convivir: to **live together**	conviviendo conviviendo	3-R-Discutir
convocar: to **convoke,** to **summon**	convocando convocado	9-O-Tocar
coronar : to crown	coronando coronado	1-R-Hablar
corregir: to **correct,** to **reprimand**	corrigiendo corregido	36-S-Colegir-Elegir
correr : to run	corriendo corrido	2-R-Beber
cortar: to cut, to **crop**	cortando cortado	1-R-Hablar
cosechar: to **harvest, to crop**	cosechando cosechado	1-R-Hablar
coser: to sew, to **stitch**	cosiendo cosido	2-R-Beber
costar: to cost	costando costado	D 26-S-Aprobar-Acortar
crear: to create, to make	creando creado	1-R-Hablar
crecer: to grow, to increase	creciendo crecido	18-O-Conocer
creer: to believe	creyendo creído	8-O-Creer
criar: to raise, to breed, to bring up	criando criado	91-Ú/Í-Ampliar
cruzar: to cross	cruzando cruzado	7-O-Rezar
cubrir: to cover	cubriendo cubierto	3-R-Discutir

cuidar: to take care of, to look after	cuidando cuidado	1-R-Hablar
cuidarse: to take care of oneself	cuidándose cuidado	49-R-RF-Levantarse
culpar: to blame, to accuse	culpando culpado	1-R-Hablar
cultivar: to cultivate, to grow	cultivando cultivado	1-R-Hablar
cumplir: to comply, to fulfill	cumpliendo cumplido	3-R-Discutir
curar: to cure, to remedy	curando curado	1-R-Hablar
cursar: to take a course, to study	cursando cursado	1-R-Hablar
dañar: to damage	dañando dañado	1-R-Hablar
dar: to give	dando dado	59-I-Dar
deber: to owe, to have to	debiendo debido	2-R-Beber
decidir: to decide, to determine	decidiendo decidido	3-R-Discutir
decir: to say, to tell	diciendo dicho	60-I-Decir
declarar: to declare, to state	declarando declarado	1-R-Hablar
declararse: to make one's view known	declarándose declarado	49-R-RF-Levantarse
dedicar: to devote, to dedicate	dedicando dedicado	9-O-Tocar
dedicarse: to devote oneself	dedicándose dedicado	RF O/W 9-O-Tocar
deducir: to deduce, to deduct	deduciendo deducido	20-M-Producir
defender: to defend	defendiendo defendido	25-S-Perder-Entender
defenderse: to defend oneself	defendiéndose defendido	41-S-RF-Defenderse

212

degustar: to taste, to sample	degustando degustado	1-R-Hablar
dejar: to leave, to let	dejando dejado	1-R-Hablar
delinquir: to commit an offence	delinquiendo delinquido	15-O-Delinquir
demostrar : to prove, to demonstrate	demostrando demostrado	26-S-Aprobar-Acortar
depender: to depend	dependiendo dependido	2-R-Beber
deponer: to lay down, remove, to depose	deponiendo depuesto	68-I-Poner
deportar: to deport	deportando deportado	1-R-Hablar
derivar: to derive	derivando derivado	1-R-Hablar
derrumbar: to pull down	derrumbando derrumbado	1-R-Hablar
desafiar: to challenge	desafiando desafiado	91-Ú/Í-Ampliar
desaparecer: to disappear	desapareciendo desaparecido	18-O-Conocer
desarmar: to disarm	desarmando desarmado	1-R-Hablar
desarrollar: to develop, to roll out	desarrollando desarrollado	1-R-Hablar
desayunar: to breakfast	desayunando desayunado	1-R-Hablar
descansar: to rest	descansado descansado	1-R-Hablar
descartar: to discard	descartando descartado	1-R-Hablar
descolgar: to unhook, to take down	descolgando descolgado	84-M-Colgar
describir: to desribe	describiendo descrito	3-R-Discutir

213

descubrir: to discover	descubriendo descubierto	3-R-Discutir
desear: to desire, to wish	deseando deseado	1-R-Hablar
desdeñar: to disdain	desdeñando desdeñado	1-R-Hablar
desempeñar: to play a part, to perform	desempeñado desempeñando	1-R-Hablar
desenchufar: to disconnect, to unplug	desenchufando desenchufado	1-R-Hablar
deshacer: to undo	deshaciendo deshecho	98-DC-Deshacer
deshacerse: to come undone, to get rid of	deshaciéndose deshecho	RF O/W 98-DC-Deshacer
desistir: to desist	desistiendo desistido	3-R-Discutir
deslizarse: to slip, to slide	deslizándose deslizado	RF O/W 7-O-Rezar
deslucir: to tarnish, to spoil	desluciendo deslucido	19-O-Lucir
desparramar: to scatter, to spill	desparramando desparramado	1-R-Hablar
despedir: to say goodbye to	despidiendo despedido	31-S-Servir-Competir
despedirse: to say goodbye, to take leave	despidiéndose despedido	42-S-RF-Despedirse
despegar: to take off, to unstick/detach	despegando despegado	10-O-Pagar
despertar: to wake up, to rouse	despertando despertado	24-S-Alentar-Acertar
despertarse: to wake oneself up	despertándose despertado	RF O/W 24-S-Alentar-Acertar
desplazarse: to travel, to move	desplazando desplazado	RF O/W 7-O-Rezar

214

destacar: to stand out, to highlight	destacando destacado	9-O-Tocar
desterrar: to banish	desterrando desterrado	24-S-Alentar-Acertar
destruir: to destroy	destruyendo destruido	21-O-Instruir
desvestirse: to undress oneself	desvistiéndose desvestido	43-S-RF-Desvestirse
desviar: to divert, to deflect	desviando desviado	91-Ú/Í-Ampliar
detener: to stop, to detain	deteniendo detenido	75-I-Tener
detenerse: to stop, to delay	deteniéndose detenido	RF O/W 75-I-Tener
detestar: to detest, to hate	detestando detestado	1-R-Hablar
devolver: to return, to give back	devolviendo devuelto	27-S-Morder-Remover
dibujar: to draw, to sketch	dibujando dibujado	1-R-Hablar
diferenciar: to distinguish	diferenciando diferenciado	1-R-Hablar
dimitir: to resign, to quit	dimitiendo dimitido	3-R-Discutir
dirigir: to direct	dirigiendo dirigido	13-O-Dirigir
dirigirse: to go to, to direct oneself	dirigiéndose dirigido	45-O-RF-Dirigirse
discernir: to discern, to distinguish	discerniendo discernido	29-S-Discernir-Cernir
disculpar: to forgive	disculpando disculpado	1-R-Hablar
discutir: to discuss, to argue	discutiendo discutido	3-R-Discutir
diseñar: to design	diseñando diseñado	1-R-Hablar
disfrutar: to enjoy	disfrutando disfrutado	1-R-Hablar

disgustar: to annoy. to upset	disgustando disgustado	1-R-Hablar
disminuir: to decrease, to diminish	disminuyendo disminuido	21-O-Instruir
disolver: to dissolve, to break up	disolviendo disuelto	27-S-Morder-Remover
disponer: to dispose, to provide/arrange	disponiendo dispuesto	68-I-Poner
distinguir: to distinguish, to discriminate	distinguiendo distinguido	14-O-Distinguir
distraer: to distract, to divert	distrayendo distraído	76-I-Traer
divertirse: to enjoy, to amuse oneself	divirtiéndose divertido	46-S-RF-Divertirse
dividir: to divide, to share	dividiendo dividido	3-R-Discutir
divorciar: to divorce, to separate	divorciando divorciado	1-R-Hablar
doblar: to fold	doblando doblado	1-R-Hablar
doler: to hurt, to ache	doliendo dolido	27-S-Morder-Remover
domar: to tame	domando domado	1-R-Hablar
dormir: to sleep	durmiendo dormido	33-S-Dormir-Morir
dormirse: to go to sleep	durmiéndose dormido	RF O/W 33-S-Dormir-Morir
ducharse: to have a shower	duchándose duchado	49-R-RF-Levantarse
dudar: to doubt	dudando dudado	1-R-Hablar
durar: to last, to continue	durando durado	1-R-Hablar

echar: to throw, to cast	echando echado	1-R-Hablar
edificar: to build	edificando edificado	9-O-Tocar
editar: to publish	editando editado	1-R-Hablar
educar: to educate	educando educado	9-O-Tocar
efectuar: to effect, to bring about	efectuando efectuado	90-Ú/Í-Evaluar
ejercer: to exercise, to exert	ejerciendo ejercido	16-O-Vencer
elaborar: to elaborate, to develop	elaborando elaborado	1-R-Hablar
elegir: to elect, to choose	eligiendo elegido	36-S-Colegir-Elegir
elevarse: to arise, to go up	elevándose elevado	49-R-RF-Levantarse
eliminar: to eliminate, to remove	eliminando eliminado	1-R-Hablar
embarcar: to embark	embarcando embarcado	9-O-Tocar
embellecer: to beautify, to embellish	embelleciendo embellecido	18-O-Conocer
embestir: to attack, to charge	embistiendo embestido	31-S-Servir-Competir
emborracharse: to get drunk	emborrachándose emborrachado	49-R-RF-Levantarse
emigrar: to emigrate	emigrando emigrado	1-R-Hablar
emitir: to emit	emitiendo emitido	3-R-Discutir
emocionar: to excite, to thrill	emocionando emocionado	1-R-Hablar
empacar: to pack	empacando empacado	9-O-Tocar

empaparse: to get soaked	empapándose empapado	49-R-RF-Levantarse
empeller (o/w empellar): to push, to impel	empellendo empellido	4-O-Bullir-Empeller
empeorar: to get worse	empeorando empeorado	1-R-Hablar
empezar: to begin, to start	empezando empezado	85-M-Empezar
emplear: to employ, to use	empleando empleado	1-R-Hablar
enamorarse: to fall in love	enamorándose enamorado	49-R-RF-Levantarse
encantar: to delight, to charm	encantando encantado	1-R-Hablar
encargar: to order, to entrust	encargando encargado	10-O-Pagar
encender: to light (fire), to switch on	encendiendo encendido	25-S-Perder-Entender
encerrar: to enclose, to shut up	encerrando encerrado	24-S-Alentar-Acertar
enchufar: to plug in	enchufando enchufado	1-R-Hablar
encontrar: to find, to encounter	encontrando encontrado	26-S-Aprobar-Acortar
encontrarse: to meet	encontrándose encontrado	RF O/W 26-S-Aprobar-Acortar
endulzar: to sweeten	endulzando endulzando	7-O-Rezar
endurecer: to harden	endureciendo endurecido	18-O-Conocer
enfadar: to anger, to annoy	enfadando enfadado	1-R-Hablar
enfadarse: to get angry	enfadándose enfadado	49-R-RF-Levantarse
enfermarse: to fall ill	enfermándose enfermado	49-R-RF-Levantarse
enfriar: to cool	enfriando enfriado	91-Ú/Í-Ampliar

218

engañar: to deceive, to trick	engañando engañado	1-R-Hablar
engañarse: to be wrong	engañándose engañado	49-R-RF-Levantarse
engordar: to fatten up, to get plump	engordando engordado	1-R-Hablar
enlazar: to tie together, to connect	enlazando enlazado	7-O-Rezar
enojarse: to get angry, to lose temper	enojándose enojado	49-R-RF-Levantarse
enraizar: to take root	enraizando enraizado	7-O-Rezar also (ai in stem) 93-Ú/Í-Airar
ensayar: to test	ensayando ensayado	1-R-Hablar
enseñar: to teach, to instruct	enseñando enseñado	1-R-Hablar
ensuciar: to make dirty	ensuciando ensuciado	1-R-Hablar
entender: to understand	entendiendo entendido	25-S-Perder-Entender
entrar: to enter	entrando entrado	1-R-Hablar
entreabrir: to half open, to leave ajar	entreabriendo entreabierto	3-R-Discutir
entregar: to hand over, to deliver	entregando entregado	10-O-Pagar
entusiasmar: to enthuse, to delight	entusiasmando entusiasmado	1-R-Hablar
envasar: to pack, to bottle	envasando envasado	1-R-Hablar
enviar: to send, to dispatch	enviando enviado	91-Ú/Í-Ampliar
envidiar: to envy	envidiando envidiado	1-R-Hablar
envolver: to wrap up, to envelop	envolviendo envuelto	27-S-Morder-Remover

equivaler: to be equal to, to rank the same as	equivaliendo equivalido	104-DC-Equivaler
equivocarse: to make a mistake,	equivocándose equivocado	RF O/W 9-O-Tocar
erguir: to raise, to lift	irguiendo erguido	14-O-Distinguir
erigir: to erect, to build	erigiendo erigido	13-O-Dirigir
errar: to miss, to mistake	errando errado	1-R-Hablar
escaparse: to escape, to get away	escapándose escapado	49-R-RF-Levantarse
escoger: to choose, to select	escogiendo escogido	12-O-Escoger
escribir: to write	escribiendo escrito	3-R-Discutir
escuchar: to listen, to hear	escuchando escuchado	1-R-Hablar
escupir: to spit	escupiendo escupido	3-R-Discutir
esforzarse: to make an effort, to strive	esforzándose esforzado	RF O/W 86-M-Forzar
esparcir: to scatter, to spread	esparciendo esparcido	17-O-Esparcir
esperar: to hope, to wait, to expect	esperando esperado	1-R-Hablar
esquiar: to ski	esquiando esquiado	91-Ú/Í-Ampliar
establecer: to establish, to set up	estableciendo establecido	18-O-Conocer
estallar: to burst, to explode	estallando estallado	1-R-Hablar
estar: to be	estando estando	62-I-Estar
estremecer: to shake	estremeciendo estremecido	18-O-Conocer
estrenar: to show for first time,	estrenando estrenado	1-R-Hablar

estropear: to ruin, to spoil	estropeando estropeado	1-R-Hablar
estudiar: to study	estudiando estudiado	1-R-Hablar
evadir: to evade	evadiendo evadido	3-R-Discutir
evaluar: to evaluate	evaluando evaluado	90-Ú/Í-Evaluar
evitar: to avoid, to prevent	evitando evitado	1-R-Hablar
exaltar: to exalt, to excite	exaltando exaltado	1-R-Hablar
exigir: to demand, to require	exigiendo exigido	13-O-Dirigir
existir: to exist	existiendo existido	3-R-Discutir
experimentar: to experience, to try out	experimentando experimentado	1-R-Hablar
explicar: to explain	explicando explicado	9-O-Tocar
exponer: to expose, to exhibit	exponiendo expuesto	68-I-Poner
extender: to extend, to enlarge	extendiendo extendido	25-S-Perder-Entender
extinguir: to extinguish, to putout	extinguiendo extinguido	14-O-Distinguir
extraer: to extract	extrayendo extraído	76-I-Traer
extrañar: to surprise, to find strange	extrañando extrañado	1-R-Hablar
fabricar: to make	fabricando fabricado	9-O-Tocar
facturar: to invoice, to register	facturando facturado	1-R-Hablar
fallar: to fail, to miss	fallando fallado	1-R-Hablar

fallecer: to die, to pass away	falleciendo fallecido	18-O-Conocer
faltar: to lack, to fail	faltando faltado	1-R-Hablar
fascinar: to fascinate, to enthral	fascinando fascinado	1-R-Hablar
fastidiar: to annoy	fastidiando fastidiado	1-R-Hablar
fatigar: to fatigue	fatigando fatigado	10-O-Pagar
favorecer: to favour	favoreciendo favorecido	18-O-Conocer
felicitar: to congratulate	felicitando felicitado	1-R-Hablar
fermentar: to ferment	fermentando fermentado	1-R-Hablar
festejar: to celebrate	festejando festejado	1-R-Hablar
fiar: to entrust, to confide	fiando fiado	91-Ú/Í-Ampliar
figurar: to represent	figurando figurado	1-R-Hablar
fijar: to fix, to set	fijando fijado	1-R-Hablar
fijarse: to be fixed, to pay attention	fijándose fijado	49-R-RF-Levantarse
filtrar: to filter	filtrando filtrado	1-R-Hablar
finalizar: to finish	finalizando finalizado	7-O-Rezar
fingir: to fake, to pretend	fingiendo fingido	13-O-Dirigir
firmar: to sign	firmando firmado	1-R-Hablar
fluir: to flow, to run	fluyendo fluido	21-O-Instruir
formar: to form, to shape, to educate	formando formado	1-R-Hablar

222

forzar: to force, to compel	forzando forzado	86-M-Forzar
fracasar: to fail, to fall through	fracasando fracasado	1-R-Hablar
fregar: to scrub, to wash up	fregando fregado	87-M-Regar
freir: to fry	friendo frito	35-S-Reir-Freir
frenar: to brake	frenando frenado	1-R-Hablar
frotar: to rub	frotando frotado	1-R-Hablar
fulgurar: to glow, to shine	fulgurando fulgurado	1-R-Hablar
fumar: to smoke	fumando fumado	1-R-Hablar
funcionar: to function, to work	funcionando funcionado	1-R-Hablar
fundar: to found, to establish	fundando fundado	1-R-Hablar
ganar: to gain, to earn, to win	ganando ganado	1-R-Hablar
garantizar: to guarantee	garantizando garantizado	7-O-Rezar
gastar: to spend, to consume	gastando gastado	1-R-Hablar
gatear: to crawl	gateando gateado	1-R-Hablar
gemir: to moan, to groan	gimiendo gemido	Present-P: gimiendo+31-S-Servir-Competir
girar: to turn, to twist, to rotate	girando girado	1-R-Hablar
glorificar: to glorify	glorificando glorificado	9-O-Tocar
gobernar: to govern, to rule	gobernando gobernado	24-S-Alentar-Acertar
golpear: to strike, to beat	golpeando golpeado	1-R-Hablar

223

gorgotear: to gurgle	gorgoteando gorgoteado	1-R-Hablar
gozar: to enjoy	gozando gozado	7-O-Rezar
grabar: to engrave, to record	grabando grabado	1-R-Hablar
granizar: to hail (ie storm)	granizando granizado	D 7-O-Rezar
gravitar: to gravitate	gravitando gravitado	1-R-Hablar
gritar: to shout, to yell	gritando gritado	1-R-Hablar
gruñir: to grunt, to growl	gruñendo gruñido	5-O-Bruñir-Tañer
guardar: to guard, to protect	guardando guardado	1-R-Hablar
guiar: to guide, to lead	guiando guiado	91-Ú/Í-Ampliar
guiñar: to wink	guiñando guiñado	1-R-Hablar
gustar: to please (to like), to taste	gustando gustado	D 1-R-Hablar
haber: to have (auxillary verb)	habiendo habido	63-I-Haber
habitar: to inhabit, to live in	habitando habitado	1-R-Hablar
habituarse: to get accustomed to	habituándose habituado	RF O/W 90-Ú/Í-Evaluar
hablar : to talk, to speak	hablando hablado	1-R-Hablar
hacer: to make, to create	haciendo hecho	64-I-Hacer
halagar: to flatter	halagando halagado	10-O-Pagar
hallar: to find, to discover	hallando hallado	1-R-Hablar
hallarse: to find oneself	hallándose hallado	49-R-RF-Levantarse
hambrear: to starve	hambreando hambreado	1-R-Hablar

224

henchir: to stuff, to cram	hinchendo henchido	6-O-Henchir
herir: to injure, to wound	hiriendo herido	Present-P: hiriendo O/W 30-S-Sentir-Advertir
hervir: to boil	hirviendo hervido	Present-P: hirviendo O/W 30-S-Sentir-Advertir
hincharse: to swell, to bulge	hinchándose hinchado	49-R-RF-Levantarse
hipnotizar: to hypnotize	hipnotizando hipnotizado	7-O-Rezar
hipotecar: to mortgage	hipotecando hipotecado	9-O-Tocar
hospedar: to accommodate, to lodge	hospedando hospedado	1-R-Hablar
hospedarse: to stay with, to lodge with	hospedándose hospedado	49-R-RF-Levantarse
huir: to run away, to escape	huyendo huido	21-O-Instruir
humillar: to humiliate	humillando humillado	1-R-Hablar
hundir: to sink, to submerge	hundiendo hundido	3-R-Discutir
identificar: to identify	identificando identificado	9-O-Tocar
ilusionar:to give false hopes	ilusionando ilusionado	1-R-Hablar
imaginar: to imagine, to think up	imaginando imaginado	1-R-Hablar
imaginarse: to imagine, to fancy	imaginándose imaginado	49-R-RF-Levantarse
imbuir: to infuse	imbuyendo imbuido	21-O-Instruir
impartir: to impart	impartiendo impartido	3-R-Discutir

impedir: to prevent, to impede	impidiendo impedido	31-S-Servir-Competir
implicar: to implicate, to involve	implicando implicado	9-O-Tocar
implorar: to implore	implorando implorado	1-R-Hablar
imponer: to impose, to enforce upon	imponiendo impuesto	68-I-Poner
importar: to matter, to be important,	importando importado	1-R-Hablar
imprecar: to curse	imprecando imprecado	9-O-Tocar
impresionar: to impress	impresionando impresionado	1-R-Hablar
improvisar: to improvise	improvisando improvisado	1-R-Hablar
impulsar: to impel	impulsando impulsado	1-R-Hablar
incitar: to encourage, to rouse	incitando incitado	1-R-Hablar
incluir: to include	incluyendo incluido	21-O-Instruir
indicar: to indicate	indicando indicado	9-O-Tocar
indignar: to anger, to make indignant	indignando indignado	1-R-Hablar
inducir: to induce, to persuade	induciendo inducido	20-M-Producir
influir: to influence	influyendo influido	21-O-Instruir
ingerir: to swallow, to take in	ingiriendo ingerido	Present-P: ingiriendo O/W 30-S-Sentir-Advertir
ingresar: to go in, to enter, to enrol	ingresando ingresado	1-R-Hablar

inhalar: to inhale	inhalando inhalado	1-R-Hablar
iniciar: to start, to initiate	iniciando iniciado	1-R-Hablar
inquirir: to investigate, to enquire into	inquiriendo inquirido	32-S-Adquirir-Inquirir
inscribirse: to enrol, to enscribe	inscribiéndose inscrito	47-R-RF-Inscribirse
insistir: to insist	insistiendo insistido	3-R-Discutir
inspirar: to inspire	inspirando inspirado	1-R-Hablar
instalar: to install, to set up	instalando instalado	1-R-Hablar
instruir: to instruct, to teach	instruyendo nstruido	21-O-Instruir
integrar: to integrate, to make up	integrando integrado	1-R-Hablar
intentar: to try, to attempt	intentando intentado	1-R-Hablar
interesar: to interest	interesando interesado	1-R-Hablar
interesarse: to be interested,	interesándose interesado	49-R-RF-Levantarse
interrumpir: to interupt, to cut off	interrumpiendo interrumpido	3-R-Discutir
intimar: to intimate, to announce	intimando intimado	1-R-Hablar
intimarse: to become friendly	intimándose intimado	49-R-RF-Levantarse
intimidar: to intimidate	intimidando intimidado	1-R-Hablar
introducir: to introduce, to bring in	introduciendo introducido	20-M-Producir

227

invertir: to invest, to turn upside down	invirtiendo invertido	30-S-Sentir-Advertir
investigar: to investigate, to research	investigando investigado	10-O-Pagar
invitar: to invite	invitando invitado	1-R-Hablar
ir: to go	yendo ido	65-I-Ir
irritar: to irritate, to annoy	irritando irritado	1-R-Hablar
irse: to go away, to leave	yéndose ido	48-I-RF-Irse
izar: to hoist	izando izado	7-O-Rezar
jactarse: to boast	jactándose jactado	49-R-RF-Levantarse
jadear: to gasp, to pant	jadeando jadeado	1-R-Hablar
jubilar: to retire	jubilando jubilado	1-R-Hablar
jugar: to play, to gamble	jugando jugado	34-S-Jugar
juntarse: to come together	juntándose juntado	49-R-RF-Levantarse
justificar: to justify, to substantiate	justificando justificado	9-O-Tocar
juzgar: to judge	juzgando juzgado	10-O-Pagar
laborar: to work	laborando laborado	1-R-Hablar
labrar: to work, to carve	labrando labrado	1-R-Hablar
ladrar: to bark	ladrando ladrado	1-R-Hablar
lagrimear: to shed tears easily	lagrimeando lagrimeado	1-R-Hablar

lamentar: to lament, to regret	lamentando lamentado	1-R-Hablar
lamer: to lick	lamiendo lamido	2-R-Beber
lanzar: to launch, to throw	lanzando lanzado	7-O-Rezar
lastimar: to hurt, to injure	lastimando lastimado	1-R-Hablar
latir: to beat, to pulsate	latiendo latido	3-R-Discutir
lavar: to wash	lavando lavado	1-R-Hablar
lavarse: to wash oneself	lavándose lavado	49-R-RF-Levantarse
leer: to read	leyendo leído	8-O-Creer
legalizar: to legalize	legalizando legalizado	7-O-Rezar
levantar: to lift up, to raise	levantando levantado	1-R-Hablar
levantarse: to get up, to stand up	levantándose levantado	49-R-RF-Levantarse
liar: to tie	liando liado	91-Ú/Í-Ampliar
librar: to save, to free	librando librado	1-R-Hablar
licenciarse: to graduate	licenciándose licenciado	49-R-RF-Levantarse
lidiar: to fight	lidiando lidiado	1-R-Hablar
limitar: to limit	limitando limitado	1-R-Hablar
limpiar: to clean	limpiando limpiado	1-R-Hablar
llamar: to call	llamando llamado	1-R-Hablar
llamarse: to be called	llamándose llamado	49-R-RF-Levantarse
llegar: to arrive, to reach	llegando llegado	10-O-Pagar

229

llenar: to fill	llenando llenado	1-R-Hablar
llevar: to carry, to lead, to wear	llevando llevado	1-R-Hablar
llevarse: to carry off	llevándose llevado	49-R-RF-Levantarse
llorar: to weep, to cry	llorando llorado	1-R-Hablar
llover: to rain	lloviendo llovido	D 27-S-Morder-Remover
lograr: to obtain, to achieve	logrando logrado	1-R-Hablar
luchar: to fight, to struggle	luchando luchado	1-R-Hablar
lucir: to illuminate, to shine	luciendo lucido	19-O-Lucir
machacar: to crush, to grind	machacando machacado	9-O-Tocar
madrugar: to get up early	madrugando madrugado	10-O-Pagar
madurar: to mature	madurando madurado	1-R-Hablar
maldecir: to curse, to swear	maldiciendo maldecido	60-I-Decir
maltratar: to ill-treat, to abuse	maltratando maltratado	1-R-Hablar
malversar: to embezzle, to misappropriate	malversando malversado	1-R-Hablar
mandar: to order, to command	mandando mandado	1-R-Hablar
manejar: to handle, to operate	manejando manejado	1-R-Hablar
mantener: to maintain, to support	manteniendo mantenido	75-I-Tener
maquillarse: to make up	maquillándose maquillado	49-R-RF-Levantarse

maravillar: to wonder	maravillando maravillado	1-R-Hablar
marcar: to mark, to indicate	marcando marcado	9-O-Tocar
marearse: to feel sick, to feel dizzy	mareándose mareado	49-R-RF-Levantarse
martillar: to hammer	martillando martillado	1-R-Hablar
mascar: to chew, to mumble	mascando mascado	9-O-Tocar
masticar: to chew, to masticate	masticando masticado	9-O-Tocar
matar: to kill, to murder	matando matado	1-R-Hablar
matricular: to enroll	matriculando matriculado	1-R-Hablar
mecer: to rock, to swing	meciendo mecido	16-O-Vencer
medir: to measure	midiendo medido	31-S-Servir-Competir
meditar: to meditate	meditando meditado	1-R-Hablar
mejorar: to improve, to make better	mejorando mejorado	1-R-Hablar
mentir: to lie	mintiendo mentido	30-S-Sentir-Advertir
merecer: to deserve, to merit	mereciendo merecido	18-O-Conocer
merendar: to have afternoon tea/snack	merendando merendado	24-S-Alentar-Acertar
meter: to put, to insert, to introduce	metiendo metido	2-R-Beber
mezclar: to mix, to blend	mezclando mezclado	1-R-Hablar
mirar: to look at	mirando mirado	1-R-Hablar

231

mirarse to look at oneself	mirándose mirado	49-R-RF-Levantarse
modificar: to modify	modificando modificado	9-O-Tocar
mojar: to wet	mojando mojado	1-R-Hablar
moler: to grind, to mill, to crush	moliendo molido	27-S-Morder-Remover
molestar: to bother, to annoy, to disturb	molestando molestado	1-R-Hablar
montar: to mount, to ride	montando montado	1-R-Hablar
morder: to bite	mordiendo mordido	27-S-Morder-Remover
morderse: to bite oneself	mordiéndose mordido	50-S-RF-Morderse
morir: to die	muriendo muerto	33-S-Dormir-Morir
mostrar: to show, to display	mostrando mostrado	26-S-Aprobar-Acortar
mover: to move, to shift, to drive	moviendo movido	27-S-Morder-Remover
mullir: to beat, to soften	mullendo mullido	4-O-Bullir-Empeller
muñir: to summon	muñendo muñido	5-O-Bruñir-Tañer
nacer: to be born	naciendo nacido	18-O-Conocer
nadar: to swim	nadando nadado	1-R-Hablar
narrar: to narrate	narrando narrado	1-R-Hablar
navegar: to sail, to navegate	navegando navegado	10-O-Pagar
necesitar: to need	necesitando necesitado	1-R-Hablar
negar: to deny	negando negado	87-M-Regar

negarse: to refuse to do, to decline	negándose negado	RF O/W 87-M-Regar
negociar: to negotiate, to bargain	negociando negociado	1-R-Hablar
nevar: to snow	nevando nevado	D 24-S-Alentar-Acertar
nombrar: to name, to nominate,	nombrando nombrado	1-R-Hablar
notar: to notice, to see, to note	notando notado	1-R-Hablar
notificar: to notify	notificando notificado	9-O-Tocar
obedecer: to obey	obedeciendo obedecido	18-O-Conocer
obligar: to oblige, to force	obligando obligado	10-O-Pagar
obrar: to work	obrando obrado	1-R-Hablar
observar: to observe	observando observado	1-R-Hablar
obsesionar: to obsess, to haunt	obsesionando obsesionado	1-R-Hablar
obstruir: to obstruct	obstruyendo obstruido	21-O-Instruir
obtener: to get, to obtain, to secure	obteniendo obtenido	75-I-Tener
ocultar: to hide, to conceal	ocultando ocultado	1-R-Hablar
ocultarse: to hide oneself	ocultándose ocultado	49-R-RF-Levantarse
ocupar: to occupy, to fill	ocupando ocupado	1-R-Hablar
ocurrir: to occur, to happen	ocurriendo ocurrido	D 3-R-Discutir
odiar: to hate	odiando odiado	1-R-Hablar
ofender: to offend	ofendiendo ofendido	2-R-Beber

ofertar: to offer/tender	ofertando ofertado	1-R-Hablar
ofrecer: to offer, to give, to present	ofreciendo ofrecido	18-O-Conocer
oir: to hear, to listen to	oyendo oído	66-I-Oir
oler: to smell, to sniff out	oliendo olido	28-S-Oler
olfatear: to smell/sniff	olfateando olfateado	1-R-Hablar
olvidar: to forget	olvidando olvidado	1-R-Hablar
olvidarse: to forget	olvidándose olvidado	49-R-RF-Levantarse
ondear: to wave/ripple	ondeando ondeado	1-R-Hablar
opinar: to think/opine	opinando opinado	1-R-Hablar
oponer: to pit against, to oppose	oponiendo opuesto	68-I-Poner
oponerse: to be opposed, to object	oponiéndose opuesto	68-I-Poner
optar: to choose, to opt	optando optado	1-R-Hablar
ordeñar: to milk,	ordeñando ordeñado	1-R-Hablar
ordenar: to put in order, to arrange	ordenando ordenado	1-R-Hablar
organizar: to organize, to arrange	organizando organizado	7-O-Rezar
ornar: to adorn	ornando ornado	1-R-Hablar
ostentar: to show (off)	ostentando ostentado	1-R-Hablar
pagar: to pay	pagando pagado	10-O-Pagar
palmear: to pat/clap	palmeando palmeado	1-R-Hablar

palpar: to touch/feel	palpando palpado	1-R-Hablar
parar: to stop,	parando parado	1-R-Hablar
pararse: to stop, to come to a stop	parándose parado	49-R-RF-Levantarse
parecer: to seem, to appear	pareciendo parecido	18-O-Conocer
parecerse: to look alike, to appear like	pareciéndose parecido	RF O/W 18-O-Conocer
parpadear: to blink	parpadeando parpadeado	1-R-Hablar
participar: to parcipate, to take part	participando participado	1-R-Hablar
partir: to set of, to go away, to depart	partir partido	3-R-Discutir
pasar: to pass, to happen,	pasando pasando	1-R-Hablar
pasear: to walk	paseando paseado	1-R-Hablar
pasearse: to go for a walk	paseándose paseado	49-R-RF-Levantarse
pastar: to pasture	pastando pastado	1-R-Hablar
patear: to kick	pateando pateado	1-R-Hablar
pedalear: to pedal	pedaleando pedaleado	1-R-Hablar
pedir: to ask for, to request	pidiendo pedido	31-S-Servir-Competir
pegar: to stick onto, to beat, to hit	pegando pegado	10-O-Pagar
peinar: to comb	peinando peinado	1-R-Hablar
peinarse: to comb one's hair	peinándose peinado	49-R-RF-Levantarse
pelar: to peel, to shell, to skin	pelando pelado	1-R-Hablar

235

pelear: to quarrel, to brawl,	peleando peleado	1-R-Hablar
pelearse: to quarrel over	peleándose peleado	49-R-RF-Levantarse
pensar: to think	pensando pensado	24-S-Alentar-Acertar
percibir: to perceive, to notice	percibiendo percibido	3-R-Discutir
perder: to lose, to waste	perdiendo perdido	25-S-Perder-Entender
peregrinar: to trave/ pilgrimage	peregrinando peregrinado	1-R-Hablar
perfeccionar: to perfect	perfeccionando perfeccionado	1-R-Hablar
permanecer: to remain, to stay	permaneciendo permanecido	18-O-Conocer
permitir: to permit, to allow	permitiendo permitido	3-R-Discutir
perseguir: to pursue,to chase,to persecute	persiguiendo perseguido	88-M-Seguir
pertenecer: to belong to	perteneciendo pertenecido	18-O-Conocer
pervertir: to pervert	pervirtiendo pervertido	30-S-Sentir-Advertir
pesar: to weigh,	pesando pesado	1-R-Hablar
pescar: to fish, to catch	pescando pescado	9-O-Tocar
picar: to sting, to prick, to chop	picando picado	9-O-Tocar
pinchar: to prick/jab	pinchando	1-R-Hablar
pintar: to paint, to paint	pintando pintado	1-R-Hablar
pisar: to step, to tread	pisando pisado	1-R-Hablar
placer: to please	placiendo placido	18-O-Conocer

planchar: to iron, to press	planchando planchado	1-R-Hablar
planificar: to plan	planificando planificado	9-O-Tocar
platicar: to talk, to converse	platicando platicado	9-O-Tocar
poblar: to populate, to colonize	poblando poblado	26-S-Aprobar-Acortar
poder: to be able	pudiendo podido	67-I-Poder
poner: to put, to place	poniendo puesto	68-I-Poner
ponerse: to place/put oneself	poniéndose puesto	68-I-Poner
poseer: to possess, to own	poseyendo poseído	8-O-Creer
practicar: to practise, to go in for	practicando practicado	9-O-Tocar
precisar: to need, to identify clearly	precisando precisado	1-R-Hablar
predecir: to foretell, to predict	prediciendo predicho	60-I-Decir
predicar: to preach	predicando predicado	9-O-Tocar
preferir: to prefer,	prefiriendo preferido	30-S-Sentir-Advertir
preguntar: to ask, to enquire	preguntando preguntado	1-R-Hablar
preocuparse: to care/ to worry about	preocupándose preocupado	49-R-RF-Levantarse
preparar: to prepare, to make ready	preparando preparado	1-R-Hablar
presentar: to present, to introduce	presentando presentado	1-R-Hablar

prestar: to lend, to render	prestando prestado	1-R-Hablar
prevenir: to provide, to forestall	previniendo prevenido	78-I-Venir
prever: to foresee, to anticipate	previendo previsto	104-DC-Prever
probar: to prove, to test, to sample,	probando probado	26-S-Aprobar-Acortar
probarse: to try on (eg clothing)	probándose probado	RF O/W 26-S-Aprobar-Acortar
proceder: to proceed	procediendo procedido	2-R-Beber
procesar: to prosecute, to case against	procesando procesado	1-R-Hablar
proclamar: to proclaim	proclamando proclamado	1-R-Hablar
producir: to produce, to generate	produciendo producido	20-M-Producir
programar: to program	programando programado	1-R-Hablar
prohibir: to prohibit, to ban	prohibiendo prohibido	95-Ú/Í-Prohibir
prometer: to promise, to pledge	prometiendo prometido	2-R-Beber
promover: to promote, to advance	promoviendo promovido	27-S-Morder-Remover
pronosticar: to predict, to forecast	pronosticando pronosticado	9-O-Tocar
pronunciar: to pronounce, to deliver	pronunciando pronunciado	1-R-Hablar
proponer: to propose, to put forward	proponiendo propuesto	68-I-Poner
proteger: to protect	protegiendo protegido	12-O-Escoger

protegerse: to **protect oneself**	protegiéndose protegido	RF O/W 12-O-Escoger
protestar: to **protest**	protestando protestado	1-R-Hablar
proveer: to **provide, to supply**	proveyendo proveido	8-O-Creer
provocar: to **provoke, to tempt**	provocando provocado	9-O-Tocar
publicar: to **publish**	publicando publicado	9-O-Tocar
pudrir: to rot, to putrify	pudriendo podrido	3-R-Discutir
pulir: to polish	puliendo pulido	3-R-Discutir
quebrar: to smash, to break	quebrando quebrado	24-S-Alentar-Acertar
quedar: to stay, to remain	quedando quedado	1-R-Hablar
quedarse: to stay, to remain	quedándose quedado	49-R-RF-Levantarse
quejarse: to **complain**	quejándose quejado	49-R-RF-Levantarse
quemar: to burn	quemando quemado	1-R-Hablar
querer: to want, to wish, to like	queriendo querido	69-I-Querer
quitar: to remove, to take away	quitando quitado	1-R-Hablar
quitarse: to **withdraw from, to take off**	quitándose quitado	49-R-RF-Levantarse
racionar: to ration	racionando racionado	1-R-Hablar
radicar: to tske root, to be rooted in	radicando radicado	9-O-Tocar
raer: to fray, to scape	rayendo raído	23-O-Caer
rallar: to grate,	rallando rallado	1-R-Hablar

rascar: to scratch	rascando rascado	9-O-Tocar
ratificar: to ratify	ratificando ratificado	9-O-Tocar
rayar: to make lines on	rayando rayado	1-R-Hablar
realizar: to realize/achieve, to carry out	realizando realizado	7-O-Rezar
rebasar: to exceed, to overtake, to pass	rebasando rebasado	1-R-Hablar
rebuscar: to search carefully	rebuscando rebuscado	9-O-Tocar
recaer: to relapse	recayendo recaído	23-O-Caer
rechazar: to reject, to repel, to refuse	rechazando rechazado	7-O-Rezar
recibir: to receive, to welcome	recibiendo recibido	3-R-Discutir
reciclar: to recycle	reciclando reciclado	1-R-Hablar
reclamar: to claim/demand	reclamando reclamado	1-R-Hablar
recobrar: to recover	recobrando recobrado	1-R-Hablar
recoger: to collect, to pick up	recogiendo recogido	12-O-Escoger
recomendar: to recommend, to suggest	recomendando recomendado	24-S-Alentar-Acertar
reconciliarse: to become reconciled	reconciliándose reconciliado	49-R-RF-Levantarse
reconocer: to recognise, to admit	reconociendo reconocido	18-O-Conocer
reconquistar: to reconquer, to recapture	reconquistando reconquistado	1-R-Hablar

recordar: to remember, to recall	recordando recordado	26-S-Aprobar-Acortar
recorrer: to travel, to go around	recorriendo recorrido	2-R-Beber
recriminar: to reproach, to recriminate	recriminando recriminado	1-R-Hablar
reducir: to reduce	reduciendo reducido	20-M-Producir
referir: to refer, to recount	refiriendo referido	30-S-Sentir-Advertir
referirse: to refer to	refiriéndose referido	40-S-RF-Convertirse
reflejar: to reflect	reflejando reflejado	1-R-Hablar
reflejarse: to be reflected	reflejándose reflejado	49-R-RF-Levantarse
refluir: to flow back	refluyendo refluido	21-O-Instruir
refrescar: to refresh	refrescando refrescado	9-O-Tocar
regalar: to give away, to give a present	regalando regalado	1-R-Hablar
regar: to water, to irrigate	regando regado	87-M-Regar
regresar: to go back, to return	regresando regresado	1-R-Hablar
rehacer: to redo, to remake	rehaciendo rehecho	64-I-Hacer
rehusar: to refuse	rehusando rehusado	94-Ú/Í-Rehusar
reir: to laugh	riendo reído	35-S-Reir-Freir
reirse: to laugh at	riéndose reído	52-S-RF-Reírse
relacionarse: to be related, to be connected	relacionándose relacionado	49-R-RF-Levantarse

241

releer: to reread	releyendo releído	8-O-Creer
remitir: to remit, to send, to refer	remitiendo remitido	3-R-Discutir
remontarse: to rise, to soar, to go back to	remontándose remontado	49-R-RF- Levantarse
remover: to stir, to move, to turn over	removiendo removido	27-S-Morder- Remover
reñir: to quarrel, to argue	riñendo reñido	31-S-Servir- Competir
reparar: to repair, to mend	reparando reparado	1-R-Hablar
repartir: to distribute, to divide up	repartiendo repartido	3-R-Discutir
repetir: to repeat, to replay	repitiendo repetido	31-S-Servir- Competir
replicar: to retort, to answer back	replicando replicado	9-O-Tocar
reponer: to replace, to put back	reponiendo repuesto	68-I-Poner
rescatar: to rescue, to recover	rescatando rescatado	1-R-Hablar
reservar: to book, to reserve	reservando reservado	1-R-Hablar
reservarse: to reserve for oneself	reservando reservado	49-R-RF- Levantarse
resfriarse: to catch a chill, to cool down	resfriándose resfriado	RF O/W 91-Ú/Í- Ampliar
resolver: to resolve/solve, to settle	resolviendo resuelto	27-S-Morder- Remover
respetar: to respect,	respetando respetado	1-R-Hablar
responder: to answer, to reply to	respondiendo respondido	2-R-Beber

restituir: **to restore, to return**	restituyendo restituido	21-O-Instruir
resultar: to result, to prove to be	resultando resultado	1-R-Hablar
retirar: **to withdraw,** **to remove**	retirando retirado	1-R-Hablar
retraer: to retract	retrayendo retraído	102-DC-Retraer
retrasar: to slow down, to retard	retrasando retrasado	1-R-Hablar
retrasarse: to be delayed, to be held up	retrasándose retrasado	49-R-RF- Levantarse
reunir: to reunite, to gather	reuniendo reunido	96-Ú/Í-Reunir
reunirse: to join together, to gather	reuniéndose reunido	RF O/W 96-Ú/Í- Reunir
revenir: to shrink, to come back	reviniendo revenido	78-I-Venir
rever: to see again, to review	reviendo revisto	79-I-Ver
revisar: to revise, to review	revisando revisado	1-R-Hablar
revocar: to revoke, to repeal	revocando revocado	9-O-Tocar
revolver: to mix, to turn over	revolviendo revuelto	27-S-Morder- Remover
rezar: to pray	rezando rezado	7-O-Rezar
robar: to rob,	robando robado	1-R-Hablar
rodar: to roll, to roll camera/film	rodando rodado	26-S-Aprobar- Acortar
rodear: **to surround,** **to encircle**	rodeando rodeado	1-R-Hablar
roer: to gnaw, to nibble	royendo roído	70-I-Roer

rogar: to petition, to pray	rogando rogado	M 26-S-Aprobar-Acortar + 10-O-Pagar
romper: to break	rompiendo roto	2-R-Beber
saber: to know	sabiendo sabido	71-I-Saber
sacar: to take out, to withdraw	sacando sacado	9-O-Tocar
salar: to salt	salando salado	1-R-Hablar
salir: to go out, to leave	saliendo salido	72-I-Salir
salivar: to salivate	salivando salivado	1-R-Hablar
saltar: to jump, to leap	saltando saltado	1-R-Hablar
saludar: to greet, to salute	saludando saludado	1-R-Hablar
salvar: to rescue, to save	salvando salvado	1-R-Hablar
santiguarse: to cross/bless o.s.	santiguándose santiguado	RF O/W 11-O-Averiguar
satisfacer: to satisfy, to please	satisfaciendo satisfecho	73-I-Satisfacer
sazonar: to season, to flavour	sazonando sazonado	1-R-Hablar
secar: to dry	secando secado	9-O-Tocar
segar: to mow, to reap	segando segado	87-M-Regar
seguir: to follow, to continue	siguiendo seguido	88-M-Seguir
sembrar: to sow, to plant	sembrando sembrado	24-S-Alentar-Acertar
señalar: to mark, to show, to indicate	señalando señalado	1-R-Hablar
sentarse: to sit down	sentándose sentado	53-S-RF-Sentarse

sentir: to feel, to sense	sintiendo sentido	30-S-Sentir-Advertir
sentirse: to feel regret, to be sorry for	sintiéndose sentido	54-S-RF-Sentirse
ser: to be	siendo sido	74-I-Ser
serrar: to saw	serrando serrado	24-S-Alentar-Acertar
servir: to serve, to help	sirviendo servido	31-S-Servir-Competir
significar: to signify, to mean	significando significado	9-O-Tocar
silbar: to whistle	silbando silbado	1-R-Hablar
simbolizar: to simbolize, to typify	simbolizando simbolizado	7-O-Rezar
sitiar: to besiege	sitiando sitiado	1-R-Hablar
situar: to place/situate	situando situado	90-Ú/Í-Evaluar
sobrar: to exceed, to remain	sobrando sobrado	1-R-Hablar
sobresalir: to project, to stand out	sobresalido sobresalido	100-DC-Sobresalir
sobrevivir: to survive, to outlive	sobreviviendo sobrevivido	3-R-Discutir
soldar: to solder/weld	soldando soldado	26-S-Aprobar-Acortar
soler: to be in the habit of doing	soliendo solido	27-S-Morder-Remover
solicitar: to request, to ask, to seek	solicitando solicitado	1-R-Hablar
sollozar: to sob	sollozando sollozado	7-O-Rezar
soltar: to release, to drop	soltando soltado	26-S-Aprobar-Acortar

solucionar: to solve, to sort out	solucionar solucionado	1-R-Hablar
soñar: to dream	soñando soñado	26-S-Aprobar-Acortar
sonar: to sound, to ring, to play	sonando sonado	26-S-Aprobar-Acortar
sonreír: to smile	sonriendo sonreído	35-S-Reir-Freir
sorprender: to surprise, to astonish	sorprendiendo sorprendido	2-R-Beber
sorprenderse: to be surprised/astonished	sorprendiéndose sorprendido	RF O/W 2-R-Beber
sortear: to raffle/draw	sorteando sorteado	1-R-Hablar
sostener: to hold up, to support/sustain	sosteniendo sostenido	75-I-Tener
subir: to go up, to climb, to raise	subiendo subido	3-R-Discutir
suceder: to happen, to occur	sucediendo sucedido	D O/W 2-R-Beber
sufrir: to suffer/sustain, to experience	sucediendo sucedido	3-R-Discutir
sugerir: to suggest, to prompt	sugiriendo sugerido	30-S-Sentir-Advertir
sumergir: to submerge, to immerse	sumergiendo sumergido	13-O-Dirigir
superar: to overcome, to surpass	superando superado	1-R-Hablar
suponer: to suppose, involve, to entail	suponiendo supuesto	68-I-Poner
surgir: to arise, to emerge	surgiendo surgido	13-O-Dirigir

sustituir: to **substitute,** to **replace**	sustituyendo sustituido	21-O-Instruir
sustraer: to **remove,** to **subtract**	sustrayendo sustraído	76-I-Traer
susurrar: to **whisper,** to **murmur**	susurrando susurrado	1-R-Hablar
tañer: to play **(music)**	tañendo tañido	5-O-Bruñir-Tañer
tapar: to cover, to **cap**	tapando tapado	1-R-Hablar
tardar: to delay, to take time	tardando tardado	1-R-Hablar
tejar: to tile	tejando tejado	1-R-Hablar
telefonear: to **telephone**	telefoneando telefoneado	1-R-Hablar
temblar: to **tremble, to shake**	temblando temblado	24-S-Alentar-Acertar
temer: to fear	temiendo temido	2-R-Beber
tender: to tend, to spread	tendiendo tendido	25-S-Perder-Entender
tener: to have, to possess	teniendo tenido	75-I-Tener
teñir: to dye	tiñendo teñido	83-M-Ceñir
terminar: to end, to finish	terminando terminado	1-R-Hablar
testar: to make a will	testando testado	1-R-Hablar
tirar: to throw, to throw away	tirando tirado	1-R-Hablar
tiritar: to shiver	tiritando tiritado	1-R-Hablar
tocar: to touch, to play	tocando tocado	9-O-Tocar

tomar: to take, to have	tomando tomado	1-R-Hablar
topar: to bump into	topando topado	1-R-Hablar
torcer: to turn, to twist	torciendo torcido	M 27-S-Morder-Remover+ 16-O-Vencer
torear: to fight bulls	toreando toreado	1-R-Hablar
toser: to cough	tosiendo tosido	2-R-Beber
tostar: to toast,to roast, to tan	tostando tostado	26-S-Aprobar-Acortar
trabajar: to work	trabajando trabajado	1-R-Hablar
traducir: to translate	traduciendo traducido	20-M-Producir
traer: to bring, to carry	trayendo traído	76-I-Traer
tragar: to swallow	tragando tragado	10-O-Pagar
tranqilizarse: to calm down	tranqilizándose tranqilizado	RF O/W 7-O-Rezar
transcurrir: to elapse	transcurriendo transcurrido	3-R-Discutir
transformar: to transform, to change	transformando transformado	1-R-Hablar
transportar: to transport, to carry	transportando transportado	1-R-Hablar
trasladar: to move, to transfer	trasladando trasladado	1-R-Hablar
trasladarse: to move, to go	trasladándose trasladado	49-R-RF-Levantarse
tratar: to treat, to handle	tratando tratado	1-R-Hablar
tratarse: to be about/to concern oneself	tratándose tratado	49-R-RF-Levantarse

trazar: to trace, to draw, to sketch	trazando trazado	7-O-Rezar
trepar: to climb	trepando trepado	1-R-Hablar
triunfar: to triumph, to suceed, to win	triunfando triunfado	1-R-Hablar
trocar: to barter, to exchange	trocando trocado	89-M-Trocar
tropezar: to encounter, to come across	tropezando tropezado	85-M-Empezar
tumbar: to knock over	tumbando tumbado	1-R-Hablar
tutear: to address as 'tu'	tuteando tuteado	1-R-Hablar
ubicar: to locate, to situate, to place	ubicando ubicado	9-O-Tocar
unir: to connect, to unite, to join	uniendo unido	3-R-Discutir
unirse: to join/come/unite together	uniéndose unido	47-R-RF-Inscribirse
untar: to smear/rub on	untando untado	1-R-Hablar
urdir: to weave	urdiendo urdido	3-R-Discutir
usar: to use	usando usado	1-R-Hablar
usurpar: to usurp	usurpando usurpado	1-R-Hablar
utilizar: to utilize, to use	utilizando utilizado	7-O-Rezar
vaciar: to empty	vaciando vaciado	91-Ú/Í-Ampliar
vagar: to wander, to roam	vagando vagado	10-O-Pagar
valer: to be worth, to avail, to help	valiendo valido	77-I-Valer

valorar: to value, to assess, to appraise	valorando valorado	1-R-Hablar
variar: to vary, to alter	variando variado	91-Ú/Í-Ampliar
velar: to keep watch	velando velado	1-R-Hablar
vencer: to conquer, to defeat,	venciendo vencido	16-O-Vencer
vender: to sell	vendiendo vendido	2-R-Beber
vengar: to avenge	vengando vengado	10-O-Pagar
venir: to come	viniendo venido	78-I-Venir
ver: to see	viendo visto	79-I-Ver
verter: to empty, to dump	vertiendo vertido	25-S-Perder-Entender
vestir: to dress, to clothe	vistiendo vestido	31-S-Servir-Competir
vestirse: to dress oneself	vistiéndose vestido	43-S-RF-Desvestirse
viajar: to journey, to journey	viajando viajado	1-R-Hablar
vigilar: to watch over, to guard	vigilando vigilado	1-R-Hablar
visitar : to visit	visitando visitado	1-R-Hablar
visualizar: to visualize	visualizando visualizado	7-O-Rezar
vivir: to live	viviendo vivido	3-R-Discutir
volar : to fly, to blow up	volando volado	26-S-Aprobar-Acortar
volver: to return, to turn	volviendo vuelto	27-S-Morder-Remover
vomitar: to vomit, to throw up	vomitando vomitado	1-R-Hablar

votar: to vote, to vow, to promise	votando votado	1-R-Hablar
yacer : to lie down, to be lying down	yaciendo yacido	18-O-Conocer
zurcir: to darn, to mend	zurciendo zurcido	17-O-Esparcir

Chapter 24
The 151 Best Spanish Verbs to Study First
Learn these and you will be able make yourself understood in the majority of everyday situations.

The prospect of studying all the 1001 verbs may be a little daunting for those who are just beginning to study Spanish.

This chapter then provides a list of the 151 best verbs to study for those anxious to keep their work at first to a minimum. The list is designed to provide enough to make oneself understood and to get by in the majority of everyday situations (travel, easy conversations, etc.) in the language. By using the memorising methods explained in the remaining chapters of this book you should not find it difficult to master the 151 and you will then have a excellent foundation from which to go on to the wider range of the 1001.

With each verb there is a letter, A, B or C. The A verbs are more or less the most important to learn initially, then the B verbs and finally the Cs, but really all should be learned.

The 151 list also provides a very good range of the different verb types that will be encountered generally. When you can understand and can conjugate the 151 verbs you should be able to cope with very nearly every type of verb however it may be conjugated, although not for example those that would be encountered only infrequently. The 104 fully conjugated verbs however covers all possible variations of conjugations.

Verb	Participles	Conjugation Guide
Abandonar: to leave to abandon - C	abandonando abandonado	1-R-Hablar
Abrazar: to embrace, to hug - C	abrazando abrazado	7-O-Rezar
Abrir: to open - B	abriendo abierto	3-R-Discutir
Acabar: to finish, to end - B	acabando acabado	1-R-Hablar

Aceptar: to accept, to take - B	aceptando aceptado	1-R-Hablar
Admirar: to admire - C	admirando admirado	1-R-Hablar
Aguardar: to wait for - C	aguardando aguardado	1-R-Hablar
Andar: to walk - A	andando andado	55-I-Andar
Aprender: to learn - A	aprendiendo aprendido	2-R-Beber
Asistir: to assist, to attend - B	asistiendo asistido	3-R-Discutir
Bailar: to dance - C	bailando bailado	1-R-Hablar
Bajar: to go down, to descend - C	bajando bajado	1-R-Hablar
Beber: to drink - A	bebiendo bebido	2-R-Beber
Besar: to kiss - C	besando besado	1-R-Hablar
Burlar: to deceive, to trick - C	burlando burlado	1-R-Hablar
Buscar: to look for - A	buscando buscado	9-O-Tocar
Caber: to fit, to accommodate A	cabiendo cabido	57-I-Caber
Caer: to fall - A	cayendo caído	23-O-Caer
Caerse: to fall - A	cayéndose caído	39-I-RF-Caerse
Cambiar: to change - B	cambiando cambiado	1-R-Hablar
Cantar: to sing - B	cantando cantado	1-R-Hablar
Callarse:to shut up/to be silent B	callándose callado	49-R-RF-Levantarse
Carecer: to lack - C	careciendo carecido	18-O-Conocer
Casarse: to marry - C	casándose casado	49-R-RF-Levantarse

Cerrar: to close - A	cerrando cerrado	24-S-Alentar-Acertar
Cobrar: to charge, to collect - C	cobrando cobrado	1-R-Hablar
Cocinar: to cook - B	cocinando cocinado	1-R-Hablar
Coger: to take, to catch, to seize - A	cogiendo cogido	12-O-Escoger
Comenzar: to commence, to begin - B	comenzando comenzado	M 24-S-Alentar-Acertar+ 7-O-Rezar
Comer: to eat - A	comiendo comido	2-R-Beber
Compartir: to share, to divide up - C	compartiendo compartido	3-R-Discutir
Comprar: to buy - A	comprando comprado	1-R-Hablar
Conducir: to lead, to conduct - B	conduciendo conducido	20-M-Producir
Conocer: to know, to meet - B	conociendo conocido	18-O-Conocer
Construir: to build, to construct - B	construyendo construido	21-O-Instruir
Contar: to tell, to relate - A	contando contado	26-S-Aprobar-Acortar
Correr: to run - B	corriendo corrido	2-R-Beber
Cortar: to cut, to crop - B	cortando cortado	1-R-Hablar
Costar: to cost - A	costando costado	D 26-S-Aprobar-Acortar
Creer: to believe - A	creyendo creído	8-O-Creer
Cuidarse: to take care of oneself - B	cuidándose cuidado	49-R-RF-Levantarse
Dar: to give - A	dando dado	59-I-Dar
Deber: to owe, to have to - A	debiendo debido	2-R-Beber
Decidir: to decide, to determine - B	decidiendo decidido	3-R-Discutir

Decir: to say, to tell - A	diciendo dicho	60-I-Decir
Defenderse: to defend oneself - C	defendiéndose defendido	41-S-RF-Defenderse
Descansar: to rest - B	descansado descansado	1-R-Hablar
Desear: to desire, to wish - B	deseando deseado	1-R-Hablar
Despedir -C	despidiendo despedido	31-S-Servir-Competir
Despedirse -C	despidiéndose despedido	42-S-RF-Despedirse
Despertar -C	despertando despertado	24-S-Alentar-Acertar
Despertarse -C	despertándose despertado	RF O/W 24-S-Alentar-Acertar
Desvestirse -C	desvistiéndose desvestido	43-S-RF-Desvestirse
Detener: to stop, to detain - C	deteniendo detenido	75-I-Tener
Dormir: to sleep - A	durmiendo dormido	33-S-Dormir-Morir
Dudar: to doubt - B	dudando dudado	1-R-Hablar
Echar: to throw, to cast - B	echando echado	1-R-Hablar
Empezar: to employ, to use - A	empezando empezado	85-M-Empezar
Emplear: to employ, to use - B	empleando empleado	1-R-Hablar
Encantar: to delight, to charm - B	encantando encantado	1-R-Hablar
Encontrar: to find, to encounter - A	encontrando encontrado	26-S-Aprobar-Acortar
Enseñar: to teach, to instruct - B	enseñando enseñado	1-R-Hablar
Entender: to understand - A	entendiendo entendido	25-S-Perder-Entender
Entrar: to enter - B	entrando entrado	1-R-Hablar

255

Enviar: to send, to dispatch - B	enviando enviado	91-Ú/Í-Ampliar
Escribir: to write - A	escribiendo escrito	3-R-Discutir
Escuchar: to listen, to hear - B	escuchando escuchado	1-R-Hablar
Esperar: to hope, to wait, to expect - A	esperando esperado	1-R-Hablar
Estar: to be - A	estando estando	62-I-Estar
Estudiar: to study - B	estudiando estudiado	1-R-Hablar
Fiar: to entrust, to confide - C	fiando fiado	91-Ú/Í-Ampliar
Firmar: to sign - B	firmando firmado	1-R-Hablar
Ganar: to gain, to earn, to win - B	ganando ganado	1-R-Hablar
Gastar: to spend, to consume - B	gastando gastado	1-R-Hablar
Gozar: to enjoy - C	gozando gozado	7-O-Rezar
Gustar: to please (to like), to taste - A	gustando gustado	D 1-R-Hablar
Haber:to have(auxillary verb)- A	habiendo habido	63-I-Haber
Hablar: to talk, to speak - A	hablando hablado	1-R-Hablar
Hacer: to make, to create - A	haciendo hecho	64-I-Hacer
Hambrear: to starve - C	hambreando hambreado	1-R-Hablar
Imaginarse: to imagine, to fancy - C	imaginándose imaginado	49-R-RF-Levantarse
Intentar: to try, to attempt - B	intentando intentado	1-R-Hablar
Ir: to go/to go away - A	yendo ido	65-I-Ir
Irse: to go/to go away - A	yéndose ido	48-I-RF-Irse

256

Jugar: to play, to gamble - B	jugando jugado	34-S-Jugar
Labrar: to work, to carve - C	labrando labrado	1-R-Hablar
Lavarse: to wash/: o.s - C	lavándose lavado	49-R-RF-Levantarse
Leer: to read - A	leyendo leído	8-O-Creer
Llenar: to fill - C	llenando llenado	1-R-Hablar
Llegar: to arrive, to reach - A	llegando llegado	10-O-Pagar
Llevar: to carry, to lead, to wear - B	llevando llevado	1-R-Hablar
Llover: to rain - C	lloviendo llovido	D 27-S-Morder-Remover
Mentir: to lie - B	mintiendo mentido	30-S-Sentir-Advertir
Mirar: to look at. - A	mirando mirado	1-R-Hablar
Mirarse: to look at. o.s- A	mirándose mirado	49-R-RF-Levantarse
Morir: to die - C	muriendo muerto	33-S-Dormir-Morir
Mostrar: to show, to display - B	mostrando mostrado	26-S-Aprobar-Acortar
Nacer: to be born - C	naciendo nacido	18-O-Conocer
Necesitar: to need - B	necesitando necesitado	1-R-Hablar
Oir: to hear, to listen to - A	oyendo oído	66-I-Oir
Olvidar: to forget - C	olvidando olvidado	1-R-Hablar
Pagar: to pay - A	pagando pagado	10-O-Pagar
Parrar: to stop - C	parando parado	1-R-Hablar
Partir: to set of, to go away, to depart - B	partir partido	3-R-Discutir
Pasar: to pass, to happen - A	pasando pasando	1-R-Hablar
Pasearse: to walk/: to go for a walk - C	paseándose paseado	49-R-RF-Levantarse

Pedir: to ask for, to request - B	pidiendo pedido	31-S-Servir-Competir
Pensar: to think - A	pensando pensado	24-S-Alentar-Acertar
Perder: to lose, to waste - B	perdiendo perdido	25-S-Perder-Entender
Permitir: to permit, to allow - C	permitiendo permitido	3-R-Discutir
Placer: to please - C	placiendo placido	18-O-Conocer
Poder: to be able - A	pudiendo podido	67-I-Poder
Poner: to put, to place - B	poniendo puesto	68-I-Poner
Practicar: to practise, to go in for - C	practicando practicado	9-O-Tocar
Preferir: to prefer - C	prefiriendo preferido	30-S-Sentir-Advertir
Preguntar: to ask, to enquire - A	preguntando preguntado	1-R-Hablar
Preocuparse: to care/ to worry about - C	preocupándose preocupado	49-R-RF-Levantarse
Prohibir: to prohibit, to ban - C	prohibiendo prohibido	95-Ú/Í-Prohibir
Quedar: to stay, to remain - C	quedando quedado	1-R-Hablar
Quedarse: to stay, to remain - C	quedándose quedado	49-R-RF-Levantarse
Quejarse: to complain - B	quejándose quejado	49-R-RF-Levantarse
Querer: to want, to wish, to like - A	queriendo querido	69-I-Querer
Recibir: to receive, to welcome - C	recibiendo recibido	3-R-Discutir
Regalar: to give away, to give a present -B	regalando regalado	1-R-Hablar
Regresar: to go back, to return - C	regresando regresado	1-R-Hablar
Reirse: to laugh at - B	riéndose reído	52-S-RF-Reírse

Responder: to answer, to reply to - B	respondiendo respondido	2-R-Beber
Robar: to rob - C	robando robado	1-R-Hablar
Romper: to break - C	rompiendo roto	2-R-Beber
Saber: to know - A	sabiendo sabido	71-I-Saber
Sacar: to take out/to withdraw C	sacando sacado	9-O-Tocar
Salir: to go out, to leave - A	saliendo salido	72-I-Salir
Seguir: to follow, to continue -B	siguiendo seguido	88-M-Seguir
Sentirse: to feel, to sense/ to feel regret - B	sintiéndose sentido	54-S-RF-Sentirse
Sentarse: to sit o.s. down - C	sentándose sentado	53-S-RF-Sentarse
Ser: to be - A	siendo sido	74-I-Ser
Servir: to serve, to help - C	sirviendo servido	31-S-Servir-Competir
Sorprender: to surprise, to astonish - C	sorprendiendo sorprendido	2-R-Beber
Subir: to go up, to climb, to raise - B	subiendo subido	3-R-Discutir
Tardar: to delay, to take time - C	tardando tardado	1-R-Hablar
Tener: to have, to possess - A	teniendo tenido	75-I-Tener
Terminar: to end, to finish - B	terminando terminado	1-R-Hablar
Tirar: to throw, to throw away - C	tirando tirado	1-R-Hablar
Tocar: to touch, to play - B	tocando tocado	9-O-Tocar
Tomar: to take, to have - B	tomando tomado	1-R-Hablar
Trabajar: to work - A	trabajando trabajado	1-R-Hablar

Traer: to bring, to carry - C	trayendo traído	76-I-Traer
Usar: to use - B	usando usado	1-R-Hablar
Valer: to be worth, to avail, to help - A	valiendo valido	77-I-Valer
Vencer: to conquer, to defeat - C	venciendo vencido	16-O-Vencer
Vender: to sell - B	vendiendo vendido	2-R-Beber
Venir: to come - A	viniendo venido	78-I-Venir
Ver: to see - A	viendo visto	79-I-Ver
Viajar: to journey, to travel - A	viajando viajado	1-R-Hablar
Vivir: to live - A	viviendo vivido	3-R-Discutir
Volver: to return, to turn - A	volviendo vuelto	27-S-Morder-Remover

Part Four: Mastering, Memorising and Recalling Spanish Verbs and Tenses

Chapter 25
Essential Memorizing Techniques For Spanish Verbs

So far this book has detailed what has to be learned to become a Spanish verb wizard. The remainder of this book will show you how to learn everything quickly and efficiently. This chapter 25 deals specifically with memory reinforcement techniques to be used at every stage in your learning of Spanish verbs. The next chapter will explain a learning method to be used with the techniques. A final chapter provides a number of valuable tips, and pointers to aid your memory of Spanish verb conjugations.

As you begin to study individual verbs remember that despite the value of any rules or patterns for the verbs, the rules are not themselves the language. The use of a language by its speakers gives rise to the rules and not vice versa. It is more important to learn actual conjugations and the practical use of the verbs than any background technical comments as to their formation.

The 9 Rs for Spanish verb learning
The learning of Spanish verbs, like any subject worth studying, must involve some effort and it is desirable that the efforts to be expended should secure the maximum results in proportion to the time spent. The following Memory 9 Rs will help you to achieve that.

Reading Aloud: Read aloud the conjugations of the verb to be learned verb.

Reflection: Think about the verb, it's meaning, and any similarities with the conjugations of other verbs and any variations that it may have from the regular rules. Also reflect on the pronunciation of the verb conjugations. It is important always to try and speak with an authentic Spanish sound, but being aware of the correct pronunciation is also an aid to understanding and recalling the conjugations. As has been seen many of the apparent irregularities of some verbs are due entirely to euphonic and spelling requirements. The basic sound of the particular conjugation may in fact follow the regular rule, but to achieve it, the spelling may vary from the regular.

Additionally it is essential always know the right place for the accent, so as to express or understand the meaning intended.

wRiting: Writing down the verb and it's conjugations is an aid to concentration and to re-enforcing your memory of them.

Repetition: Repeating the verb conjugations by frequent use, speaking, writing and re-reading. Simple repetition is desireable especially in the early stages of learning so as to begin to impose the verb and it's conjugations on your memory.

Other Repitition methods
1. Chant the verb conjugations to yourself frequently in the same way that probably you learned the times tables at school. In this way their use will more easily become second nature and should not be something that you have to think about..

2. Keep a notebook, both of the current selection of verbs that you are learning and of any other verbs that may be encountered and which might be useful. Alternatively make some flashcards (postcard size) with a selection of the weeks verbs to be studied; for example one verb and it's conjugation set out on each side of the card. These have to be written out but this itself is a helpful aid to concentration and memory as has been seen. The cards or notebook can be carried around and taken out to study in spare moments during the day.

Regular study: A little and often is the way to study the verbs. A long period of study carried out infrequently will not yield the same results. Aim at studying your Spanish verbs for a short period every day; just 10 or 15 minutes a day will produce remarkable results within a short time.

Reinforcement: The verbs that you learn should be put to use as much as possible. Practice, practice and practice again, employing the verbs and making up sentences and speaking with them, so as to reinforce your memory of the verbs and so to make your command of them become second nature.

Risking: It is important to take the chance with Spanish conversation and use the verbs with (hopefully) the correct conjugations whenever an opportunity presents itself. Take the risk and speak with any Spanish speaker you may meet. You are bound to get your verbs wrong from time to time, but you should not allow anxiety about this to be a cause of failure to seize the chance to speak. As you use the verbs you will quickly become proficient.

Reference: As a further aid to impressing a new verb on the memory try looking it up it up in a dictionary (preferably a monolingual Spanish Dictionary) and checking the meaning. The translation of each verb provided in this book is necessarily brief and you may find from a dictionary that some other interpretations are possible.

Recitation: Recitation of the verb conjugations is similar to repetition in that it involves going over the verb several times, but with this difference: with recitation there is an attempt to recollect the verb conjugations and to repeat them just from memory. Recitation is important because it challenges the memory and in doing so makes a deeper impression upon it. You may not be successful all at once when trying to recite the verb conjugations, but by making the effort to remember (checking the original text version of the verb as need be to see if the effort was accurate and then trying again, as often as necessary) you will start to create a satisfactory strong memory of the verb.

After an initial period of reading and reflection on the verb and the conjugations you should be ready to start to try and memorize them.

Read over each tense of the selected verb in turn again and then try immediately to recall the conjugation of the tense from memory, repeating as necessary checking and correcting yourself when it error.: (Recitation). Work through each of the tenses for the selected verb in the same way.

Repeat a small selection of verbs every day over a period of several days and presently you will begin to remember the selection satisfactorily. Once you have few verbs at your fingertips, provided you are persistent, other verbs will begin to be easier to command.

Chapter 26.
The Lock-Step Method
for Mastering and Recalling Spanish Verbs & Tenses

Follow the easy steps explained below you will soon become fluent with any and every Spanish verb.

The steps are based on the object of gaining an understanding of all the different tenses together as soon as possible, instead of spending undue amounts of time trying to be perfect with the use of one tense, before moving on the next, and so on. The traditional way to learn verbs in a foreign language is to take one tense, for example the present, and then to learn how to use the present tense with each of the various verb types, before proceeding to the next tense. Consequently beginners learning Spanish tend to overlearn the present tense and the future because these often appear early in text books and also are perceived to be easier.

The lock step method provides a different approach. It requires you to start learning **all** the tenses for a single verb type at once (and not on the learning thoroughly of one tense at a time for all verbs types). This alternative approach is more active and avoids the risk of acquiring a mind-set for the obvious first tenses generally taught, and so becoming more proficient with these tenses than with others and relying unduly on them. The only variation to this learning method is with regard to the compound tenses that will be left to Step 4. This is because the compound tenses require the verb haber to be learned and that is the subject of Step 4.

Following the steps also makes learning easier because as well as starting to see all tenses equally, you will begin to notice patterns in the way a verb may develop. Additionally the step method reinforces what has been learned at each stage and emphasises the need to keep on learning and practising by conjugating further verbs.

Daily Preliminary.
Each day make a rapid skim reading of the chapters covering the explanations as to how **all** the different verb tense forms and conjugations work and are used. The object with this reading is not to try and learn the material fully, but to develop an overview and to gain an understanding of where your study is going to take you. In

this way when you start to learn the different tenses you will be able to see them in context, and that will be a powerful aid to learning.

Next read in depth the explanation of at least one single different verb type and tenses. Start a new subject each day even though you may feel that the previous days study has not been fully grasped. Keep the cycle of a new subject per day going, until all have been covered and then return to the beginning and start again; in this way you will soon have an opportunity of revisiting any matters you may have found tricky.

Step 1.
Learn all the conjugations for the regular AR verbs using Hablar as your reference verb; but leaving out the compound verbs for the time being. Remember always to aim for accuracy and not speed.

Also take a different selection of other AR verbs each day and conjugate them in all their tenses. If you get stuck then look at the example verb in the 104 Fully Conjugated Spanish Verbs.

Step 2.
Repeat Step 1 for regular ER verbs using Beber as your reference verb.

Step 3.
Repeat Step 1 for regular IR verbs using Discutir as your reference verb.

Step 4.
Learn the verb Haber and the use of the compound tenses. As you will see, you should immediately be able to conjugate the compound forms for Hablar, Beber, Discutir and for every other Spanish verb. Your daily selection of Spanish verbs can now cover all regular AR, ER and IR verbs as well as the compound tenses for all these verbs.

Step 5.
Learn about the verbs that have changes or irregularities for orthographic or euphonic reasons. In fact these types of verbs largely conform to obvious rules and the reasons for the changes will be obvious. With a good knowledge of the regular verb forms you should not find these verbs difficult to master. These types of verbs can now be added to your daily selection of verbs to conjugate.

Step 6.
Learn the verbs that are irregular due to Stem/Stress changes. Whilst these are not quite so easy as the verbs that change for orthographic or euphonic reasons, nonetheless there is often an underlying pattern to the irregularities. These types of verbs can also now be added to your daily selection of verbs to conjugate.

Step 7.
Learn the reflexive verb forms and add these to your daily selection.

Step 8.
Learn the verbs from the 104 that are completely irregular without any obvious pattern or rule. Your understanding of the regular verb forms will again be an aid, because even the truly irregular verbs may have something in common with the regular forms. With these irregular verbs learned you will be able to cope with any Spanish verb whether spoken or written.

Step 9.
When you have a good grasp of all verb forms, take a selection of verbs at random each day to study and conjugate. Always aim for accuracy and not for speed. Practice, more practice, patience and experience will bring perfection, and will also bring increased speed without any effort or need to worry about being quick. Make sure you are accurate and the speed will take care of itself.

Remember that the verbs should be used, not just learned. Do not let them become merely an intellectual exercise, instead press them into active service in conversations and writing as often as possible.

Chapter 27
Memory-tips, patterns and pointers
for remembering Spanish verb conjugations.

1. The accent. The accent is a guide both to pronunciation and to the relevant tense. The correct accents should be considered in every conjugation. It is important always to get these right, so as to learn correctly, to understand correctly and to be understood when speaking.

2. O. The ending for the first person singular of nearly all present tense verb types (AR, ER, IR) is O. The letter O is only otherwise used as the final letter of a verb ending in the preterite (past historic) tense where it always takes the accent (ó) except with some irregular verbs.

3. S, The second person singular of all tenses (other than the preterite/past historic and the imperative) and with all verb types (AR, ER, IR) has S as the final letter; (with other letters in the endings relevant to the particular tense/mood).

4. MOS. The first person plural (we/nosotros) in all verbs types (AR, ER, IR) and in all tenses/moods, has MOS as the final letters. (with other letters in the endings relevant to the particular tense/mood).

5. IS. The second person plural (you/vosotros) has IS as the final letters in all verb types (AR, ER, IR) and all tenses/moods other than the imperative (with other letters in the endings relevant to the particular tense/mood).

6. N. The third person plural (they/ellos) in in all tenses and with all verb types (AR, ER, IR) has N as the final letter. (with other letters in the endings relevant to the particular tense/mood).

7. ER and IR verbs. Verbs ending in ER and IR have identical endings in all tenses/moods and persons other than the first and second persons plural in the present tense and in the second person plural in the imperative.

8. The Imperfect. The imperfect tense is completely regular for all verbs except for Ir (to go), Ver (to see) and Ser (to be).

267

9. The Preterite (past historic). Note the similarity between the singular and the plural endings, the O ending that only occurs with this tense and with the present tense (the third person singular in the preterite tense and the first person singular in the present tense); also the MOS, the IS and the N endings, etc.

10. The Preterite (past historic). The first person plural (nosotros) is the same for the preterite as for the present tense with regular AR verbs and also with regular IR verbs. (This is not the case with regular ER verbs because they are the same as the IR verbs in the preterite).

11. The Preterite (past historic). Unless the pronouns are spoken as well, the only way to tell the difference between (Yo) hablo (present tense) and (Él) habló (preterite) is by noting the accent: and of course the pronouns are not always spoken if the person speaking is obvious from the conjugation (and correct pronunciation) of the verb.

12. The Future tense. The endings for the future tense are always regular, and only with the infinitive stem, to which they are added, are there ever any irregularities. These future tense irregularities are limited to the 12 irregular verbs following: DECIR, PONER, SALIR, VALER, QUERER, TENER, HACER, HABER, PODER, SABER, CABER, VENIR. For details of the future tense stem irregularities with these verbs see the chapter on the future tense.

Even with these 12 a pattern is evident. Note that the sound of the 12 irregular verbs in the future tense is made more comfortable by the irregularities. Try speaking them as they would otherwise be and the phonetic reason for the irregularities will be obvious. So the 12 irregular verbs should be easy to learn.

13. The Future tense and Haber. The present tense of haber is as follows: he, has, ha, hemos, habéis, han. The h is silent is Spanish, and when the h and the hab are deleted, you have the endings for the future tense.

14 The Conditional tense. The endings are the same for all verb types (AR, ER, IR).

15. The Conditional tense. The irregular verb stems are the same 12 as for the future tense (see above).

16. The Conditional tense and ER and IR verbs. The endings, although in a different place (ie attached to the infinitive) are the same as with the imperfect tense for er and ir verbs.

17. The Progressive tenses. Learn the Estar conjugations first.

18. The Progressive tenses. When learning the conjugations of any verb learn the participles at the same time. You will need the Present-Participle to form progressive tenses and the Past-Participle to form the compound Haber tenses.

19. The Progressive tenses. The progressive tenses are easy to learn and use and have the advantage of flexibilty in that they can be used with the Present-Participle of any verb; and this is particularly helpful if perhaps the present or imperfect form of the relevant verb cannot be recalled.

20. The Present Subjunctive. Remember the clue generally given by the first person present indicative, Nearly always the irregular or stem changing verbs in the present subjunctive have the same stem as the verb in the first person present indicative.

21. The Present Subjunctive. AR verbs change their A for an E; and that ER and IR verbs change their E or I, for an A.

22. The Subjunctive. Whenever a sentence as to anything that is not a simple statement as to fact, is required, then consider whether the subjunctive should be used.

23. The Subjunctive. When reading anything in Spanish, if the subjunctive is encountered then always pause and work out why it was appropriate, and why the particular subjunctive tense was used. Keep a note book and make a list of the sentences found in this way, for future revision purposes.

24 The Imperfect Subjunctive. The imperfect subjunctive is formed by taking the third person plural (Ellos) of the preterite tense of the verb, removing the ending (which will be ARON for AR verbs and

IERON for ER and IR verbs) and then applying the relevant endings. As to these see the chapter dealing with the Imperfect subjunctive.

25. The Future Subjunctive. This is not used at all now, so although you may come across it when reading older books, do not bother to learn it.

26. The Imperative. The accent for the imperative stays in the same place when pronouns are added on to the verb, as it would be if they had not been added.

27. The Imperative. Apart from the Tú and Vosotros forms, the imperative borrows from the present subjunctive. So it will be helpful to master the present subjunctive before learning the imperative.

28. The Imperative. The dropping of the S from MOS in reflexive verb forms for Nosotros and the dropping of the D in the reflexive verb forms for Vosotros are clearly the result of the more comfortable sound achieved. For example: 'Peinémosnos' and 'Peinados' would feel somewhat clumsy.

Printed in Great Britain
by Amazon